Open versus Closed

Debates over redistribution, social insurance, and market regulation are central to American politics. Why do some citizens prefer a large role for government in the economic life of the nation while others wish to limit its reach? In *Open versus Closed*, the authors argue that these preferences are not always what they seem. They show how deep-seated personality traits underpinning the culture wars over race, immigration, law and order, sexuality, gender roles, and religion shape how citizens think about economics, binding cultural and economic inclinations together in unexpected ways. Integrating insights from both psychology and political science – and twenty years of observational and experimental data – the authors reveal the deeper motivations driving attitudes toward government. They find that for politically active citizens these attitudes are not driven by self-interest, but by a desire to express the traits and cultural commitments that define their identities.

Christopher D. Johnston is an assistant professor of political science at Duke University. He is coauthor of *The Ambivalent Partisan: How Critical Loyalty Promotes Democracy* (2012), which won both the David O. Sears award from the International Society of Political Psychology and the Robert E. Lane award from the American Political Science Association. His peer-reviewed research has been published in the *American Journal of Political Science*, *Journal of Politics*, *Public Opinion Quarterly*, *Political Psychology*, *American Politics Research*, and elsewhere.

Howard G. Lavine is Arleen C. Carlson Professor of Political Science at the University of Minnesota and director of the Center for the Study of Political Psychology. He is coauthor of *The Ambivalent Partisan: How Critical Loyalty Promotes Democracy* (2012), which won both the David O. Sears and Robert E. Lane book awards. He has published articles in *The American Political Science Review*, *American Journal of Political Science*, *Journal of Personality and Social Psychology*, the *New York Times*, and elsewhere. He is past editor of *Political Psychology* and current editor of *Advances in Political Psychology* and *Routledge Studies in Political Psychology*.

Christopher M. Federico is a professor of psychology and political science at the University of Minnesota. His research interests include ideology and belief systems, the psychological foundations of political preferences, and intergroup attitudes. He is the recipient of numerous awards, including the 2007 ISPP Erik Erikson Award for Early Career Achievements, the 2007 ISPP Roberta Sigel Junior Scholar Paper Award, and the International Society for Justice Research's 2009 Morton Deutsch Award. His research has been published in the *Journal of Personality and Social Psychology*, *American Journal of Political Science*, *Public Opinion Quarterly*, *Political Psychology*, and elsewhere.

Open versus Closed

Personality, Identity, and the Politics of Redistribution

CHRISTOPHER D. JOHNSTON

Duke University

HOWARD G. LAVINE

University of Minnesota

CHRISTOPHER M. FEDERICO

University of Minnesota

CAMBRIDGE
UNIVERSITY PRESS

CAMBRIDGE
UNIVERSITY PRESS

University Printing House, Cambridge CB2 8BS, United Kingdom

One Liberty Plaza, 20th Floor, New York, NY 10006, USA

477 Williamstown Road, Port Melbourne, VIC 3207, Australia

314-321, 3rd Floor, Plot 3, Splendor Forum, Jasola District Centre, New Delhi - 110025, India

79 Anson Road, #06-04/06, Singapore 079906

Cambridge University Press is part of the University of Cambridge.

It furthers the University's mission by disseminating knowledge in the pursuit of education, learning and research at the highest international levels of excellence.

www.cambridge.org
Information on this title: www.cambridge.org/9781107546424
DOI: 10.1017/9781316341452

First published 2017

A catalogue record for this publication is available from the British Library

ISBN 978-1-107-12046-4 Hardback
ISBN 978-1-107-54642-4 Paperback

Cambridge University Press has no responsibility for the persistence or accuracy of URLs for external or third-party internet websites referred to in this publication, and does not guarantee that any content on such websites is, or will remain, accurate or appropriate.

CJ: *For Amy and Hannah*
HL: *For my fathers, Ira S. Somerson and Edward W. Lavine*
CF: *For my mother*

*We're born to be righteous, but we have to learn
what, exactly, people like us should be righteous about.*

Jonathan Haidt, The Righteous Mind (2012: 26)
We do not see things as they are; we see them as we are.

The Talmud

Contents

Figures

Tables

Acknowledgments

This book has taken a winding path, and we owe a debt of gratitude to a number of people who have directly and indirectly contributed to it. First, a special thank you to Stanley Feldman, who was the primary advisor on Johnston's dissertation. We would also like to thank our home departments at Duke and Minnesota, which have provided both intellectual nourishment and financial resources that enabled us to complete our research and writing. From Duke, special thanks go to Sunshine Hillygus and John Aldrich for help in obtaining data used in two chapters. From Minnesota, we are grateful to our colleagues in political psychology – Gene Borgida, Paul Goren, Joanne Miller, Dan Myers, and Wendy Rahn – who provide a wise and steady sounding board for all of our ideas.

We are also grateful to Jamie Druckman and Jeremy Freese for administering the National Science Foundation–funded Time-Sharing Experiments for the Social Sciences, and for their help with the study on libertarianism reported in Chapter 6. The NSF provided support to Johnston for the first experiment in Chapter 6, and to Federico for the need for closure data analyzed in Chapters 4 and 5. The data for the first experiment in Chapter 6 first appeared in an article in *Political Psychology* coauthored with Julie Wronski. Thank you to Robert Dreeson at Cambridge for his support of this project, as well as Brianda Reyes and Cassi Roberts for their work on production. Three anonymous reviewers also provided very helpful comments on early drafts. We owe intellectual debts to colleagues too numerous to list here, but let us name a few. Thank you to John Alford, Jamie Druckman, Stanley Feldman, Marc Hetherington, John Hibbing, Leonie Huddy, John Jost, Dan Kahan, Cindy Kam, Milt Lodge, Ariel Malka, Jeffery Mondak, David Sears, Rune Slothuus, Kevin

Smith, Paul Sniderman, and Chuck Taber for their path-breaking work on personality, partisanship, motivated reasoning, and the biological bases of political attitudes. To the extent we are successful, it is due in large part to what we have learned from these individuals. All failures, errors, and omissions, of course, are ours alone.

On a more personal note, Johnston would like to thank Amy Lee Johnston for being his best friend, partner, and travel companion, for the sacrifices she has made and continues to make for his career, and for Hannah, who is perfect. He would also like to thank his immediate and extended families for their love and support. To mom Eileen, and siblings Erin, Jeff, Cory, and Sarah; and to Rita, Chuck, Mark, Sharon, Brendan, Logan, Carey, and Casey: thank you for all you do for Amy, Hannah, and me.

Lavine thanks the Carlson Family Foundation, as well as the College of Liberal Arts and the Department of Political Science at the University of Minnesota for financial support during the writing of this book. He also thanks his former chairs, Bud Duvall and Joan Tronto, who provided invaluable professional and personal counsel. Finally, Lavine thanks his children, Seamus and Finnian Lavine, for providing a daily dose of wonderment, joy, challenge, and love, and his wife, JaneAnne Murray, who gives so much to so many.

Federico thanks his parents, Valerie Federico and the late Kenneth Federico. Much of his success is due to the support, encouragement, and guidance they have provided. Chris also thanks his wife, Penny Nichol, for her love and her willingness to share her quantitative expertise with him; and his sons, Paul and Adam, for their patience while he was occupied with this project. In addition, he thanks his many wonderful students and coauthors, in particular Grace Deason, Damla Ergun, Emily Fisher, Corrie Hunt, and Michal Reifen Tagar, for their contributions to earlier work that influenced some of the ideas we develop in this book. Finally, he would be remiss not to thank Mark Edward Smith, David Robert Jones, and James Newell Osterberg Jr. for creative energy and inspiration over the years.

And a final thank you to the reader: the following pages are far from perfect, but we hope you find them worthy of your time.

Personality and the Foundations of Economic Preferences

Following a series of highly contentious debates in Congress, the people's representatives returned home in the summer of 2009 to reconnect with voters in town-hall-style meetings. Traditionally, these interactions are a forum for constituents to provide input into the policy-making process and for lawmakers to explain and generate support for their decisions. While such democratic give-and-take sessions are typically cordial and low-key, in August 2009 they were anything but. Across the country, voter outrage was focused on the new health care reform bill then making its way through Congress, the Affordable Care Act (ACA) – or "Obamacare," as it became known. At one meeting in Lebanon, Pennsylvania, held by Democratic Senator Arlen Specter, a man denounced the bill by shouting: "One day, God's gonna stand before you, and he's gonna judge you and the rest of your damn cronies up on the Hill, and then you will get your just desserts."[1] At another meeting in Tampa, Florida, Representative Kathy Castor faced a crowd of hundreds "banging on the door and drowning out the congresswoman's remarks."[2] Across the nation, these forums descended into disruption, and occasionally even violence. The ensuing debate about the expansion of health insurance was marked by anger, with each side seeing malign intent on the part of the other. The Democrats wanted to put Grandma in front of "death panels," and the Republicans

---

[1] http://talkingpointsmemo.com/dc/town-hall-attendee-tells-specter-one-day-god-s-gonna-stand-before-you

[2] www.npr.org/sections/itsallpolitics/2013/08/07/209919206/5-memorable-moments-when-town-hall-meetings-turned-to-rage

wanted the poor to "die quickly," or so it seemed to their political adversaries.[3]

The heated debates over the Affordable Care Act are a microcosm of twenty-first-century American politics. What is the source of such vitriol? Political scientists have emphasized the role of polarization – both in terms of the growing ideological gap between Democrats and Republicans, and the growing economic gap between the rich on one hand and the middle class and the poor on the other (e.g., Abramowitz 2010; McCarty, Poole, and Rosenthal 2006). In this view, American politics has become more acrimonious over the past few decades because conflicts rooted in ideology and class have become more pronounced. In a society of deep – and growing – economic inequality, we should expect people to experience strong feelings because the policy stakes are high. However, the evidence suggests this cannot be the whole story. First, despite partisan polarization among *elites*, the average citizen remains relatively moderate (Hill and Tausanovitch 2015). Rhetoric notwithstanding, rank-and-file Republicans support major elements of the welfare state and their Democratic counterparts support a generally free market economy. Second, household income and other indicators of material interest turn out to have only a modest impact on economic policy preferences, especially on highly salient issues like health insurance reform. In a 2012 survey, for example, low- and high-income individuals supported the ACA at similar rates, as did those with and without health insurance.[4] These findings signal that public opinion on bread-and-butter issues may not always be rooted in instrumental motives related to self-interest.

In light of these considerations, recent work in political psychology proposes a very different explanation for the nature of the debate over the ACA (and other issues): the red and the blue of American politics increasingly reflect a gap between fundamentally different kinds of people (e.g., Hetherington and Weiler 2009; Hibbing, Smith, and Alford 2014a). In this view, citizens are divided by considerations that cut deeper than debates about the proper scope of government intervention in the economy. They are divided to the core by personality. With the rise of cultural and lifestyle politics, Democrats and Republicans are now sharply distinguished by a

---

[3] www.cbsnews.com/news/grassley-warns-of-government-pulling-plug-on-grandma/, http://www.cbsnews.com/news/alan-grayson-die-quickly-comment-prompts-uproar/

[4] Here we are referring to the 2012 American National Election Study, which is the premier survey of the American public during election years. The data are publicly accessible at www.electionstudies.org/studypages/anes_timeseries_2012/anes_timeseries_2012.htm.

set of basic psychological dispositions related to experiential *openness* – a general dimension of personality tapping tolerance for threat and uncertainty in one's environment. As a result of this psychological sorting process, political debates have come to seem more personal and less reconcilable, even when ideological polarization is actually quite minimal. From this perspective, the nature of contemporary American politics is one of *social* distance and *affective* polarization (Iyengar, Sood, and Lelkes 2012; Iyengar and Westwood 2014).

Yet, despite a large literature linking personality to political preferences (see Jost et al. 2003), there is also a problem with this account: dispositions related to openness reliably predict attitudes on the issues at the heart of the culture wars – like gay marriage, gender roles, and immigration – but not on bread-and-butter economic issues like the ACA. When it comes to preferences on taxes, spending, and the role of government in markets – which constitute the primary ideological dimension in American politics – most studies find that such traits possess little explanatory value (e.g., Feldman and Johnston 2014). We believe this to be an important gap in our understanding of the psychology of mass belief systems. As Harold Lasswell (1936) famously wrote, politics at its core is about "who gets what, when, and how." Despite the rise of cultural division over the past few decades, economic issues remain the focus of public concern and political debate in American politics (Smith 2007).[5] In an era of rising inequality, questions related to the nature, origins, and quality of mass opinion on these issues – where such preferences come from, what they represent, whether they are "rational," and how they are maintained and changed – are central to the study of American democracy. If the political impact of openness does not extend to opinion in the realm of who gets what, psychological perspectives on ideology may be of limited relevance in understanding the bulk of what contemporary American politics is really about.

Thus, we have a puzzle. People react strongly to debates about economic policy, but material interests account for only a modest portion of the variation in economic preferences, and the personality divide that political psychologists emphasize does not pick up the slack. Still, the level of affective intensity calls out for an explanation. This book is an attempt to resolve this puzzle. In short, we find that personality openness *is* a powerful determinant of the public's policy opinions on economic

---

[5] Economic issues also garner both more media coverage and more legislative activity than social issues (Hayes and Lawless 2016; Lee 2009).

issues. However, its impact is complex and conditional. It is bound up with the increasingly culture-laden nature of partisan competition at an institutional level, and with the way that citizens engage – or do not engage – with American party politics at an individual level. We argue that openness influences economic preferences through two distinct and *opposing* pathways, one for politically engaged citizens – those who know and care about politics – and one for the politically unengaged. Among the engaged, we claim that openness influences economic opinion indirectly by shaping how citizens sort into political groups and use information from elite actors. As partisan conflict has been extended to cultural and lifestyle issues, engaged citizens have organized themselves into parties by personality, a process we refer to as "dispositional sorting." In particular, those with "closed" personality traits have moved into the Republican column over the past few decades, and those with "open" traits have become Democrats. More generally, open citizens now take their economic policy cues from trusted elites on the cultural left, while closed citizens adopt the positions of those on the cultural right. In this way, personality has become politically meaningful because it shapes how engaged citizens seek out policy-related information from elites.

For unengaged citizens, the process is quite different. Among those who pay only sporadic attention to politics, there has been little dispositional sorting over the past two decades: personality and political identity remain largely independent. However, this does not mean that openness is irrelevant in this stratum of the electorate. Rather, we propose that among unengaged citizens, openness influences economic attitudes directly by shaping desired levels of social protection from the government against the inherent uncertainties of free market capitalism. Specifically, we expect those who are less comfortable with risk and uncertainty (closed citizens) to prefer higher levels of redistribution, social insurance, and market regulation than those who are tolerant of risk and uncertainty (open citizens). Thus, openness is likely to be a powerful determinant of mass preferences on matters of economic policy, but in precisely opposite ways for different groups of citizens: for the engaged, openness follows the ideological structure of elite politics and leads to *liberal* economic preferences; but for the unengaged, openness leads to *conservative* economic preferences. The sign reversal this heterogeneity produces has obscured the central role that commonly studied personality traits play in economic preference formation. Scholars who look only for "main" or unconditional effects will fail to find an important role for openness, because the two effects largely cancel out in the aggregate considered as a whole. Political psychologists were right to look to this dimension of personality for insight into contemporary polarization, but extant theories are underspecified and fail to capture the conditional nature of its influence.

To account for this reversal effect, we propose that engaged and unengaged citizens think about economic policy in fundamentally different ways. Among the unengaged, policies related to taxes and spending are evaluated instrumentally in terms of their tangible consequences. In forming an opinion, the question for the unengaged citizen is: what will this policy *do for* me? Among the engaged, however, reactions to economic issues are better understood as expressively motivated signals of identity. The question for the engaged citizen is: what does support for this policy position *say about* me? In addition to clarifying the political impact of personality, this functional analysis can help us understand the dynamics of self-interest in the economic domain. The standard view in this regard is that informed individuals are more capable of weighing the costs and benefits of different courses of action and choosing the policy that best promotes their personal economic interests. If, however, engaged citizens hold their economic opinions for largely expressive reasons – as a reflection of cultural commitments rooted in personality – they may be largely indifferent to a policy's instrumental consequences (that is, what it actually does). Variables related to economic class may therefore have little bearing on how engaged citizens view economic issues.

According to our model, self-interest effects should be most evident among the *least* engaged. Politically unengaged individuals typically care less about the politics of identity and culture, leading them to focus on more concrete and "close to home" aspects of economic policies, including whether and how they may be personally affected (Converse 1964). As we will demonstrate in Chapter 7, this framework helps to explain why many working-class citizens – especially those who are politically well informed – take policy positions that seem to conflict with their economic interests. Simply put, they are motivated by other concerns altogether. Indeed, we find that typical indicators of self-interest matter much more for uninformed than informed citizens.

In sum, this is a book about how personality shapes mass opinion on issues related to social insurance, redistribution, and the regulation of markets. In particular, it is a book about how a broad dimension of personality related to experiential openness structures the public's preferences about who gets what, and what this tells us about the nature of contemporary American democracy. Our framework integrates two seemingly contradictory but central features of contemporary mass politics: that the current partisan vitriol is rooted in deep-seated differences of personality, lifestyle, and culture (Hetherington and Weiler 2009), and that debate over economic redistribution, social insurance, and government regulation remains the dominant dimension of American political conflict (Ansolabehere, Rodden, and Snyder 2006; Bartels 2006; Gelman 2008). Our most important conclusion is that cultural and lifestyle politics have reshaped the bases of economic preferences among politically engaged citizens, such that they are best understood as expressively motivated signals of personality and identity, rather than instrumentally motivated beliefs about what policies will bring about optimal outcomes. In contemporary mass politics, economic debates – at least among the most aware and active citizens – are often not in the main about *where we stand* on society's economic ladder; they are about *who we are* as individuals.

Personality and Ideology

Political theorists and social scientists have long reflected on the link between personality and politics. In *The Protestant Ethic and the Spirit of Capitalism*, Max Weber provided a foundation for the psychological study of ideology with his concept of *elective affinities*, or "the forces of mutual attraction that exist between the structure and contents of belief systems and the underlying needs and motives of individuals and groups who subscribe to them" (Jost, Federico, and Napier 2009: 308). A half-century later the authors of *The Authoritarian Personality* provided the first systematic evidence that political convictions are rooted in deep-seated psychological dispositions (Adorno et al. 1950). Working in the immediate aftermath of World War II, Adorno and his colleagues focused on the traits of people who were susceptible to antidemocratic propaganda. They found such individuals to be submissive to idealized authorities, aggressive toward nonconformists, and rigid in their style of thinking. Over the succeeding decades, the connections between psychological dispositions and political preferences have been subject to persistent theoretical refinement and empirical scrutiny, and this field is now one of the most active areas of research in political psychology (Jost et al. 2003).[6]

Despite the diversity of work in this area, it appears that much of it is converging on a common idea, which is that liberalism and conservatism

[6] See, e.g., Alford, Funk, and Hibbing 2005; Ahn et al. 2014; Amodio et al. 2007; Block and Block 2006; Carney et al. 2008; Dodd et al. 2012; Eysenck 1954; Federico, Deason, and Fisher 2012; Gerber et al. 2010; Graham, Haidt, and Nosek 2009; Jost, Federico, and

are rooted in stable individual differences in the ways people perceive, interpret, and cope with *threat* and *uncertainty* (e.g., Hibbing et al. 2014b; Jost et al. 2003). Some people are highly sensitive to potential threats in the environment, and focus on preventing negative outcomes. These individuals tend to prioritize order, certainty, and security in their lives. As a result, they value tradition, self-discipline, group cohesion, and respect for authority, and they tend to have conventional cultural tastes in things like music, food, and art. We refer to people with such qualities as "low in openness" or "dispositionally closed." Other people are less sensitive to threat, and focus more on achieving positive outcomes. They are attracted by novelty and the unknown; they are skeptical of traditional sources of authority, prioritize self-direction and individualism, and pride themselves on having unique and unconventional tastes and preferences. We refer to people with these qualities as "high in openness" or "dispositionally open." One might think of an open or closed door as an analogy to understand these differences: a closed door is secure against threats but limiting in opportunities, while an open door is inviting of possibilities but vulnerable and exposed.

The omnibus concept of openness is a useful shorthand for thinking about people's general proclivities when dealing with an uncertain world, from the initial processing and evaluation of stimuli to the core values and moral inclinations that guide behavior in a consistent way across time.[7] In setting out this distinction, we acknowledge that people are complex, and no one is a perfect match for either description. Nevertheless, most people can be placed closer to one side than the other, and they will readily – and reliably – characterize themselves as such when given the opportunity. Thus, while we will often use the categorical terms "open" and "closed" for expository purposes, we think of openness as a continuum.

Instrumental Motives Linking Personality and Politics

How and why do personality traits influence political attitudes? To answer this question, we consider the different functions that political attitudes serve for citizens (Katz 1960). The most influential theoretical approach

Napier 2009; Lavine et al. 2002; McClosky 1958; Mondak 2010, Oxley et al. 2008; Rokeach 1960; Schreiber et al. 2013; Settle et al. 2010; Sniderman 1975; Weber and Federico 2013; Wilson 1973.

[7] See Carney and colleagues (2008) for a similar argument. We will review this literature extensively in Chapter 2.

suggests an *instrumental* motive linking personality and political preferences. It assumes that certain policies – because of the outcomes they
bring about and the benefits they provide – are a natural fit to the psychological needs and goals that characterize people with different personalities (Adorno et al. 1950; Jost et al. 2003, 2009). For example, a common
claim is that citizens with closed personalities prefer culturally conservative policies (e.g., less immigration) because they promote certainty,
group cohesion, and stability in social norms and values (Kruglanski et
al. 2006). Various indicators of openness are indeed strongly related to
cultural values and policy preferences. For example, people who exhibit
strong cognitive and physiological reactions to threatening stimuli – indicating low openness – tend to be more supportive of traditional norms
and values, such as rigidly defined gender roles and the restriction of marriage to one man and one woman (Oxley et al. 2008; Smith et al. 2011a).
Similarly, people who place a high priority on the open values of self-
direction and stimulation tend to be more supportive of nontraditional
lifestyles than those who place a higher priority on the closed values of
security and social order (e.g., Malka et al. 2014).

But our primary concern in this book is with *economic* preferences –
that is, those related to redistribution, social insurance, and market regulation. Here, we believe that instrumental theories predict the opposite
relationship between openness and ideology. Economic liberalism – in
the American sense of "liberal" – seeks a more active government role in
the economy as a way to reduce the risks associated with free markets,
while economic conservatism entails a reduction of government, and a
transfer of responsibility for risk management to individuals and communities. The largest social welfare programs in the United States – Social
Security, Medicare, Medicaid, unemployment insurance, food aid, and
the like – all reduce the downside risks of capitalism by providing a social
safety net. These policies set a limit on how far one can fall in difficult
economic circumstances. Economic liberals also tend to support a strong
government role in regulating markets, such as in occupational licensing requirements (e.g., for taxi drivers or hairdressers), regulation of the
financial industry, and government oversight of new drugs, foods, and
services. Thus, government intervention in markets is, on its face, about
social insurance and protection: some individual freedom, diversity, and
choice is sacrificed to provide a measure of economic order, certainty, and
security. Given this reasoning, we would expect dispositionally closed
citizens to be attracted to economic liberalism, since liberalism in the
economic domain reduces uncertainty and risk. By contrast, we would

expect dispositionally open citizens to be attracted to economic conservatism, since conservatism in the economic domain allows for more individualism and self-direction. The problem is that – with a few exceptions that we will review in Chapters 2 and 3 – research has generally failed to find evidence for this hypothesis. Rather, studies indicate that openness strongly predicts cultural but *not* economic preferences.

Expressive Motives Linking Personality and Politics

An instrumental analysis provides one pathway by which personality and economic preferences may be connected. However, to account for the lack of empirical support for this theory, we consider a second approach, one that emphasizes the *expressive* dimension of people's policy preferences (Katz 1960). By expressive, we mean that political attitudes serve to reinforce and signal to others important aspects of one's self-concept. In this view, the influence of personality on economic opinion arises not because the expected outcomes of a policy match an individual's traits (as in the instrumental approach), but because those traits resonate with the social meaning a policy has acquired through party competition. In other words, citizens care less about the outcomes a policy *produces* and more about the groups and symbols with which a policy is *associated*.

A simple example may help to make this clear. Imagine that a person high in openness is exposed to a political advertisement in which the voiceover states: "Representative Smith has long been a staunch advocate for gay marriage. Representative Smith is also fighting against the Trans-Pacific Partnership (TPP) deal." On what basis might the individual form an opinion of the TPP? It is a complex issue; indeed, most people have probably given it little if any consideration. Therefore, it is unlikely that openness will have a *direct* influence on attitudes. But what about a *mediated* influence? We posit a two-step process whereby openness initially promotes positive feelings toward Representative Smith on the basis of cultural affinity, leading to an indirect link between openness and opposition to the TPP. This is a contrived example, but in similar ways political elites construct the broader social significance of economic policy positions by tying them to symbols to which citizens already have strong emotional reactions. In this way elites forge a link between openness and economic opinion. In this view, openness determines how citizens assimilate information from elites, thereby influencing what policies citizens believe reflect their self-concepts and social identities. In this sense, economic preferences become a symbolic expression of one's identity; they are a way of signaling "who I am" through politics.

This expressive approach suggests that the relationship between personality and economic preferences is not one of simple elective affinity. Rather, it critically depends on how elite political actors – such as elected officials, candidates vying for office, and pundits – construct the social meaning of an issue. Consider, for example, that the "individual mandate" for purchasing health insurance was originally associated with conservatism in the early 1990s, proposed as part of a market-oriented Republican alternative to the health care reform plan developed by the Clinton administration. However, the same policy has taken on a liberal cast as part of the Affordable Care Act that President Obama eventually signed into law. When psychological dispositions influence economic preferences in a mediated fashion – that is, through elite construction – the instrumental implications of a policy may be less important than the appeal of the social, cultural, and political symbols grafted onto it.

Choosing Whom to Believe

To expand on these ideas, we turn to a fundamental point Lupia and McCubbins made in their study of mass political reasoning, namely, that "to understand how people learn from others, we must be able to explain *how people choose whom to believe*" (1998: 8).[8] In their discussion of the nature of learning, Lupia and McCubbins argue that individuals may acquire knowledge directly (i.e., through personal experience) or indirectly by learning from others. When it comes to politics, however, they contend that only the second option may be available, as "politics is often abstract and its consequences are remote" (p. 9). This should be especially true for economic issues, which are technical, means-oriented, and unlikely to invite the visceral responses associated with cultural issues like gay marriage and immigration (Carmines and Stimson 1980). For example, how can average citizens adjudicate a technical debate about whether tax cuts or deficit spending would better stimulate economic growth during a recession? Rather than attempting to sort out such things for themselves, people often seek out the advice of others whom they perceive as knowledgeable and trustworthy, including the media, experts, friends and family, and the crowd at the proverbial water cooler. In practice, however, it is the two parties that provide structure to American politics

---

[8] Emphasis original. See also Kahan and Braman (2006).

by discursively linking technical issues to broader symbols. In this way, partisan affinity serves as a primary anchor as citizens attempt to make sense of technical policy debates (Cohen 2003; Goren 2005; Lavine, Johnston, and Steenbergen 2012).

If, as much research suggests, partisan loyalty exerts a strong influence on political reasoning, understanding how citizens decide whom to believe is tantamount to understanding why they are attracted to one political party or the other. In turn, understanding the roots of partisan affinity is central to understanding the nature of mass preferences about the role of government. Normatively, insofar as people hold principled, exogenous beliefs about the proper size and scope of government intervention in the economy, and insofar as they use those beliefs to sort themselves into parties, American democracy rests on a reasonably sound footing (e.g., Goren 2013). These conditions are unlikely to have been satisfied a half century ago, when the parties were ideologically heterogeneous coalitions. In a party system without well-known, easily identifiable ideological brands, citizens are unlikely to perceive and evaluate partisan conflict in terms of abstractions like liberalism or conservatism (Nie, Verba and Petrocik 1976). Today, however, as the parties have become more homogeneous and distinctive, many have argued that party identification among ordinary citizens has become more ideological, particularly among politically engaged citizens. As Abramowitz writes, "the Democratic and Republican parties today offer voters a clear-cut choice between coherent policy packages, one liberal and one conservative, and most voters appear to have little difficulty choosing the party whose package is more to their liking" (2010: 159).

We agree that the contemporary parties offer voters a clear-cut choice between liberal and conservative policy packages, and that most voters choose the party whose ideological symbols are more to their liking. If, however, these packages are understood in predominantly *cultural* terms – in terms of what the left and right are generally like as people, rather than what they signify about the proper role and scope of the federal government – then choosing a party identification on the basis of ideological resonance does not tell us much about the nature and meaning of the public's *economic* views. We argue that as emotionally laden cultural and lifestyle issues have become more central to partisan branding, two fundamental changes have occurred in the nature of partisanship. First, the extension of partisan conflict to issues touching on race, ethnicity, gender, sexuality, nationalism, and religion has created an alignment between political identity and dispositional openness (Hetherington and

Weiler 2009). Second, the notion of partisan identities as *social* identities – defining what Democrats and Republicans are stereotypically like as people – has intensified, leading the two partisan groups to hold increasingly negative feelings about each other (Iyengar et al. 2012; Mason 2015a). Indeed, Iyengar and Westwood (2014) find that partisan prejudice – in terms of both negative feelings and behavioral discrimination – may now be larger in magnitude than *racial* prejudice.[9] As Mason writes, "We are a nation of partisans who are prejudiced against each other, active just for the sake of winning, and increasingly angry. We might believe that we are responding to specific policy disputes, but to a very real extent we are also being driven by an automatic, basic need to defend our social group" (2015b: 58).

This has created a context in which partisan contests (even those over objective facts) are increasingly viewed as a struggle between in-group and out-group, animated by the desire for "positive distinctiveness" – a belief that one's party is different and better than the other party (Tajfel and Turner 1979). This suggests that citizens may use economic policy conflict as an arena for more basic conflicts over the relative status of competing cultural groups. In this view, personality does not directly constrain policy attitudes – as the instrumental approach suggests it does. Rather, it shapes how citizens respond to the prominent symbols of elite conflict. Open citizens identify with the cultural liberalism of the left and adopt the associated economic policy positions of liberals and Democrats, while closed citizens identify with the cultural conservatism of the right and adopt the positions of conservatives and Republicans. Viewed in this way, economic preferences are ultimately expressive rather than instrumental in nature. They reflect the primacy of group loyalty rather than judgments about the desirability of tangible policy outcomes.

In sum, the expressive approach suggests that citizens form partisan attachments on the basis of cultural affinities rooted in dispositional openness, and then proceed to take cues from partisan elites on technical issues related to taxes, spending, and government regulation of the economy. Through attention to elite discourse, open and closed citizens learn what economic opinions are appropriate for people like them. By expressing these opinions – on surveys, to friends, on social media, and elsewhere – citizens signal that they are a member in good standing of one cultural group or the other. The content of the opinion matters less

---

[9] For example, an increasingly large number of partisans say they would be upset if their child married a member of the other party (Iyengar et al. 2012). Thus, the *social* distance between partisans has grown substantially.

than the fact that it is "our" opinion. As Haidt (2012) explains in the epigraph to this book, "We're born to be righteous, but we have to learn what, exactly, people like us should be righteous about."

Openness, Political Engagement, and the Reversal Effect

To this point we have presented two pathways by which dispositional openness may influence economic preferences. The first is an instrumental pathway by which a closed personality orientation (relative to an open one) promotes support for activist government for reasons related to the perceived value of social protection. The second is an expressive pathway by which this same personality orientation promotes support for *limiting* government for reasons related to cultural identification.[10] We believe that both pathways are operative in the formation of economic opinion, but that each one predominates among different sets of individuals. Specifically, we argue that *political engagement* is associated with a shift in the primary motivation underlying political preference formation, from instrumental at low levels of engagement to expressive at high levels.

Political scientists have long noted that many Americans are uninterested in politics and know comparatively little about it. However, there is a great deal of variation, such that there are some people who do closely track political events, form stable political identities, and hold strong opinions about what the government should do. Why are some people highly engaged in politics while others are not? This is one of the most frustrating puzzles in political science, because intensive political engagement seems to run counter to the expectations of rational choice theory. Why? The core problem is that citizens typically have no good *instrumental* reason to become engaged, as their individual opinions have nary a chance of swaying policy outcomes (Downs 1957). Perhaps, however, people engage in politics for other reasons. Perhaps engagement promotes a sense of social identity, thus facilitating the attainment of other gratifications such as social belongingness and validation, positive self-regard, and the reduction of uncertainty (Brennan and Lomasky 1993; Brown 2000; Hogg 2007; Turner et al. 1987). Somin likens the motivation to acquire political information to that of a sports fan: "Fans who acquire extensive knowledge of their favorite teams and players do not

---

[10] And we expect the opposite for those with an open personality orientation.

do so because they can thereby influence the outcome of games. They do it because it increases the enjoyment they get from rooting for their favorite teams" (2006: 261) (see also Abrams, Iversen, and Soskice 2011; Groenendyk 2013).

Political engagement may thus be rooted – at least in large part – in the pleasure derived from expressing something akin to team spirit. In an ideal world, citizens would be engaged in politics without exhibiting the biases of passionate partisans. They would consider alternative views, consider new and contradictory perspectives, and privilege instrumental over expressive concerns (Kam 2006; Schudson 1998; Taber and Lodge 2006). It appears, however, that if their stake in the game is lowered, citizen involvement in public affairs plummets. The price for more engagement and enthusiasm is a heightened partisan spirit in the electorate (Levendusky 2009). This, we think, is the real democratic dilemma: instrumentally motivated citizens do not participate at high rates, and thus people who do participate are typically more concerned with gratifying their identities than achieving good policy outcomes.

In line with these considerations, we argue that political engagement is associated with a shift in the primary motivation underlying economic preference formation. Among citizens who pay little attention to politics, bread-and-butter economic issues are viewed through the lens of instrumentalism – "what will this policy *do for* me?" For the politically engaged, by contrast, the relevant question is "what does support for this policy *say about* me?" Based on this reasoning, we predict a "reversal" of the influence of openness on economic opinion across levels of political engagement. Among the unengaged, we argue that there is a natural tendency for closed citizens to support an active role for government in the economy and for open citizens to oppose it. This relationship is similar to that between risk and insurance preferences (e.g., Duch and Rueda 2014). By contrast, among the engaged, we suggest that openness is channeled into support for an interventionist approach to economic policy through expressive motives related to social identity. Open individuals identify with the cultural liberalism of the Democratic Party and adopt its approach to economic matters as a package deal, while closed citizens identify with the cultural conservatism of the Republican Party and adopt *its* approach to economic policy. This *reversal hypothesis* can account for the mixed empirical evidence in previous work on personality and economic opinion. As we have noted, and as we will show in Chapter 2, past work on the link between openness and economic opinion is highly inconsistent. As we will show in Chapter 4, once heterogeneity across political engagement is explicitly modeled, openness becomes one of the most important predictors of economic preferences, rivaling, and often exceeding the influence of other key variables such as income, race, and employment.

The Importance of Cultural Conflict

Our framework reconciles two seemingly contradictory but central features of contemporary mass politics: that current partisan polarization is cultural and affective in nature (Hetherington and Weiler 2009; Iyengar et al. 2012), and that the economy and economic issues remain the focus of most political debate and the "most important problems" of the average citizen (e.g., Smith 2007). According to many analysts of American politics, the Republican Party's success in presidential elections in the latter part of the twentieth century was abetted by taking populist positions on cultural issues, thereby *displacing* the economic domain from its central position in mass politics. For example, Huckfeldt and Kohfeld argue in their book *Race and the Decline of Class in American Politics*:

Quality of life issues have replaced quantity of life issues. Concerns of minimum wage laws, workplace safety, social security, and unemployment compensation have frequently given way to a lengthy agenda of nonmaterial issues concerns: energy, the environment, pro-life versus pro-choice and so on. (1989)

We do not subscribe to the view that cultural division has displaced economic issues on the public agenda. Whether the government defends or dismantles the welfare state remains a key concern for the vast majority of Americans. Rather, our core argument is that the preferences of politically active citizens on economic issues are *endogenous* to a basic cultural division in the electorate, a division rooted in deep-seated personality differences.[11] Engaged citizens forge long-term political identities on the basis of cultural affinity, and take cues from co-partisan elites about the "correct" positions on economic issues. Thus, the perspective we offer integrates economic and cultural arguments about the nature of contemporary American politics. While economic issues remain the

---

[11] See Kahan (2015), Kahan and Braman (2006), and Walsh (2012) for related perspectives on how cultural divisions can become intertwined with preferences in seemingly unrelated domains.

primary focus of day-to-day politics, engaged citizens anchor and orient themselves politically on the basis of identities rooted in openness.

In sum, the rise of lifestyle politics has not displaced economic conflict; rather, it has *shaped* economic preferences by fundamentally altering the basis of partisan sorting, political information seeking, and delegation. More broadly, we conclude that among engaged citizens, economic preferences cannot be interpreted at face value – that is, as exogenous beliefs about the degree to which the government should act to redistribute wealth or regulate economic activity. Rather, they are an expression of a more basic cultural division in the electorate. The primacy of economic debate in American politics thus obscures an important truth: economic policy conflict is not simply about economics per se; it is just as much about cultural conflict. To a large extent, then, economic divisions *are* cultural divisions in contemporary American politics.

Overview of Chapters

The remainder of this volume unpacks and empirically tests these ideas in detail. In the next two chapters, we lay out a theoretical framework for how dispositional openness provides a basis for political identity and economic opinion. In Chapter 2, we expand on the concept of openness and review past work on the psychological roots of political ideology. We then identify two key limitations of this literature. First, we note that although openness consistently predicts cultural preferences and political identity, it is only minimally related to preferences on social welfare policy, redistribution, and government regulation of the economy. Second, we argue that prior work devotes little theoretical or empirical attention to the *processes* by which personality factors are translated into political preferences. In particular, we note that past work fails to incorporate factors central to standard theories of mass politics, including political engagement, the behavior of political elites, and citizen–elite interactions (Zaller 1992).

In Chapter 3, we lay out the central elements of our theoretical model. We argue that dispositions linked to openness translate into economic preferences through two distinct and opposing pathways, and that the sign of the relationship depends on which pathway is operative. Among unengaged citizens, we claim that a closed personality orientation promotes a preference for activist government for instrumental reasons related to the attractiveness of publicly provided social protection.

Among engaged citizens, by contrast, we claim that the same orientation promotes a preference for limited government in economic matters for expressive reasons related to cultural identification.

In Chapters 4 through 7, we present empirical tests of the various components of the theory. In Chapter 4, we present an extensive set of tests of the *reversal hypothesis* using six distinct indicators of openness and ten nationally representative datasets spanning more than two decades of American politics. We find that the reversal dynamic is a highly reliable phenomenon, and that the influence of openness on economic opinion competes with, and often exceeds standard predictors of economic preferences such as income.

In Chapter 5, we examine the conditional impact of openness on partisan, ideological, and informational sorting. We find that engaged citizens who score low on openness forge right-leaning political identities, sort into right-leaning political information environments, and privilege messages from right-leaning elite groups and actors, whereas those who score high on openness do the opposite. By contrast, the politically unengaged do not translate psychological orientations into political orientations. Among these citizens, personality is almost entirely unrelated to political identity and information seeking.

In Chapter 6, we present several national survey experiments to examine the importance of elite behavior in linking personality to economic attitudes. Specifically, we show that among engaged – but not unengaged – citizens, dispositional openness guides the reception and assimilation of political information about economic issues, thereby structuring economic beliefs and preferences indirectly. Here, we demonstrate that the relationship between openness and economic preferences among engaged citizens is neither psychologically inherent nor inevitable; rather, it is forged by elites. We also show that the dynamics we have witnessed thus far – on hard-fought *domestic* economic issues – do not pertain to economic issues with an international component, such as support for international trade, over which elite partisans are less clearly divided. In the latter case, we find strong evidence that dispositional openness promotes a free-market orientation for all citizens, but most strongly for the engaged.

In Chapter 7, we test the key claim that political engagement shifts the way citizens think about economic issues from an instrumental to an expressive mode. Specifically, we show that the engaged (relative to the unengaged) are much less likely to use their personal financial circumstances (e.g., income, employment status, health insurance coverage) to form beliefs and preferences about issues of redistribution and social insurance.

Finally, in Chapter 8, we take stock of our findings, raise a number of potential objections to our theory and empirics, and discuss their implications for the quality of democratic citizenship, the contingent relevance of psychological dispositions, and the evolution of partisan competition in the United States.

2

The Psychology of Ideology

In this book, we attempt to shed light on citizens' economic values and policy preferences through an exploration of how they relate to the enduring characteristics that define people as individuals. Our focus is thus on personality rather than the socioeconomic characteristics – such as income or labor market position – that constitute the dominant approach in much of political science. While we do not deny the influence of such factors (see Chapter 7), their explanatory power is limited, leaving a wide gap in our understanding of mass politics. We believe that a substantial portion of that gap is filled by enduring needs, motives, and traits. In the next chapter, we develop our key arguments. In particular, we suggest that the relationship between dispositions and political preferences depends on the increasingly culture-laden nature of partisan political competition at an *institutional* level and on whether economic issues are considered in expressive or instrumental terms at an *individual* level. Before turning to a detailed treatment of our own model, however, we take stock of what political scientists, psychologists, and others have learned about the interface between personality and political attitudes. Here, we use the term *personality* broadly to encompass a wide range of dispositional qualities that shape the character of individuals, from the standard traits of the Big Five to stable individual differences in information processing and physiology.

We begin by reviewing the extensive literature on relationships between psychological variables and political preferences. Integrating findings from previous research, we argue that these relationships reflect a common tendency for political preferences to vary as a function of dispositional openness. We then identify two key limitations of this literature. First, we observe that while variables related to open and closed personalities consistently predict political identification and cultural preferences, they do a poor job in predicting preferences on the primary, economic dimension of political conflict. Second, we contend that extant work provides little theoretical or empirical attention to the *political* processes through which psychological dispositions are translated into preferences. In particular, we argue that this work largely ignores factors central to classic theories of opinion formation in political science, including parties, the strategic behavior of political elites, and citizens' engagement (or not) with elite politics.

Open and Closed

Our own thinking has a long intellectual lineage in the psychological bases of ideological division. Modern social scientific interest in this question can be traced back to Max Weber's interest in the "elective affinities" – or inherent resonances – that link the appeal of certain ideas to individual characteristics (Gerth and Mills 1948/1970: 62–3; see also Jost et al. 2009: 308). However, systematic empirical research on the topic did not begin in earnest until the postwar era. Scholars as diverse as Lasswell (1930), Adorno, Frenkel-Brunswik, Levinson, and Sanford (1950), Allport (1954), Eysenck (1954), Smith, Bruner, and White (1956), McClosky (1958), Lipset (1959), Rokeach (1960), Lane (1962), Tomkins (1963), Sanford (1966), Greenstein (1969), Wilson (1973), and Sniderman (1975) crafted theoretical frameworks in which personality characteristics predispose individuals to certain kinds of political beliefs. Although the field of personality and politics later languished, it has recently experienced a notable revival (for reviews, see Federico 2012; Gerber et al. 2011; Hibbing et al. 2014a; Jost et al. 2003, 2009; Mondak 2010). Perhaps as a result of rising polarization, in which the left and right often seem like fundamentally different types of people, psychologists have placed a renewed emphasis on uncovering the deeper determinants of political tastes. Indeed, contemporary research suggests that the predictive power of psychological dispositions often rivals or exceeds that of demographic variables central to models of political attitudes and behavior, such as income, race, and education (e.g., Gerber et al. 2010).

While this literature is diverse, we agree with others (e.g., Janoff-Bulman 2009; Jost et al. 2003, 2009; Hibbing et al. 2014b) that the field is converging on a common idea, which is that liberalism and conservatism are rooted in stable differences in the ways people perceive and deal with threat and uncertainty in their environments. Specifically, scholars have identified two opposing personality types: an *open* type typically associated with political liberalism and a *closed* type typically associated with political conservatism (Carney et al. 2008). As described in Chapter 1, closed people are more sensitive to potential threats in the environment and tend to experience uncertainty as aversive. In turn, they emphasize values and moral principles that promote order, certainty, and security in their environments. In contrast, open people are less sensitive to threat, and focus more on promoting gains relative to the status quo. They are attracted to rather than repelled by novelty and the unknown. In turn, they tend to be more skeptical of traditional sources of authority, and prioritize values and moral principles that promote individualism and cultural diversity. As we noted in Chapter 1, it is important to emphasize that these are idealized endpoints of a continuum, and we focus on *relative* differences in openness in our analyses. Few people fall at the extremes of this dimension, but we will show that it matters a great deal to political attitudes whether one is closer to one side or the other.

Before we turn to a more extensive review of this literature, we would like to clarify our terminology. First, we use the terms *open* and *closed* as a way of describing what is common or latent in previous research on this topic, not to define a new dimension of personality (see Carney et al. 2008 for a similar approach). These terms simply provide a useful and, we think, conceptually appropriate shorthand for referring to the clusters of traits that define the personality types typically associated with liberalism and conservatism. Indeed, the words *open* and *closed* are constituents of some of the most common predictors of political ideology, including "openness to experience," "openness to change," and "the need for cognitive closure." Other commonly used constructs make reference to synonyms and related terms, such as "binding" moral principles (Haidt 2012) and "novelty-seeking" (Settle et al. 2010). Throughout this book, we will refer to "openness," the "open-closed dimension," or "open and closed citizens" so that we do not have to constantly reiterate the defining traits of these two clusters.

To be clear, we are *not* claiming that all of the dispositional variables we will consider later in this volume – constructs ranging from loss aversion to conscientiousness – are identical or wholly interchangeable. We acknowledge that the numerous personality variables that have been linked to political preferences are distinct in some respects (e.g., level of abstraction), and are not perfectly coterminous in empirical terms. Nevertheless, these variables are clearly linked conceptually and theoretically, and they share much common variance empirically.[1] It is this common content that defines what we refer to as "openness." We believe that to avoid fragmentation into several sub-literatures that make only superficially different claims about the psychological bases of political preferences, it is important to work toward an integrative framework. Despite using diverse personality constructs, most of this work is, at its core, making a common claim: liberals and conservatives are divided by the way they deal with an uncertain and potentially threatening world, from the initial processing and evaluation of stimuli (e.g., Oxley et al. 2008) to the core values and moral inclinations that guide behavior in a consistent way across time (e.g., Caprara et al. 2006; Haidt 2012). The use of the summary term *openness* reflects our pursuit of theoretical integration. We would be perfectly happy to replace *openness* with a better term should one emerge that serves a similar function. For now, *open* and *closed* are useful summary terms, and reflect the core of what unifies this wide-ranging literature.

Second, we do not view either cluster of traits as normatively superior. Rather, the two orientations have unique sets of advantages and disadvantages. For example, common synonyms of the term *open* include those with a generally positive connotation – such as *receptive* or *unprejudiced* – as well as those with a generally negative connotation – such as *exposed* or *vulnerable*. The same is true of the term *closed*. It is natural that people vary in their basic tastes, and there are few dimensions more fundamental and broadly influential in social life than orientations toward threat and uncertainty (e.g., Camerer 2005; Kruglanski 1989; McDermott, Fowler, and Smirnov 2008; Pietri, Fazio, and Shook 2013).

Finally, we do not intend the term *closed* to imply political closedmindedness or bias at the expense of facts or new information. As previous research suggests, and as we will explain more fully in Chapter 3, this type of bias arises primarily from a psychological investment in one's political identity, not from differences in personality (e.g., Huddy, Mason, and Aarøe 2015). In Kruglanski's (1989: 14–16) terms, the open-closed dimension is related to needs for *nonspecific* closure, while political bias emerges from needs for *specific* closure, that is, the need to see one's own political group as better than competing groups (Tajfel and Turner 1979). Indeed, empirical evidence suggests that the left and right are both prone to political tribalism and motivated reasoning (e.g., Conway et al. 2015; Kahan et al. 2013).

---

[1] See Jost and colleagues (2003) for a highly influential statement of this position.

Research on Personality and Political Preferences

In the remainder of this chapter, we provide a review of the major areas of research on the dispositional foundations of political preferences. The final sections of this chapter turn a critical eye on this literature, describe its shortcomings, and set the stage for our own contribution, which we describe in Chapter 3.

Existential Motives, Epistemic Needs, and Political Preferences

A common theme that emerges from both classic and contemporary work on the relationship between psychology and politics is the idea that people are attracted to conservative (vs. liberal) political attitudes and identifications because they satisfy "*existential needs* to maintain safety and security and to minimize danger and threat," and "*epistemic needs* to attain certainty, order, and structure" (Jost, Federico, and Napier 2013: 236). The most comprehensive version of this argument is made by social psychologist John Jost and his colleagues (including one of us), who offer a "motivated social cognition" perspective on the roots of ideology (Jost, Nosek, and Gosling 2008; Jost et al. 2003, 2009, 2013). In a meta-analysis of more than eighty studies, Jost and colleagues (2003) argue that two "core" aspects of political conservatism, opposition to change and acceptance of inequality, are driven by chronic or situationally induced needs to reduce insecurity and uncertainty in one's social environment. From this perspective, conservatism embodies support for the status quo – for long-standing values, institutions, and socioeconomic hierarchies. By its very nature, then, conservatism represents support for the known over the unknown, for the "tried and true" over the insecurity and uncertainty intrinsic to social change.

In their work, Jost and his colleagues (2003, 2009) find that many psychological variables tapping the closed personality type are associated with conservative political orientations. For example, to cite one of the oldest variables in this literature, *authoritarianism* emerges as a clear predictor of political conservatism (see also Federico, Fisher, and Deason 2011; Federico, Hunt, and Ergun 2009; Hetherington and Weiler 2009). Authoritarianism is typically defined as a general attitude of deference to authority and convention, coupled with punitiveness and animosity toward "deviant" outgroups, and a skeptical view of democracy (Adorno et al. 1950; Altemeyer 1996; Stenner 2005). Contemporary views consider authoritarian attitudes and behavior to be rooted in chronic differences in sensitivity to threat and uncertainty aversion (Feldman 2003;

Feldman and Stenner 1997; Hetherington and Weiler 2009; Lavine et al. 1999, 2002; Marcus et al. 1995; Sullivan, Piereson, and Marcus 1982). In line with this view, numerous studies find that authoritarianism is strongly associated with the belief that the world is threatening and dangerous (Altemeyer 1998; Duckitt 2001; Duckitt and Sibley 2009; McFarland 2005).[2] Indeed, threat sensitivity among authoritarians is even detectable at an unconscious level. For example, Lavine, Lodge, Polichak and Taber (2002) found that authoritarians responded more quickly than non-authoritarians to threatening (but not neutral or positive) words on an automatic word recognition task. Authoritarianism has also been consistently linked to variables tapping an aversion to uncertainty and ambiguity (Jost et al. 2003). More recently, Hetherington and Weiler (2009) have provided evidence that the authoritarian predisposition is closely tied to conservative policy preferences. Specifically, they show that citizens who value obedience and order over individuality and self-reliance lean to the right on a range of policy issues, from gay marriage to the war on terrorism (see also Hetherington and Suhay 2011).

Jost and others also find a strong relationship between individual differences in the *need for nonspecific cognitive closure* and political conservatism (Jost et al. 2009). People with a strong need for closure place a high value on certainty and prefer to reach conclusions quickly and decisively. This tendency leads them to "seize" quickly on available information, and to "freeze" on conclusions once they are reached.[3] Consistent with this description, the need for closure is associated with an increased reliance on stereotypes, a rejection of out-groups, and a desire for consensus within groups (Kruglanski 2004; Kruglanski and Webster 1996; Kruglanski et al. 2006; Webster and Kruglanski 1994). Accordingly, multiple lines of research reveal an affinity between the need for closure and support for the certainty provided by a politics of the status quo (e.g., conservative ideological identifications and policy attitudes).[4]

---

[2] See also Cohrs and Asbrock (2009); Feldman (2003); Feldman and Stenner (1997); Greenberg et al. (1990); Lavine, Lodge and Freitas (2005); McFarland (2005); Stenner (2005).

[3] People who are high in need for closure agree with items such as "when I am confronted with a problem, I'm dying to reach a solution very quickly"; and "I don't like to be with people who are capable of unexpected actions."

[4] See Chirumbolo, Areni, and Sensales (2004); Federico et al. (2012); Federico and Goren (2009); Jost et al. (2008); Kemmelmeier (1997); Shook and Fazio (2009); Van Hiel, Onraet, and Pauw (2010); Van Hiel, Pandelaere, and Duriez (2004). Similarly, the need for closure is positively associated with other variables that conceptually relate to conservatism, such as a preference for high-status in-groups (Kruglanski et al. 2006; Kruglanski et al. 2002) and greater cultural traditionalism (Feldman and Johnston 2014; Van Hiel et

Conceptually similar findings emerge from research on *regulatory focus theory* (Higgins 1998). This theory examines basic individual differences in the tendency to focus more on preventing losses from a reference point (a closed orientation) or promoting gains (an open orientation). Cornwell and Higgins (2013), for example, find that a tendency to focus on preventing losses is associated with the endorsement of moral principles typically associated with conservatism, such as respect for authority and in-group loyalty, while a focus on promoting gains is associated with the endorsement of stereotypically liberal principles. These findings echo research in behavioral decision theory in which "loss aversion" – the tendency for a potential loss to be viewed as more aversive than a nominally equivalent potential gain is viewed as positive – creates a preference for sure things over mixed gambles and a general preference for the reference point or status quo (e.g., Kahneman and Tversky 1979; Quattrone and Tversky 1988; see also Janoff-Bulman, Sheikh, and Baldacci 2008).

Recent research by Shook and Fazio (2009) strongly supports this idea. They examined behavior in a computer game called *Beanfest* in which participants are presented with a series of stimuli ("beans") that vary physically on two dimensions: shape and number of spots. Each bean is associated with a positive or negative payoff that is, at first, unknown to participants. On each round of the game the participant is asked to "accept" the bean and receive its associated payoff, or "reject" the bean, in which case she does not learn its value. *Beanfest* is thus a nice analogy to the choices over prospects that often confront people in their daily lives: should you approach a novel stimulus and take the chance that it results in a negative experience, or should you simply avoid it altogether, and forego the possible gain but also prevent the possible loss? Shook and Fazio find that liberals play an open strategy and tend to sample a large number of novel beans, while conservatives play a closed strategy and sample many fewer beans. Importantly, they also find that conservatives *remember* a disproportionately greater number of the negative beans they do sample. This suggests that conservatives are more attentive to losses than gains, which results in a deeper encoding of the negative

al. 2004). Parallel results have also been found with other measures of cognitive motivation. One such variable is the *need for cognition* – a dispositional variable tapping the extent to which a person enjoys effortful thinking and seeks out new information, including counter-attitudinal information (Cacioppo et al. 1996). It correlates negatively with the need for closure and other variables indicative of uncertainty aversion, such that those high in the need for cognition tend to be *more* tolerant of uncertainty. Accordingly, the need for cognition often shows an inverse relation with various forms of conservatism (Feldman and Johnston 2014; Johnston 2013; Sargent 2004).

stimuli they actually experience. Taken as a whole, these results suggest that conservatives will, on average, restrict themselves to a smaller set of known, positive experiences relative to liberals. Liberals, by contrast, will tend to be more exploratory and open to novel experiences.

Other studies indicate that concerns about threat and uncertainty may vary contextually as well as across individuals. For example, situational inductions of the most fundamental existential insecurity of all – an awareness of one's mortality – appear to boost conservatism. Bonanno and Jost (2006) found that direct exposure to the terrorist attacks on September 11 in New York City was associated with a "conservative shift" in political ideology (see also Nail and McGregor 2009). Thórisdóttir and Jost (2011) directly manipulated threat by having participants think about what will happen to them as they die (the standard "mortality salience" manipulation from terror management theory; see Pyszczynski et al. 2004). They found that participants randomly assigned to think about their own mortality were more likely to identify as conservative, and that the experimental effect was mediated by temporary increases in need for closure. Studies conducted in the context of the 2004 presidential election similarly demonstrated that reminders of one's mortality were associated with increased support for Republican President George W. Bush over Democratic candidate John Kerry, even among those not predisposed to support conservative candidates (Cohen et al. 2005; Landau et al. 2004). Finally, manipulations that increase cognitive load and curtail the ability to engage in cognitive effort – which should produce mental states akin to a high need for closure – elicit increased conservatism (Eidelman et al. 2012; see also Kruglanski et al. 2002). The political significance of existential and epistemic needs thus extends beyond differences among individuals to differences among social contexts. This type of experimental work also provides leverage for drawing causal inferences about the relationship between epistemic and existential needs and political preferences.

Values and Moral Foundations

Basic psychological needs are embodied in enduring goal structures such as core human values and moral principles, and the connection between openness and political preferences is reflected in the study of these more abstract constructs as well. Much research in this area suggests that individuals differ in the extent to which they emphasize values and moral concerns that reflect a closed orientation aimed at protecting security and order versus a more open orientation focused on promoting individual rights and freedom, and diversity. For example, in his influential model of human values, psychologist Shalom Schwartz (1992, 1994) highlights ten basic value domains that are seen in nearly all cultures. Of particular relevance here are the values of tradition, conformity, security, self-direction, stimulation, and hedonism. The first three form a cluster of *conservation values* that serve the common preventive goals of safety, self-restraint, social stability, and group cohesion. Opposing these, the latter three cluster as *openness values* that serve the promotive goals of "independent thought and action – choosing, creating, exploring" (Schwartz 1992: 43). Schwartz describes this higher-order value dimension, *openness to change versus conservation*, as arraying "values in terms of the extent to which they motivate people to follow their own intellectual and emotional interests in unpredictable and uncertain directions versus to preserve the status quo and the certainty it provides in relationships with close others, institutions, and traditions." Endorsement of these values is linked to other measures of aversion to insecurity and uncertainty, as well as to political conservatism (Bilsky and Schwartz 1994; Duckitt and Sibley 2009; Olver and Mooradian 2003). For example, Thórisdóttir and her colleagues (2007) find that the importance of "security" as a general value correlates reliably with right-wing tendencies in Western Europe (see also Caprara et al. 2006; Malka et al. 2014; Schwartz 2007b), and Goren (2013) finds that tradition and conformity predict a conservative policy orientation among Americans (especially with respect to matters of public morality and military strength).

Work inspired by Haidt's (2012; Graham et al. 2013) *moral foundations theory* provides similar insights. According to the theory, moral judgments rest on five "adaptive challenges," including protecting and caring for other people (harm/care), reaping the benefits of two-way partnerships (fairness/cheating), forming cohesive coalitions (loyalty/betrayal), forming status hierarchies (authority/subversion), and avoiding contaminants (sanctity/degradation).[5] The first two foundations – related to caring and fairness – are considered "individualizing," as their function is to protect individual rights and welfare. The other foundations – related to loyalty, authority, and sanctity – are considered "binding," as their function is to protect the integrity and cohesion of the in-group. Haidt and his colleagues (Graham et al. 2009; Haidt 2012) have shown that conservatives place more weight on the

---

[5] Haidt (2012) has recently discussed a sixth foundation – liberty versus oppression – but we do not consider it here, as it is not directly relevant to our theoretical model, and is not yet formally accepted as a part of moral foundations theory (Graham et al. 2013).

binding foundations than liberals. This makes sense: the binding foundations bear a strong resemblance to Schwartz's (1992) conservation values of tradition, conformity, and security, as both are focused on protecting in-group values and maintaining social order. A preference for binding over individualizing foundations also converges with research on authoritarianism and its emphasis on respect for authority and adherence to group norms (e.g., Altemeyer 1988; Federico et al. 2013; Feldman 2003; Kruglanski et al. 2006; Stenner 2005). As mentioned earlier, the relative importance of binding moral foundations is also related to dispositional loss aversion and a focus on prevention rather than promotion (Cornwell and Higgins 2013).

The Big Five Traits and Politics

The political implications of the open-closed dimension are also evident in research on characteristics even more abstract than values – namely, the core traits that make up the basic structure of human personality.[6] The trait-based approach is perhaps the one most familiar to political scientists, as it dominates the recent surge of interest in the study of personality and political behavior in the discipline (e.g., Gerber et al. 2010; Mondak 2010). The assumption in this literature is that people vary in terms of a small number of stable behavioral tendencies that are reflected in the language we use to talk about individual differences. In personality psychology, the dominant model is the so-called Big Five (Goldberg 1990; McCrae 1996; McCrae and Costa 1999, 2003). Based on detailed analyses of trait adjectives found in everyday language, this model reduces variation in personality to five overarching dimensions: *extraversion*, one's level of sociability and assertiveness; *agreeableness*, one's level of altruism and concern for others; *conscientiousness*, one's level of concern for social duty, responsibility, and impulse control; *emotional stability*, one's level of even-temperedness or freedom from negative emotion; and *openness to experience*, one's level of interest in novelty, complexity, and originality.

Research on the political correlates of the Big Five converges on the conclusion that openness to experience promotes political liberalism, and, to a lesser extent, that conscientiousness promotes political conservatism (Carney et al. 2008; Gerber et al 2010, 2011; McCrae 1996; Mondak 2010; Van Hiel and Mervielde 2004). For example, Carney and her

---

[6] For a theoretical and empirical treatment of the relationship of values to personality, see Caprara et al. (2006) and Caprara and Vecchione (2013).

colleagues (2008) find significant associations between openness to experience and liberalism and between conscientiousness and conservatism, but weak and inconsistent results for the other Big Five traits. They also find that the possession of a wide array of personal "artifacts" related to openness – books, music, travel photos, and the like – is correlated with political liberalism in undergraduates. Similarly, in a recent study using a national sample, Gerber and colleagues (2010) found that openness to experience and conscientiousness were the strongest predictors of general ideology and preferences over both social and economic policy.

Mondak defines openness to experience as "a willingness to seek new paths, and a corresponding weak attachment to familiar ways" (2010: 51), and defines "conscientiousness" in terms of industriousness, order, and responsibility, and, to a lesser extent, self-control, traditionalism, and virtue. From these definitions, it is clear that these two traits reflect the general concerns tapped in other work on the psychology of ideology. Specifically, openness to experience – with its implications for individual self-direction and the attractiveness of novelty and diversity in experience – bears a clear conceptual relation to one's willingness to tolerate insecurity and uncertainty, while conscientiousness taps a preference for restraint and discipline that relates closely to societal mechanisms aimed at warding off insecurity and social disorder (i.e., rules, morality, traditional social codes). For example, recent research by Boyce, Wood and Ferguson (2016) suggests that people high in conscientiousness are more loss averse than people low in conscientiousness (e.g., they react more strongly to losses of income).

Do Dispositional Influences on Politics Have a Biological Foundation?

With increasing evidence that personality and political orientation are in part heritable (e.g., Alford et al. 2005),[7] scholars have sought to determine whether the connection between psychology and

[7] This literature, at present, is more controversial than the others we discuss. Our own position is that the evidence to date strongly suggests at least some heritable component to political preferences. Our primary argument in this book, however, does not rest on the issue of heritability, and would be unchanged if the dispositions with which we are concerned turn out to be entirely environmentally determined (though it is hard to imagine this would be true). For reviews of the relevant positions of each side of this debate, see Alford, Funk, and Hibbing (2008), Charney (2008), Charney and English (2012), Hannagan and Hatemi (2008), and Smith et al. (2012). It is also important to note that the question of heritability is distinct from the issue of whether physiological traits (e.g., threat sensitivity) influence political attitudes (see Hibbing et al. 2014a).

political preferences has deeper *physiological* roots (for a review, see Jost et al. 2014). While the field of biopolitics remains in its infancy, several recent studies have identified intriguing physiological differ- ences between liberals and conservatives that seem to map closely to the open-closed distinction. In one study, Amodio and his colleagues (2007) hypothesized that liberals and conservatives differ with respect to activity in the anterior cingulate cortex (ACC), a region of the brain involved in monitoring conflict between habitual response patterns and the requirements of one's immediate context, and detecting complexity, ambiguity, and novelty more generally (Botvinick, Cohen, and Carter, 2004; Cunningham et al. 2003; Kerns et al. 2004; Lieberman 2007; see also Schreiber et al. 2013). Given their greater attraction to novelty, Amodio and colleagues expected to find greater ACC activity during interrupted tasks among liberals. In their experiment, participants were required to make a "go" response by indicating the presence of a spe- cific stimulus using a key press. The task is repeated until the point that the response becomes habitual. On a small number of trials, however, a different "no-go" stimulus appears which indicates that one's habitual response should be inhibited. Amodio and colleagues (2007) examined the association of ACC activity in response to "no-go" trials with ideo- logical self-identification, and found a large and significant correlation ($r = 0.59$) such that liberals showed substantially more ACC activity in response to the "no-go" trials than conservatives. This finding is consis- tent with the notion that liberals have a weaker attachment to what is familiar and known relative to conservatives.

Physiological indicators of threat sensitivity have also been linked to conservatism. In one study, Oxley and colleagues (2008) measured changes in participants' skin conductance – a general measure of arousal – in response to briefly presented threatening images (e.g., a large spider on the face of a frightened person). On trials in which threaten- ing images appeared, changes in skin conductance were larger among conservatives than liberals, indicating greater threat sensitivity. Related work indicates that conservatives show greater sensitivity to disgusting stimuli (e.g., a person eating a handful of worms), suggesting that evolved affective mechanisms that serve to alert people to the risk of biological contamination may be more active among those who lean right.[8] This latter finding is consistent with Haidt's work on morality and the relative

---

[8] See Helzer and Pizarro (2011); Hodson and Costello (2007); Inbar et al. (2009); Smith et al. (2011a); Terrizzi, Shook, and Ventis (2010).

importance of the "purity" foundation to conservatives, as the emotional concomitant of purity violations (biological or socio-moral) is disgust.

These findings are strongly reinforced by research examining actual differences in brain structure. For example, Kanai and colleagues (2011) find that political ideology in young adults is significantly correlated with gray matter volume in the ACC (liberals have more) and the amygdala (conservatives have more). As described previously, the ACC is implicated in the processing of conflict and uncertainty in one's immediate environment, whereas the amygdala is associated with fear and the processing of threatening stimuli (Lazarus 1991; LeDoux 1998). In a replication study, these authors were able to correctly classify 72 percent of their subjects in ideological terms using gray matter volume in the ACC alone. Thus, tendencies for liberals to engage more with uncertain or unfamiliar stimuli and for conservatives to be more sensitive to threatening stimuli may be reflected in brain anatomy.

While this literature remains controversial, work on the neurophysiological bases of ideology converges with other work on the psychological roots of political preferences. In an effort to integrate these two broad lines of inquiry, Hibbing, Smith, and Alford have argued that liberals and conservatives vary in *negativity bias*: the tendency for humans "to respond more strongly, to be more attentive, and to give more weight to negative elements of their environment" (2014b: 303). Though human beings appear generally predisposed to focus more on the negative than the positive (see Baumeister et al. 2001), there are stable individual differences in negativity bias rooted in physiology (e.g., De Martino, Camerer, and Adolphs 2010; Norris et al. 2010; Tom et al. 2007).

Hibbing and his colleagues argue that these individual differences co-vary with ideology, such that conservatives respond to and attend more closely to negative stimuli than liberals do. This implies that ideological variation derives (at least in part) from deep-seated individual differences in sensitivity to threats versus openness to opportunities (Cornwell and Higgins 2013; Janoff-Bulman 2009; Shook and Fazio 2009). Consistent with this account, studies find that conservatives are more likely to fixate on negative (versus positive) images (Dodd et al. 2012), to be distracted by threatening stimuli (Carraro, Castelli, and Machiella 2011; McLean et al. 2014; Oxley et al. 2008), and to weight negative information more heavily in opinion formation (Castelli and Carraro 2011). Conservatives are also more likely than liberals to interpret emotionally ambiguous facial expressions as indicative of anger and hostility (Vigil 2010).

Intriguingly – and consistent with Hibbing and colleagues' concept of negativity bias – research on emotions and cognitive style in psychology suggests that positive (versus negative) emotionality is associated with an open and inclusive approach to the social world (e.g., Fredrickson 2001). In summarizing this literature, Keltner and Lerner write that the "overarching function of positive emotions is to *broaden and build* thought repertoires. These basic broadening effects of positive emotion enable more creative and flexible thought, which help the individual in forming important bonds and exploring the environment" (2010: 335–6).[9] In contrast, negative emotions related to fear and anxiety are associated with cognitive "narrowing of attention and vigilance to threat." Indeed, activation of the left prefrontal cortex is typically associated with both positive emotions and approach-oriented behavior, and activation of the right cortex is associated with avoidance and withdrawal (Harmon-Jones 2007).[10] Overall, then, the concept of negativity bias dovetails with the open-closed distinction, with roots in basic neurophysiological differences.

In sum, the convergent conclusions reached by the literatures on the psychological and physiological correlates of ideology reinforce the general point that political preferences have a strong foundation in traits related to openness.[11]

Limits of Previous Research

As the preceding review indicates, a wealth of research suggests that political preferences have deep roots in psychological and physiological differences related to openness. However, a close examination of this literature reveals significant gaps and limitations, particularly with respect to (1) the ability of dispositional variables to explain political attitudes beyond mere political identification (e.g., as "liberal" or "conservative") and attitudes on cultural issues (e.g., gay rights, immigration) and (2) the processes through which dispositions are transformed into political orientations. In the following sections, we address these issues in an effort to set the stage for our own approach.

---

[9] Relevant cites are Isen (1987) and Frederickson (2001).

[10] Importantly, anger, while often considered a "negative" emotion, exhibits characteristics associated with positive emotions, such as approach behavioral tendencies and risk-taking (Lerner and Keltner 2001).

[11] For a more extended review of the literature on psychological and biological traits and ideology, see Jost et al. (2003, 2009, 2014) and Hibbing et al. (2014a).

Is the Impact of Openness Limited to Cultural Liberalism and Conservatism?

Policy disagreements among political elites fall largely along a single left-right continuum (McCarty et al. 2006); however, this is not the case among ordinary citizens. Rather, the public's preferences cluster into at *least* two ideological domains, which political scientists have traditionally referred to as "cultural" (or "social") and "economic." Cultural issues pertain to the protection of social order, security, and stability through social control, and include those related to sexuality, law and order, civil liberties, gender, religion, race, and immigration;[12] while economic issues concern the distribution of wealth and income, social insurance, and government regulation of markets. While preferences along these two dimensions are correlated, they remain statistically and conceptually distinct (e.g., Treier and Hillygus 2009). Indeed, many people are liberal in one domain and conservative in the other.[13]

Yet the majority of work on personality and political preferences – in both political science and psychology alike – has focused on cultural issues and on general political predispositions like party identification and ideological self-placement. Indeed, in their review of eighty-eight studies on the topic, Jost and colleagues (2003) report one-hundred and fifty-one tests of associations between openness-related variables and political ideology. However, as reported by Johnston (2011), only thirty-five of these ideological variables could be classified as indicators of economic preferences, and twenty-two of these thirty-five were measures of social dominance orientation, a value dimension closely associated with ethnocentrism and prejudice (Altemeyer 1998; Duckitt and Sibley 2009). More recent work has continued this tendency to focus primarily on identity and cultural preferences at the expense of the economic domain (e.g., Hetherington and Weiler 2009; Oxley et al. 2008).

This intensive focus has generated a large body of evidence in favor of the hypothesis that political identity and cultural preferences are linked to the open-closed dimension. Closed citizens are more likely to identify as conservative and Republican than open citizens, and

---

[12] While immigration is often discussed in terms of its economic implications, research suggests that immigration preferences in the mass public are driven mostly by cultural not economic concerns (e.g., Hainmueller and Hiscox 2007).

[13] See Duckitt and Sibley (2009); Ellis and Stimson (2012); Evans, Heath, and Lalljee (1996); Feldman (2013); Feldman and Johnston (2014); Fleishman (1988); Shafer and Claggett (1995); Sniderman et al. (2014); Stangor and Leary (2006); Treier and Hillygus (2009); see also Peffley and Hurwitz (1985). We do not mean to imply that there are only two

they are more conservative on specific issues related to (1) religion and traditional family values (e.g., gay marriage, abortion, school prayer, gender roles); (2) law and order (drug legalization, the death penalty); (3) civil liberties and the war on terrorism (government surveillance of U.S. citizens, support for harsh interrogation tactics); and (4) race and ethnicity (racial prejudice, immigration).[14] While this work has contributed a great deal to our understanding of the roots of ideology, openness-related traits may not play the same role in the sphere of economic preferences.

Indeed, while research on the question is limited, on the whole, extant work reveals weak and inconsistent relationships. In one recent study, Feldman and Johnston (2014) find that the need for closure, need for cognition, and authoritarianism strongly predict preferences on the issues of gay marriage, abortion, and women's role in society, but fail to predict preferences on preferred levels of government spending and services, public versus private health insurance, and employment protection (see also Crowson 2009). They also find that relations between psychological dispositions and ideological self-identification depend on the way in which the left-right continuum is subjectively construed. Among citizens who view the continuum in terms of cultural conflict, the relationship between psychological dispositions and ideological self-identification is quite strong. However, among those who view the continuum in terms of government intervention in economic matters, the two variables are unrelated. In other words, openness-related traits predict ideological identification only when citizens map cultural symbols onto the left-right space.

The greater effect of openness on cultural preferences relative to economic ones also extends to research using the Big Five personality traits (e.g., Carney et al. 2008; Van Hiel and Mervielde 2004), Schwartz's (1992) conservation values (Thórisdóttir et al. 2007), need for closure (e.g., Chirumbolo et al. 2004; Feldman and Johnston 2014; Van Hiel, Pandalaere, and Duriez 2004), intelligence (Carl 2015), and physiological measurements of disgust sensitivity (Adams, Stewart, and Blanchar 2014; Terrizzi et al. 2010). Finally, in studies that *do* find a relationship between openness and economic preferences, the sign is inconsistent: some studies

---

dimensions of preferences within the mass public, merely that research consistently identifies the cultural and the economic dimensions of public policy as the most important, accounting for a great deal, if not the bulk, of variation in public policy preferences. This is true in both the United States and Western Europe (e.g., Kriesi et al. 2006), and may be driven by the two-dimensional structure of basic human values (Feldman 2013; Schwartz 1992).

[14] For recent examples, see Federico and Goren 2009; Feldman and Johnston 2014; Hetherington and Weiler 2009; Hetherington and Suhay 2011; Johnston, Newman and Velez 2015; Jost et al. 2003; Oxley et al. 2008; Sargent 2004; Terrizzi et al. 2010.

report that open citizens are more economically liberal (as on cultural issues, e.g., Gerber et al. 2010), whereas others find that open citizens are more economically conservative.[15]

Extant research thus suggests that psychological variables tapping openness express themselves in the political domain primarily by determining cultural preferences related to "respecting tradition and social order, 'playing by the rules,' and ... endorsing conventional behaviors and appearance" (Ellis and Stimson 2012: 132). Closed citizens seek social stability and cohesion, while open citizens are more comfortable with – indeed prefer – cultural diversity and novelty. Further, to the extent that political labels like "liberal" and "conservative" have become associated with cultural preferences over time (see Ellis and Stimson 2012), openness predicts political identification as well (Feldman and Johnston 2014; Hetherington and Weiler 2009).

In sum, research on the dispositional antecedents of political preferences reveals a glaring asymmetry: individual differences indicative of the open-closed dimension predict political identifications and attitudes in the cultural domain, but they have inconsistent and typically weak predictive power in the economic domain. This presents a major challenge to the dispositional model of ideology, as it tells us very little about the psychological bases of attitudes along the central economic dimension of partisan-ideological conflict in contemporary American politics.[16]

How Does the Psychological Become Political?

Another significant gap in the literature pertains to our understanding of *how* psychological dispositions are transformed into political preferences. In particular, there has been little attention given to the *political* mechanisms that channel relatively stable psychological differences into ideological currents specific to particular political cultures. Indeed, most treatments go no further than to posit a direct process of elective affinity, whereby people choose or otherwise absorb the available ideologies that are (presumed by researchers to be) most consistent with their psychological characteristics (but see Malka et al. 2014). For example, Jost and his colleagues suggest that "a kind of matching process takes place whereby people adopt ideological belief systems ... that are most likely to satisfy their psychological needs and motives" (Jost et al 2003: 341), or a process in which "individuals gravitate toward those ideologies that

---

[15] See Aspelund, Lindeman, and Verkasalo (2013); Golec (2002); Johnston (2013); Kossowska and Van Hiel (2003); Malka et al. (2014); Thórisdóttir et al. (2007).
[16] See also Feldman (2013) and Feldman and Huddy (2014) for similar claims.

are present in the informational environment and that appeal to them, given their own psychological needs, motives, and desires" (Jost et al 2013: 235).

While work in this vein is influential and important, we believe that it leaves interesting questions unanswered. For one thing, it fails to explain why the political correlates of variables tapping the open-closed dimension are *domain specific* – with strong linkages to cultural issues but weak and inconsistent links to economic issues. To date, there has been little attempt to address this asymmetry theoretically.[17] It also fails to account for why ideological constraint between the two dimensions varies over time and across citizens. In particular, the correlation between economic and cultural conservatism has increased substantially in recent decades, and at any given point in time the size of this correlation is a positive function of political engagement. Yet standard theories connecting personality to political preferences do not contain moving parts capable of explaining such variation across time and individuals.

To address similar issues outside of the personality and politics literature, political scientists have developed models of mass belief systems that emphasize both contextual and individual heterogeneity (Campbell et al. 1960; Converse 1964; Feldman 1988; Goren 2004; McClosky and Zaller 1984; Sniderman, Brody, and Tetlock 1991; Sniderman and Stiglitz 2012; Zaller 1992).[18] Rather than focusing on psychological traits, these models focus on "predispositions" specific to the political realm – most importantly, partisanship and ideological identification. In describing the process by which citizens extrapolate from these predispositions to specific policy positions, these theories rely heavily on the notion of *elite opinion leadership* – that is, the idea that members of the mass public take cues about what positions to adopt on specific issues from elected officials who share their partisan or ideological identity. In this way, ordinary citizens are theoretically able to surmount two major challenges to the formation of political preferences – namely, the complexity of many policy debates and the public's chronic political inattentiveness (e.g., Converse 1964; Sniderman and Stiglitz 2012; Zaller 1992). That is, rather than thinking through each issue in isolation, citizens learn "appropriate" positions

---

[17] But see Gerber et al. (2010), Johnston and Wronski (2015), and Malka et al. (2014).

[18] In the context of the personality and politics literature, Jost et al. (2009) suggest that realistic models will include interactions between elite-driven and psychological sources of ideological constraint. One could view this book as fleshing out the implications of this idea in greater depth.

from elites who share their political predispositions. These models also account for the fact that individuals vary considerably in their attentiveness to politics. Only politically engaged citizens should be motivated and sufficiently attuned to communications from like-minded elites to receive and accept informative cues. A vast body of research provides support for this prediction, finding that partisanship and ideological self-placement are most likely to predict policy attitudes among those high in political engagement (e.g., interest in politics, general political knowledge; Sniderman, Brody, and Tetlock 1991; Zaller 1992; for a review, see Federico 2012).

By invoking political predispositions, elite opinion leadership and political engagement, standard models of opinion formation in political science identify the *mechanisms* through which individual characteristics are translated into specific political preferences (elite cue-taking), propose a primary source of *heterogeneity* across citizens (engagement), and implicate *political parties* as a key determinant of ideological constraint (through the bundling of issues in the context of electoral competition). That said, political science research tells us very little about the psychological dispositions that influence – but are prior to – politics. Insofar as specifically political orientations like partisanship are derivative of deeper psychological forces, the standard political science model simply raises the question of what drives variation in its own key explanatory variables – leaving a sizable gap in the discipline's understanding of mass preference formation.[19]

To sum up, research in neither discipline alone sheds much light on the mechanisms by which psychological dispositions become politicized. Psychological approaches simply assume that personality is directly linked to political preferences, and work in political science typically focuses on specifically political predispositions, the origins of which remain unexplained. As the result of a failure to communicate across disciplines, we know less than we should about the steps that intervene between biological and psychological processes on one hand and political preferences on the other, and this is especially true of preferences in the economic domain.

---

[19] Indeed, to cite one example, the long-standing assumption that partisanship is the "unmoved mover" among political preferences (*a la* Campbell et al. 1960) is itself an indicator of the extent to which established models of opinion formation make little theoretical room for the role of the dispositional variables that are clearly important antecedents of even the most general political orientations (like ideology and partisanship; see Jost 2006).

Conclusion

In this chapter, we have provided a brief tour of what social scientists know – and perhaps more importantly, what they do not know – about the interface between basic psychological dispositions and political preferences. As our review indicates, a great deal of research suggests that variables indicative of a general open-closed personality dimension are important antecedents of political preferences. This result obtains with respect to a diverse array of psychological dispositions, including authoritarianism, loss aversion, the need for closure, conservation values, moral concerns about in-group loyalty, obedience, and purity, and the openness and conscientiousness dimensions of the Big Five. Reinforcing these findings, other research suggests that these relationships are rooted in partly heritable, basic physiological differences.

However, this body of work leaves crucial issues unaddressed. First, there is little evidence to suggest that dispositions linked to the open-closed dimension have much to do with preferences over government intervention in economic matters – leaving us in the dark about the psychological bases of preferences in what remains the primary policy dimension of political debate in contemporary American life.[20] Second, extant research provides little insight into the *political* mechanisms through which these psychological dispositions become linked to political preferences; in particular, it ignores a large body of research in political science emphasizing citizen interactions with political elites. It is these shortcomings that our own model – which we introduce in the next chapter – attempts to address.

---

[20] Some evidence suggests that traits related to agreeableness and empathy may play a role in shaping economic preferences (e.g., Duckitt and Sibley 2009; Feldman and Huddy 2014; Gerber et al. 2010). Since these traits are independent of openness, this represents a theoretical approach quite distinct from our own.

3

A Dual-Pathway Model of Openness
and Economic Preferences

According to our review in Chapters 1 and 2, psychologists and political scientists have provided a compelling account of the personality dispositions that shape preferences on cultural issues related to race and ethnicity, religion, law and order, gender, and sexuality. We argued that these traits can be conceptualized as indicators of a broad dimension of personality defined by orientations toward threat and uncertainty – what we refer to as "openness." In general, those with a closed personality orientation tend toward cultural conservatism, whereas those with an open orientation tend toward cultural liberalism. We also maintained that scholars have been much less successful in explaining *economic* preferences – those related to social insurance, redistribution, and the regulation of markets – than preferences in the cultural domain. While past work has claimed that openness should promote liberalism in both the cultural and economic domains, this prediction has met with mixed, and more often, null results. Finally, we suggested that research in personality and politics has paid insufficient attention to factors that are central to standard theories of mass politics in political science, most importantly, political engagement, parties, and citizen–elite interactions.

In this chapter, we address these shortcomings. We present a new perspective on the relationship between personality and economic preferences. The core of the model, which is summarized in Figure 3.1, consists of three interacting elements: dispositional openness, political engagement, and elite position-taking. In contrast to the findings of past work, we argue that openness *is* a primary force structuring economic preferences, but in different ways for different groups of citizens. Specifically, we contend that the relationship between openness and economic

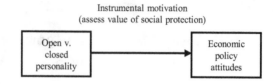

Unengaged citizens

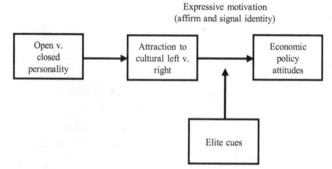

Engaged citizens

FIGURE 3.1. Two pathways from openness to economic opinion

opinion depends both on citizens' level of *political engagement* and on the ways that parties and their affiliates package *cultural* symbolism with *economic* values and policies.

Our central claim is that political engagement is associated with a shift in the primary motivation underlying economic preference formation – from instrumental to expressive – and that this shift alters the way in which psychological dispositions structure economic opinion. Among citizens who consider economic policy in terms of instrumental concerns, closed citizens prefer greater government involvement in the economy as a form of social insurance and protection, while open citizens prefer greater individual freedom at the expense of increased exposure to the downside risks of a market economy. By contrast, for those who are principally concerned with the cultural signals that economic policy position-taking sends, openness structures economic preferences conditionally through exposure to elite cues. Partisan elites construct the broader *social* meaning of economic policy by linking positions to cultural and political symbols (e.g., "Democrat"), and engaged citizens adopt the position that matches their own identities (identities that, as we will demonstrate in Chapter 5, are primarily rooted in openness). In this sense, the effect of personality among the engaged can be considered "indirect," because the connection is not intrinsic to the content of the policy options, but emerges only through exposure to elite discourse and debate. This is a very different way of thinking about the impact of personality on political preferences, but one that takes seriously (1) the expressive concerns that often drive political behavior, (2) the importance of political engagement, and (3) the guiding hand of elites in mass preference formation. Indeed, the theoretical framework presented in this chapter is an effort to integrate two seemingly unrelated literatures, one emphasizing the stable individual differences that shape preferences (e.g., Hibbing et al. 2014a; Jost et al. 2003), and one emphasizing social and political factors (e.g., Cohen 2003; Zaller 1992).

In the following sections, we elaborate on the logic of these claims, and explain why political engagement and elite messaging shape the relationship between personality and economic opinion. We begin by considering what we see as the default relationship – one that we expect to occur among politically unengaged citizens. Then, in the subsequent section, we explain how political engagement alters this relationship by shifting citizens' concerns from instrumental (what does support for this policy do for me?) to expressive (what does support for this policy say about me?). We conclude that openness is a potent force structuring both cultural *and* economic opinion, but that the nature and complexity of its role has not been fully appreciated in past research.

Personality and Economic Preferences among the Politically Unengaged[1]

Who should be most likely to support government intervention in the economy, and who should be most supportive of free markets? The answer seems straightforward enough: economically vulnerable citizens benefit from government programs while the well-off benefit from government restraint. Redistribution and social welfare take money from the relatively secure to supplement the incomes of the relatively poor. Thus, the primary determinants of economic opinion should revolve around socioeconomic status (Meltzer and Richard 1981). Although this makes abundant sense, things are not quite so simple. As Weeden and Kurzban

---

[1] Political engagement is, of course, a continuum. For expository purposes, we discuss the ideal endpoints in terms of "engaged" and "unengaged" citizens, but in the empirical chapters to come, we treat engagement as a continuous variable.

explain, "Most of the programs people think of as redistributive act as a kind of hard-times insurance. The question, then, isn't only who is experiencing hard times now, but who expects the possibility of hard times in the future" (2014: 127–8). In this view, redistribution and social welfare can also be considered as forms of publicly provided economic protection – a "safety net." When times are good, people pay into the system, and when times are bad, they collect. Social Security, Medicare, and unemployment insurance are prime examples: citizens pay into the system during their working years to insure against poverty during old age, after the death of the primary earner in the household, or when jobs are scarce. But the same goes for other programs that seem purely "redistributive," such as food stamps or Temporary Assistance for Needy Families (i.e., welfare), which reduce expected volatility in income over the lifespan (Sinn 1995). In these cases, citizens pay taxes to help fund the programs when they are doing well with the knowledge that they will benefit from them if economic times become more difficult. As should be obvious given recent events, these risks are quite real. According to one set of estimates, one-third of all Americans will experience a year or more of poverty by age thirty-five, and this rises to one-half by age sixty-five and to two-thirds by age eighty-five (Rank and Hirschl 1999). Similarly, about one-half of all Americans will draw on taxpayer-funded food aid during their prime working years (Rank and Hirschl 2005). Not everyone will ultimately be better off because of these programs. Looking back, many would have done better investing their extra wages privately. But the same is true for all insurance programs. The future is uncertain, and one pays a premium to remove some or all of the downside risk. The point is that while redistribution and social welfare programs redirect money from some people to others at a given point in time, they also insure against economic risks across time, providing some measure of economic security and peace of mind. The question for each individual is whether this decrease in risk is worth the cost as she looks forward into the future.

This view has become influential in the literature on the microfoundations of welfare states in political science. For example, research finds that citizens working in occupations with high unemployment rates (i.e., those facing a higher risk of job loss) are more supportive of redistribution than those in occupations with low unemployment rates (low risk) (Rehm 2009). Similarly, people with highly specific skills – such as those useful only in the context of one industry – are more supportive of social welfare than those with more general skills that would be useful in many different contexts (Iversen 2005; Iversen and Soskice 2001). People also seem to take into account *expected* income over the lifespan in thinking about desired levels of redistribution. Holding constant current income, individuals who expect lower income in the future prefer higher levels of government spending on employment programs compared to those who expect to be well-off in the future (Stegmueller 2013). In all of these examples, economic opinion is at least partly determined by citizens' beliefs about how government intervention in the economy benefits them over the long run by smoothing out the rough edges of a market society. This work suggests that citizens often "support welfare policy to obtain protection against risks that private insurance markets fail to cover" (Moene and Wallerstein 2001: 860).[2]

These considerations also suggest a fairly straightforward relationship between attitudes toward the role of government in the economy and openness in personality. Specifically, holding constant any objective features of one's situation that argue in favor of redistribution and social welfare, citizens who are dispositionally averse to loss and uncertainty (i.e., closed personality types) should be more supportive of government intervention than citizens who are more focused on gains and tolerant of uncertainty (i.e., open personality types). As Alesina and La Ferrara argue: "Redistributive policies constitute a form of insurance so that, for a given degree of mobility, more risk averse individuals should be more favorable to redistribution.... For sufficiently risk averse individuals, even though today's redistributive policies may bring a net loss, they may constitute a desirable means of insuring against future downward mobility" (2005: 902).

The basic idea is simple enough: people who are most concerned with downside risks are most likely to prefer a system of insurance to partially or completely remove them. Therefore, closed citizens should be more supportive of government intervention than open citizens, all else equal. This hypothesis converges with our review in Chapter 2. In study after study, closed (vs. open) citizens have been found to focus more attention on – and give greater weight to – negative outcomes and potential

---

[2] A related logic applies to issues of government regulation of goods and services, such as occupational licensing, extensive testing requirements for new drugs and treatments, or food safety and labeling standards. In these cases, citizens prefer government intervention to ensure that downside risks to participation in markets are minimized. Such intervention, of course, comes at a cost of higher prices for these goods and services (e.g., in time, supply, ease of access, cost, etc.). That is, one prefers to pay more for these goods or services in order to reduce the risk of negative outcomes. An obvious example is the additional waiting time and higher cost for new drug treatments that results from FDA safety testing requirements.

threats, and in turn, they are more averse to risk and uncertainty than their open counterparts. As previous scholars have argued, this often translates into support for socially "protective" policies that sacrifice some individual freedom for some measure of social order, certainty, and security (e.g., Feldman 2003; Hetherington and Weiler 2009; Oxley et al. 2008). For example, citizens high in threat sensitivity are more likely to support restrictions on civil liberties to reduce the risk of terrorist attacks (Hetherington and Suhay 2011). We believe this logic should extend to judgments about the desirability of government-provided *economic* protection as well.

There is some evidence to support this hypothesis. For example, using a direct measure of dispositional risk aversion, Duch and Rueda (2014) find that risk-averse individuals support redistribution to a greater extent than their risk-tolerant counterparts. Similarly, Malka and colleagues (2014) find that values tapping an open personality type (self-direction, stimulation) are typically associated with limited-government economic preferences, while values related to the closed type (security, conformity) are associated with support for redistribution and social welfare.[3] Some evidence also suggests that this relationship extends to concerns about globalization and international trade. As Scheve and Slaughter (2004, 2006) note, citizens recognize that free trade includes both benefits – such as lower prices for goods and services – and costs, such as heightened employment uncertainty and insecurity. Given these trade-offs, we should expect openness to be influential in shaping attitudes toward protectionism. For example, Ehrlich and Maestas (2010) find that risk aversion increases support for restrictions on foreign trade, and Johnston (2013) finds that personality needs for certainty and security increase support for restrictions on foreign imports into the United States.

In sum, in addition to any immediate redistributive implications, government intervention in the economy can also be understood as a means of protecting individuals against the many risks and uncertainties inherent to a market economy. Conceived in this way, there is good reason to expect closed citizens to be particularly supportive of government intervention, and open citizens to be attracted to a more individualistic, free market approach. In laying out this hypothesis, we do not deny the importance of other individual-level and contextual variables, such as income, skills, employment status, and the state of the local or national

---

[3] As our theoretical framework predicted, this was especially true of politically unengaged citizens.

economy. Our claim is simply that, all else equal, citizens with open personalities will lean toward limiting further government involvement and those with closed personalities will lean toward expanding it.

Given the intuitive nature of this hypothesis, it is surprising that political psychologists have long made precisely the opposite argument, namely that traits related to openness should promote support for a *greater* role for government in economic matters.[4] In the next section, we argue that under certain conditions, openness does in fact promote economic liberalism. However, we expect this to occur only among politically engaged citizens, and for reasons different from those given by other scholars (e.g., Jost et al. 2003). Rather than making an argument rooted in instrumental motivations, we claim that the relationship between personality and economic opinion is constructed in the context of party competition, as Democrats bundle a pro-government orientation with cultural liberalism and Republicans bundle a limited government orientation with cultural conservatism. By contrast, among those who take little notice of the cultural conflict roiling partisan debate (i.e., politically unengaged citizens), we expect to see the more intuitive relationship – whereby openness is linked to free market conservatism – as described earlier.

Openness and Economic Opinion among the Politically Engaged

The moderate correlation between the economic and cultural dimensions of mass ideology in the United States is both a relatively recent phenomenon and one largely limited to politically attentive citizens (Abramowitz 2010; Feldman 2013; Feldman and Johnston 2014; Levendusky 2009). What are the roots of this association? We argue that open and closed citizens who are engaged in politics are attracted to the left and right for cultural reasons, and experience psychological and social pressure to form opinions on economic issues that line up with those of their co-partisans and cultural affiliates.[5] In particular, the rise of cultural division between Democratic and Republican elites has created a context in which economic opinion is increasingly a means by which engaged citizens signal their allegiance to a cultural in-group. For these individuals, economic policy debates can be understood as symbolic conflict over the relative status of competing cultural groups linked to the two parties.

---

[4] Though, as described in Chapter 2, this claim has met with limited empirical success.
[5] For related arguments see Kahan (2015) and Kahan and Braman (2006).

At the elite level, Democrats have packaged cultural liberalism with a pro-interventionist economic philosophy while Republicans have packaged cultural conservatism with a limited government philosophy, creating an indirect link between openness and economic opinion that is opposite to what we expect to observe among the unengaged, as described previously.

Political Engagement and Self-Expression

We begin by noting that people do not have strong instrumental reasons to become engaged in politics, as the probability of effecting policy change through one's votes – or, for that matter, survey responses – is vanishingly small (e.g., Brennan and Lomasky 1993; Somin 2013).[6] This raises a key question: What alternative function(s) does political engagement serve? Our claim is that engaged citizens derive social-expressive

---

[6] It is often claimed that the voting act itself is irrational from an instrumental perspective. This is likely incorrect for some situations in U.S. politics. As Gelman, Silver and Edlin (2012) explain, it will often be rational to vote in expected utility terms, even in large elections, if citizens believe there is a substantial difference between candidates *and* they hold social rather than strictly "self-interested" preferences. For example, in U.S. Presidential elections the probability of being decisive in a swing state may exceed 1 in 10 million. Since the cost of voting is often low (e.g., getting to the polling place), the expected utility of voting may be positive in these situations if one believes that candidate A will be much better for the average person than candidate B. As Somin (2013: 68) argues, however, intensive political engagement is much harder to justify in instrumental terms, because the opportunity costs of information gathering, deliberation, discussion, and the like are much larger than for the voting act itself. He states, "If we conservatively estimate [the costs of voting with information acquisition] at $100 by assuming that the voter need only expend ten hours to acquire and learn the necessary information while suffering the opportunity costs of just $10 per hour," then the expected difference between the candidates in per capita benefits to make this rational is over $33,000 (this assumes a moderately altruistic individual). These values are obviously conservative with respect to the time needed to become truly informed about complex issues and the opportunity cost to the average citizen. This casts doubt on the instrumental rationality of voting when we do *not* assume that citizens have pre-existing beliefs regarding differences in utility among candidates. That is, even if the voting act itself is sometimes rational *given* a set of beliefs about candidates' relative value to society, it may not be if citizens need to spend a great deal of time and effort to uncover this information. Further, many citizens participate well beyond what is needed to determine the qualities of the candidates in election years, and in contexts where the probability of influencing the outcome is too low to generate a positive expected utility. These considerations suggest that intensive political engagement is primarily motivated by something other than achieving desirable policy outcomes, such as expressing core aspects of the self or conforming to the demands of a social identity (e.g., Brennan and Lomasky 1993). This is consistent with the work reviewed below which shows that engagement is associated with behavior that seems odd if the underlying motivation is achieving good policy outcomes, such as greater bias in political information processing and the reduction of such bias through self-affirmation.

benefits from participation that make it worth the cost (Abrams et al. 2011; Brennan and Lomasky 1993; Kahan 2015; Schuessler 2000). We view political engagement as rooted in a desire to express core aspects of the self through politics. In this view, people do not expect to change public policy by placing bumper stickers on their cars, by posting political messages on social media, or by arguing with their relatives at Thanksgiving dinner. They engage in these behaviors because they reinforce and signal an important component of their self-image (Katz 1960). While not everyone chooses to define the self through politics – there are a myriad of other ways to construct a social identity – for many it is an attractive choice.

Consider data from a nationally representative survey we conducted through Knowledge Networks' (KN)[7] web-enabled panel. Our survey included two items capturing the degree to which one's politics is rooted in expressive concerns: "My political attitudes and beliefs are an important reflection of who I am," and "In general, my political attitudes and beliefs are an important part of my self-image."[8] Our measure of political engagement – which was based on the average of nine items tapping political interest and knowledge of American politics – was strongly correlated with a scale created by averaging the two self-expression items ($r = 0.53$, $p < 0.01$).[9] This simple analysis suggests that politics is increasingly linked to expressive concerns as one ascends the ladder of engagement. This is intuitive, because the concrete costs of engagement must be outweighed by the psychological benefits if participation is to occur. Recent work in political psychology supports this contention, as engagement is associated with (1) stronger political identities and greater use of partisan cues (Berinsky 2007; Lavine et al. 2012; Zaller 1992); (2) greater motivated skepticism and bias in the evaluation of opposing viewpoints (Taber and Lodge 2006); (3) stronger moral conviction on political issues (Skitka and Bauman 2008); and (4) a heightened tendency to experience strong emotions in political contexts (Lodge and Taber 2013; Miller 2011).

At the heart of *social identity theory* (Luhtanen and Crocker 1992; Tajfel and Turner 1979) is the idea that group membership is integrated into the self-concept, thus motivating a desire for "positive distinctiveness" – a view of the "in-group" as distinct from, and better than relevant

---

[7] Knowledge Networks is now GfK.

[8] We describe this survey in greater detail in the next chapter.

[9] Each of the self-expression items was also individually associated with engagement (both $rs = 0.49$, ps < 0.01).

"out-groups." To help achieve positive distinctiveness, individuals engage in exaggerated comparisons between in-group and out-group that are designed to favor the former, particularly when the intergroup context is highly salient (Turner et al. 1987; for examples from political contexts, see Druckman, Peterson, and Slothuus 2013; Huddy et al. 2015; Kahan et al. 2013). This is one likely reason why political engagement, perhaps counterintuitively, tends to enhance – rather than diminish – bias in political judgment: the engaged are more likely to be strongly invested in their political identities, and thus they are more likely to seek positive distinctiveness and act defensively with respect to those identities (Lavine et al. 2012; Taber and Lodge 2006).[10]

In mass politics, parties are the dominant objects of affiliation. Thus, the quest for positive distinctiveness is often manifested in the expression of party-approved beliefs, attitudes, and behaviors (Cohen 2003). These expressions of loyalty signal that one is a group member in good standing, and that the in-group is superior to the out-group on an important dimension of social competition (i.e., identifying the best solutions to societal problems). In this way, policy debates can be seen as symbolic status conflicts among the social groups that define party coalitions at a given point in time. For example, rather than casting votes on the basis of preferences over complex issues, engaged citizens more often bring their issue positions into line with the candidate of their preferred party (Achen and Bartels 2016; Lavine et al. 2012; Lenz 2012).

The claim that political attitudes often serve a social-expressive function of this sort – particularly among engaged citizens – is not new. It dovetails with long-standing approaches that focus on the symbolic dimension of politics (Sears et al. 1980; Sears and Funk 1991; Tesler and Sears 2010). The authors of *The American Voter* (Campbell et al. 1960) proposed that party identification is founded on a deeply rooted affective bond, resulting in a sense of belongingness in which the partisan group is incorporated into the self-concept. They also suggested that the identification process reflects a cognitive representation of the parties in terms of linkages to salient social groups, and a matching of one's self-conception to an image of the groups associated with each party. For example, positive feelings toward evangelical Christians should facilitate identification with the Republican Party, whereas positive feelings toward racial minorities should promote identification with the Democrats. In reflecting

---

[10]   Achen and Bartels 2006; Duch, Palmer, and Anderson 2000; Evans and Anderson 2006; Gaines et al. 2007; Haider-Markel and Joslyn 2008; Jacobson 2010; Wells et al. 2009.

on whether they are Democrats or Republicans, Green and colleagues contend, people ask themselves the following questions: "What kinds of social groups come to mind as I think about Democrats, Republicans, and Independents? Which assemblage of groups (if any) best describes me?" (2002: 8).[11]

Recent empirical research also suggests that strong partisanship and political engagement may be rooted more in expressive than instrumental goals. For example, Huddy et al. (2015) compare these two motivations by examining the impact of partisan identity strength and policy positions on political participation. They find that the integration of partisanship into the self-concept[12] predicts participation more strongly than does either ideological extremity or the strength of issue positions. They also demonstrate that when partisans are threatened with electoral loss, their emotional response is driven more by strength of partisan identity than by issue preferences. On the basis of this work, it seems likely that political engagement is fueled more by the expressive benefits derived from group identification than by the instrumental pursuit of policy goals.

Research on "motivated reasoning" similarly points to the importance of expressive considerations in the formation of political preferences. Nyhan and Reifler (2015) argue that self-affirmation – a momentary bolstering of the self-concept – reduces the threat to identity posed by inconvenient political facts, allowing people to respond less defensively. They demonstrate that while biased perceptions of political facts are highly persistent, they can be corrected when people are given an opportunity to self-affirm by expressing identity-relevant values. For example, strong Republicans assigned to a self-affirmation treatment condition were more likely to acknowledge the reality of climate change than strong Republicans assigned to a control condition.[13] By momentarily bolstering self-worth through self-affirmation, expressing disloyalty to the partisan in-group would appear to be less psychologically disconcerting. Nyhan and Reifler conclude that partisan bias in reasoning about facts is not driven by the dissonance between one's political views and the evidence in question per se, but by the implications of the latter for one's self-worth (for related findings, see Cohen, Aronson and Steele 2000).

[11] Similar claims are made about ideological identification with liberals and conservatives (Conover and Feldman 1981; Ellis and Stimson 2012).
[12] E.g., "When talking about [Democrats/Republicans], how often do you use 'we' instead of 'they'?"
[13] Democrats showed similar behavior in conditions where their beliefs were threatened.

These studies imply that people engage in politics, in large part, to achieve and defend a positive social identity. Just as consumers sometimes choose products to cultivate desired images (e.g., buying a hybrid car to express environmentalism; see Snyder and DeBono 1985), citizens choose policies and leaders to express who they are. As McGraw and Tetlock write:

> If we want to understand why people often balk at the correct rational method of answering choice problems, we can adopt social-relational frameworks that focus on the identity affirming and distancing functions that judgment and choice may serve. The logic of choice often may not be consequential: What is in this for me, and how can I get as much as possible? Rather, the logic of choice often may be that of role-constrained obligation: What kind of person do I claim to be in my relations to particular others, and what types of decisions would be compatible with this image of who I am? (2005: 2)

In addition to the psychological benefits of maintaining a consistent and positive image of the self, citizens often face concrete social pressures – for example, the possibility of ostracism or loss of status within a group – to align their political attitudes with those of the in-group. As Kahan (2015) explains in the context of beliefs about climate change:

> What an ordinary person does – as consumer, voter, or participant in public discussions – is too inconsequential to affect either the climate or climate-change policymaking. Accordingly, if her actions in one of those capacities reflect a misunderstanding of the basic facts on global warming, neither she nor anyone she cares about will face any greater risk. But because positions on climate change have become such a readily identifiable indicator of ones' cultural commitments, adopting a stance toward climate change that deviates from the one that prevails among her closest associates could have devastating consequences, psychic and material. Thus, it is *perfectly rational* – perfectly consistent with promoting her happiness and well-being – for that individual to attend to information in a manner that more reliably connects her beliefs about climate change to the ones that predominate among her peers than to the best available scientific evidence.

Personality and Partisan Politics

In sum, we argue that economic preferences among politically engaged citizens are less likely to reflect beliefs about tangible policy consequences than a desire to signal information about one's social and cultural commitments. In effect, they are expressions of identity. What are the implications of this analysis for the impact of personality on economic opinion? Our theory holds that among engaged citizens, the rise of cultural and lifestyle politics has turned the open-closed dimension of personality into a primary basis of partisan sorting. As we noted in Chapter 2, personality has an especially strong influence on preferences related to religion, race and ethnicity, law and order, gender roles, sexuality, and the like, and the two parties have diverged sharply on these issues in recent decades. Given this divergence, engaged citizens with an open orientation should feel pressure to bring their economic opinions into line with those of the Democratic Party and its affiliates, whereas engaged citizens with a more closed orientation should feel pressure to conform to the positions of the Republican Party.

To better understand this process, we examine how changes in the party system over recent decades have laid the groundwork for dispositional sorting. We begin with the observation that mass partisanship has intensified as elites have polarized along a single ideological continuum (Abramowitz 2010; Hetherington 2001; Levendusky 2009). This development has created what many political scientists believe to be a "new" American voter, one whose outlook on politics is more strongly anchored in the left-right divide than in earlier eras (Abramowitz 2010; Bafumi and Shapiro 2009). According to this view, party labels now serve as easily identifiable and policy-relevant "brand names" for judgment and choice, especially among the politically attentive (Sniderman and Stiglitz 2012; Tomz and Sniderman 2005). As Sniderman and Stiglitz write:

Sometimes, the Democratic Party benefits by declaring itself the party of liberalism, sometimes by condemning the Republican Party as the party of conservatism. Ditto in political reverse for the Republican Party. The result: although few citizens know a lot about politics, a lot of citizens – on the order of seven in ten currently – know that the Democratic Party is the party of the left and the Republican Party is the party of the right. Know this and you have an ideological compass – one that partisans have good reason to know and make use of. Many of them, as a result, can tread an ideologically coherent path even if they are quite incapable of giving a definition of ideology. (2012: 20)

Thus, citizens may be able to make use of the ideological reputations of the parties without being able to formally define ideology. However, they surely need to attach *some* meaning to the labels "liberal" and "conservative" to find their own place on the continuum. We argue that liberalism and conservatism appear to be understood in largely *cultural* terms in contemporary American politics. In their in-depth investigation of the meaning of these terms over the past forty years, Ellis and Stimson conclude that people identify with ideological labels because they are attracted to and repulsed by the distinct cultural and lifestyle orientations that have come to be associated with them (2012: 116). In particular, Ellis and Stimson note a dramatic shift in the 1960s from an ideological perspective focusing on economic class conflict to one concentrating on cultural division. From the Great Depression through the 1950s, nearly half of survey respondents who placed themselves on the standard ideological self-identification scale referred to themselves as liberal. This changed suddenly and dramatically in the 1960s. As a result of the counterculture – including the new sexual morality, civil rights, urban riots, feminism, university campus insurrections, Vietnam War protests, and a general revolt against prevailing cultural norms – liberalism as a symbol increasingly acquired cultural and racial overtones (see also Carmines and Stimson 1989; Edsall and Edsall 1992; Huckfeldt and Kohfeld 1989). As Perlstein notes in *Nixonland*, these "strange new angers, anxieties and resentments wracking the nation" were coopted and politicized by Richard Nixon, who pit the cultural forces of the counterculture against the "silent majority" of Americans who stood for law and order, setting in motion the rise of race and moral traditionalism as a defining basis of societal conflict (2008: xii). As Ellis and Stimson argue, this new ideological fault line is abstract, closer to broad lifestyle orientations and personality than to specific issues of public policy:

In addition to direct religious connotations, "conservative" for many Americans connotes an approach to family and personal life, associated strongly with traditional notions of temperance, morality, and in particular obedience to authority and social norms. Along with Church on Sunday, imagine living by conventions – marriage, family, children, and work – and you have a lifestyle often called conservative. "Conservative" in this context means conventional behavior and appearance, playing by the established rules, and fitting into established social patterns. (2012: 131)

Indeed, the liberal-conservative divide, as described here, is noticeably similar to the open and closed personality orientations described in Chapter 2 (see also Alford et al. 2005; Smith et al. 2011; see Wilson 1973 for an early statement of this position).

The upshot is that as partisan elites have organized around a single ideological dimension mass partisanship has taken on strong cultural associations. Pat Buchanan's speech at the 1992 Republican National Convention is indicative:

We stand with [President Bush] for the freedom to choose religious schools, and we stand with him against the amoral idea that gay and lesbian couples should have the same standing in law as married men and women. We stand with President Bush for right-to-life and for voluntary prayer in the public schools. And we stand against putting our wives and daughters and sisters into combat units of the United States Army. And we stand, my friends, with President Bush in favor of the right of small towns and communities to control the raw sewage of pornography that so terribly pollutes our popular culture.... Friends, this election is about more than who gets what. It is about who we are. It is about what we believe and what we stand for as Americans. There is a religious war going on in this country. It is a *cultural war*, as critical to the kind of nation we shall be as the Cold War itself. For this war is for the soul of America (emphasis added).

As a more concrete demonstration, consider the relative salience of cultural considerations in the public's evaluations of the parties between 1952 and 2004.[14] The American National Election Studies (ANES) queries respondents about what they like and dislike about the Democratic and Republican parties. We coded these open-ended responses into a number of broad categories (e.g., references to contemporary party figures, economic policy considerations; see Lavine et al. 2012). Three categories were defined as *cultural*: references to cultural policy issues (e.g., "gay rights," "school prayer"), references to liberal and conservative cultural orientations and personality types ("more open to new ways of doing things," "Birchers," "Yippies"), and references to religion ("separation of Church and State").[15] We constructed a variable indicating the proportion of respondents in a given year that listed at least one cultural consideration (a like or dislike about either party). We then constructed a similar measure for economic considerations that included references to economic policy (e.g., "Social Security," "unemployment compensation") and economic ideology ("supports social welfare," "against big government"). We calculated the ratio of the two proportions – cultural to economic – as an indicator of the relative importance of cultural considerations in party evaluations over time.[16] These estimates, which are plotted in Figure 3.2, demonstrate a sharp and sustained uptick in the relative salience of cultural matters in 1992, the year coinciding with Pat Buchanan's speech and often seen as the beginning of a wider "culture war" in American politics.

Moreover – since at least September 11th, 2001 – the parties have also sharply diverged on issues related to terrorism. These are deeply intertwined with national and ethnic identity, global integration, civil liberties, law and order, and immigration, which suggests that political preferences related to the war on terror should be closely related to cultural preferences more broadly within the mass public (e.g., Hetherington and Weiler

[14] Our investigation stops in 2004 because the ANES no longer content codes the party likes and dislikes items.

[15] The code for reconstructing these measures can be found at the lead author's website.

[16] This controls for variation in the tendency to say anything at all.

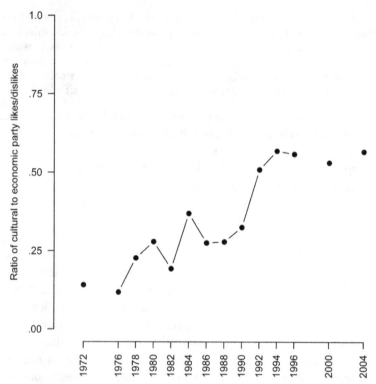

FIGURE 3.2. The rise of cultural concerns in party likes and dislikes over time

2009; Oxley et al. 2008). Indeed, the threat of terrorism is particularly evocative of concerns with social order, security, and stability.

In sum, mass partisanship is increasingly tied to cultural considerations (see also Adams 1997; Hetherington and Weiler 2009; Jacoby 2014; Layman 2001). Given the strong links between personality and cultural orientation that we reviewed in Chapter 2, citizens should thus be increasingly sorted by party as a function of personality. In line with this argument, Hetherington and Weiler (2009) demonstrate that individual differences in authoritarianism – a primary indicator of the open-closed personality dimension – have become increasingly predictive of partisan identity (see also Cizmar et al. 2014). The authors also conducted a clever experimental test of the connection between cultural and partisan divisions by making either cultural issues (i.e., LGBT rights) or New Deal issues (i.e., government spending) salient to respondents prior to having them report their perceptions of party differences. Hetherington and Weiler found that respondents assigned to the LGBT rights condition perceived the parties as substantially more polarized than did those assigned to the government spending condition.[17] Taken together, this work suggests that contemporary partisanship is strongly rooted in the emotive power of cultural disagreement. As Hetherington and Weiler explain, the increasingly partisan divide between those with contrasting cultural orientations "helps explain why politics today seems so much more acrimonious than before ... Americans are now divided over things that conjure more visceral reactions" (2009: 11).

This process of sorting should be especially pronounced among politically engaged citizens, as they are more likely to be exposed to elite rhetoric pertaining to culture-based partisan conflict (Federico and Tagar 2014; see also Federico et al. 2011; Federico and Goren 2009; Layman and Carsey 2002). Moreover, given their expressive orientation toward political life, they are also more likely to form partisan attachments based on cultural values and sympathies rooted in core aspects of personality. To summarize, we contend that elite-driven divergence in the cultural reputations of the parties has increased the extent to which dispositional openness serves as a strong input to political identity formation – a pattern that should be mainly evident among politically engaged citizens. Closed citizens should be disproportionately attracted to the Republican Party and its conservative cultural symbolism, while open citizens should gravitate toward the Democratic Party and its liberal cultural symbolism.

From Personality to Economics: The Role of Elite Messaging

Politically engaged citizens are motivated primarily by expressive goals, such that political attitudes signal broader identities. For these individuals, economic policies are not considered on their own terms – What's in it for me? How would this impact the world I live in? – but in terms of what taking one position or another on the issue signals about the self. For many economic issues, however, the social meaning of policy alternatives does not come ready-made. Instead, parties must *construct* their social meaning by linking the alternative policy options to cultural symbols and competing identity groups, thus tying economic issues to personality indirectly. In this section, we consider two processes through which personality becomes linked to economic preferences among politically engaged citizens: *partisan cue-taking* and *cultural signaling*.

---

[17] See also Bishop (2009); Feldman and Johnston (2014); Graham et al. (2009); Schwartz (2007a); Smith et al. (2011a).

First, citizens may use party identification itself as an orienting device in making policy judgments (Druckman et al. 2013; Lavine et al. 2012). In this process of partisan cue-taking, citizens adopt policy positions modeled by trusted elites who share their partisan affiliation. Indeed, this tendency is often powerful enough to lead people to ignore the ideological substance of the policies they endorse on the basis of partisan cues.[18] Dispositional factors that shape partisan attachment therefore influence how citizens perceive and evaluate economic policy debates. In particular, open citizens should seek out and accept information from Democrats and sources allied with Democrats (e.g., *The Daily Show*, *MSNBC*), while closed citizens should do the same with Republicans (e.g., Fox News, Rush Limbaugh). In this way, partisanship acts as a conduit through which personality shapes economic opinion. In effect, open and closed citizens use partisanship as a way to determine what economic positions correspond with their broader identities. As an example, Johnston and Wronski (2015) conducted an experiment to examine the relationship between three indicators of openness – authoritarianism, need for closure and conservation versus openness to change – on economic preferences. In the control condition, respondents simply reported their positions on several economic issues (e.g., privatization of Social Security), whereas in the treatment condition, stereotypical partisan cues were provided (e.g., Democrats were said to support the more liberal policy option). The authors found the link between openness and economic preferences to be significantly stronger in the presence of cues, suggesting that party labels aid citizens in linking their dispositions to concrete proposals on economic debates.[19]

Second, personality may influence economic preferences indirectly by shaping how citizens respond to cultural signals provided by elites. Cultural signaling occurs when elites make statements that reveal information about their cultural orientation in close proximity to position-taking on an economic issue. Such signals may earn the public's affection

---

[18] See Berinsky 2007; Cohen 2003; Druckman et al. 2013; Lavine et al. 2012; Lenz 2012; Samuels and Zucco 2014; Zaller 1992; c.f., Bullock 2011. It is also important to note that cue-taking may occur because party affinities allow individuals to surmount two major challenges in forming preferences: the complexity of many policy debates and the average citizen's desire to make confident political judgments without expending too much cognitive effort (Lavine et al. 2012).

[19] We explore these data more deeply in Chapter 6. Johnston and Wronski (2015) find a moderating influence of party cues for the economic, but not for the social domain of public policy (e.g., gay marriage), again suggesting that the former is particularly difficult, and thus particularly susceptible to elite influence.

and trust on the basis of cultural similarity, and these assets can then be used to sway opinion on economic issues. Cultural signaling is thus an instance of the more general concept of "affect transfer" often cited in work in the symbolic politics tradition (e.g., Lodge and Taber 2013; Sears 1993). For example, Tesler (2012) has shown that attitudes toward health insurance reform in the Obama era have been "racialized," such that anti-black affect has spilled over onto a putatively race-neutral economic issue. That is, racial attitudes primed by Obama become linked to health insurance preferences because Obama is linked to health insurance reform. These preferences become expressions of racial attitudes rather than instrumentally-motivated beliefs about the value of reform itself.

In a similar fashion, evaluations of political actors that are rooted in perceptions of cultural similarity should transfer to evaluations of economic positions. As a concrete example, on January 13, 2015, Texas State Representative Debbie Riddle posted the following for her followers on Facebook:

This is the 1st day of our Legislative Session here in Texas. I am rolling up the sleeves of my new red dress & getting to work. I have several bills I think you may like. One will protect women & children from going into a ladies restroom & finding a man who feels like he is a woman that day. Property tax is another issue we will be addressing. Of course 2nd Amendment rights & my Open Carry bill will be a major focus for me this Session. Not raising taxes is important & limiting the size of government is critical. I set politics aside & focus on getting the job done with honor & dignity. Thank you for allowing me to serve you.

In this post, Representative Riddle initially signals her endorsement of cultural conservatism by expressing disdain for transgender individuals. She then pairs this disdain with a statement about limiting the size of government. To the extent that dispositionally closed citizens are attracted to the cultural signal, this affect may spill over into judgments about property taxes and limited government.

Similarly, cultural signaling may entail framing economic issues in terms of "easier" cultural conflicts. Pollock and colleagues explain that easy issues readily call to mind relevant values and life experiences and "require only minimal political attentiveness to be understood by ordinary citizens," whereas understanding of hard issues "will depend on whether opportunistic 'cultural entrepreneurs' can successfully frame the issue as a battle over core values" (1993: 30–1). For example, Democrats helped build support for health care reform in 2009 among cultural liberals by framing the issue in terms of gender equality. Democratic House leader Nancy Pelosi explicitly connected her support for insurance reform to questions of equity for women: "It's personal for women ... my sisters here in the Congress, this was a big issue for us.... After we pass this bill, being a woman will no longer be a preexisting medical condition."[20] In a similar vein, Republican elites created opposition to health care reform among cultural conservatives by framing it as "un-American." For example, Republican House member Michele Bachmann argued on cable news program *Fox and Friends* that "socialized medicine is the crown jewel of socialism. This will change our country forever."[21] In line with this rhetoric, the belief that "the American way of doing things" needs to be protected from foreign contamination strongly predicts opposition to health care reform, especially among Republicans (Knoll and Shewmaker 2015). To the extent that cultural orientations are structured by dispositional openness, the framing of economic issues in cultural terms should strengthen the relationship between personality and economic opinion.

In sum, we expect both of these mechanisms – partisan cue-taking and cultural signaling – to play a role in connecting personality to economic preferences among politically engaged citizens. They are also likely to reinforce one another: closed individuals should gravitate to the Republican Party, take cues from Republican elites, and respond positively to conservative cultural signals, while open individuals should do the opposite. Over time, these processes should reinforce initial partisan sorting, forging stronger mutual links between personality, party identification, and economic values and policy preferences.

Summary

The crux of our argument is that the relationship between personality and economic opinion hinges critically on the manner in which citizens make sense of economic policy conflict. We expect unengaged citizens to evaluate economic debates largely in instrumental terms, asking themselves: *is this policy likely to produce outcomes that I find appealing?* In contrast, we expect politically engaged citizens to be more concerned with the social implications of their economic preferences, asking: *is this opinion consistent with who I claim to be in my social relationships, and with my broader identity and cultural commitments?* We claim that engaged citizens rely on information provided by party elites to learn what being "open" or "closed" implies with respect to economic policy. At present, Democratic

---

[20] www.washingtonpost.com/wp-dyn/content/article/2010/03/26/AR2010032602225.html
[21] *Fox and Friends*, November 3, 2009.

opinion leaders offer a combination of cultural liberalism and support for government protection in the economic realm, while Republican opinion leaders offer an amalgam of cultural conservatism and support for free markets. Given culture-based partisan sorting through personality, we expect engaged citizens with an open orientation to favor greater government intervention in the economy, and engaged citizens with a closed orientation to favor limited government. In essence, political engagement – and the expressive orientation it implies – reverses the default tendency for open citizens to support free markets and closed citizens to support a more interventionist economic stance on instrumental grounds.

The Potential for Racial and Ethnic Heterogeneity

We have now presented the basic claims of our model. However, to this point we have ignored the importance of race and ethnicity in American politics. This is consistent with previous research on personality and politics, which, with rare exceptions (Gerber et al. 2010), does not explore racial and ethnic heterogeneity in personality processes. Here, we pause to consider whether our model is more applicable to some groups than others. We think it is. Specifically, we consider potential differences among self-identified non-Latino whites, blacks, and Latinos, who, taken together, comprise more than 90 percent of the U.S. population (2014 American Community Survey).[22]

For two reasons, we believe our model may *not* apply to African Americans. First, there is far less variation in economic opinion among blacks than among other racial and ethnic groups.[23] For example, consider the "government spending and services" item in the American National Election Study surveys. In the 2012 study, non-Latino whites were spread fairly evenly over the seven categories of this item. Blacks, however, were concentrated at the liberal end of the scale. Indeed, only about 10 percent of African Americans report a conservative preference on this item. Consider also the standard three-item ANES limited government battery (i.e., which gauges preferences about whether the government or markets should play a more prominent role in economic matters).

[22] Given the relatively small numbers of respondents from other minority groups available in the surveys we rely on, statistical considerations preclude us from considering them in our analyses.

[23] We will use the terms "African-American" and "black," and the terms "Latino" and "Hispanic," interchangeably, because racial and ethnic self-identification is often measured in our data with both of the terms in each set (e.g., "Are you Hispanic or Latino?").

In 2012, only 4 percent of African Americans agreed with all three of the market-supportive statements, while 63 percent agreed with all three of the pro-government statements. The strong tendency for black Americans to reject conservative economic values and policies reduces the potential impact of personality, because there is simply much less variation to explain. Second, we have argued that personality works primarily through political identification and elite cue-taking among engaged citizens, such that open citizens identify with and take economic cues from Democrats and liberals, while closed citizens listen to Republicans and conservatives. As with preferences on economic issues, however, there is little variation in partisan affiliation among African Americans. An almost exclusive identification with the Democrats sharply constrains a primary pathway by which openness operates among engaged citizens. For these two reasons, we expect the impact of openness on economic opinion to be sharply reduced among self-identified black Americans.

To a lesser extent, these two points also apply to self-identified Hispanics. Latinos report conservative preferences on the spending and services item about 25 percent of the time, and they endorse all three limited government statements about 15 percent of the time. Thus, while Latinos are economically liberal on average, the distribution is far less skewed than for African Americans. This suggests that personality may have more leverage on Latino opinion than on black opinion. Similarly, Latinos skew toward the Democrats in terms of political identity, but much less so than do African Americans. In 2012, for example, about 22 percent of Latinos identified as Republican, while about 63 percent identified as Democrats. Overall, then, we might consider Latinos to fall somewhere between African Americans and non-Latino whites with respect to the potential for personality to influence economic preferences.

These theoretical considerations are necessarily speculative, as researchers have almost universally ignored racial and ethnic heterogeneity in building theories of personality and political preferences. This is a major gap in the literature. To address it, we will test our hypotheses using all available survey respondents, controlling for race in our analyses. This will allow us to obtain an overall test of our key hypotheses. When possible, we will follow these full-sample analyses with separate tests of our predictions among African Americans and Latinos, in an effort to catalog whatever heterogeneity exists. Although our expectations for such group-based differences are speculative, we propose that our model will apply strongly for whites and weakly (or not at all) for African Americans, with Latinos falling somewhere in the middle, and perhaps closer to whites than blacks. We see our work in this vein as a first step in a long overdue investigation, and we hope our efforts will spur more research on this topic.

Hypotheses

On the basis of the foregoing theoretical discussion, we derive four hypotheses to be tested in the following chapters. In Chapter 4, we provide an extensive empirical examination of the *reversal hypothesis*:

Among the politically *unengaged*, open citizens will be *less* supportive of government intervention in economic matters than closed citizens; among the politically *engaged*, however, open citizens will be *more* supportive of government intervention than closed citizens.

Our next set of hypotheses considers the mechanisms by which personality structures economic opinion to produce the reversal effect. First, we have argued that political identity and information seeking are tightly linked to personality among engaged citizens, but not unengaged citizens. This *dispositional sorting hypothesis* is tested in Chapter 5:

Citizens with an open orientation will identify more with left-wing ideological labels, the Democratic Party, and associated left-wing sources of political information, while citizens with a closed orientation will identify more with right-wing ideological labels, the Republican Party, and associated right-wing sources of political information. This relationship will be strong among the politically engaged, but weak or nonexistent among the politically unengaged.

Second, we expect engaged – but not unengaged – citizens to use elite cues as a means of identifying how their traits and cultural commitments map onto economic issues. We refer to these cues as "stereotypical" when Republicans and cultural conservatives oppose government intervention in economic life and cultural liberals and Democrats support such intervention. In contrast, we refer to them as "counter-stereotypical" when the opposite relationship holds (e.g., when Republicans are said to take a position on an economic issue to the left of the Democrats). By examining both stereotypical and counter-stereotypical cues, we are able to demonstrate that social and expressive concerns often trump substantive economic policy content among engaged citizens. We test this *elite influence hypothesis* in a series of experimental and observational studies in Chapter 6:

The presence of *stereotypical* partisan, ideological, and cultural cues will strengthen the positive relationship between openness and support for government intervention. By contrast, the presence of *counter-stereotypical* partisan, ideological, and cultural cues will weaken the positive relationship between openness and support for government intervention – or reverse the relationship altogether. The effect of cues will be strong among the engaged, but weak or non-existent among the unengaged.

Finally, in Chapter 7, we examine whether political engagement inhibits the use of instrumental considerations in making economic policy judgments. We do this by surveying the manner in which engagement conditions the impact of markers of self-interest such as household income, risk of unemployment, and loss of health insurance on attitudes toward economic policy. Specifically, we test the *self-interest hypothesis* in Chapter 7:

The strength of the relationship between markers of self-interest and economic opinion will *decrease* as political engagement *increases*.

Conclusion

In this chapter, we outlined a theory of personality and economic preferences that highlights the interactions among personality, political engagement, and elite messaging. Despite its multiple moving parts, the intuition behind our model is straightforward. First, we claim that citizens engage in politics because of the expressive benefits that participation affords. Second, we claim that engaged citizens with open personalities are attracted to the cultural left, and in turn adopt the interventionist economic positions of their Democratic co-partisans and cultural affiliates as a package deal. Conversely, engaged citizens with closed personalities are attracted to the cultural right and adopt the limited government economic preferences of their Republican co-partisans and affiliates. Among the engaged, parties organize policies into ideological packages, and personality organizes citizens into parties. One novel implication of these claims is that linkages between personality and economic opinion are not always rooted in direct psychological resonance or elective affinity; rather, they are constructions that follow from the manner in which elites currently compete for political power.

Third, a great many citizens show little concern for the status contests that preoccupy the nation's culture warriors. Among these politically unengaged individuals, we claim, personality and economic opinion are related in a more organic fashion. Given their strong needs for order, certainty, and security, closed citizens should support a robust government role in the economy as a means of reducing the risks and uncertainties associated with free market capitalism. By contrast, we expect unengaged citizens with open personalities – who are more willing to accept uncertainty and risk – to question the need for an activist government, and to be more attracted to the individual freedom and choice offered by relatively unfettered markets.

4

Testing the Reversal Hypothesis

In the previous chapter, we developed the logic behind the reversal hypothesis: that openness promotes support for government intervention in the economy among the politically engaged and opposition among the politically unengaged. In this chapter, we report a number of empirical tests of this dynamic, providing the strongest evidence to date that dispositional openness structures economic opinion in the United States. To ensure that our results are robust, we test the reversal hypothesis using six distinct measures of openness in ten datasets spanning twenty years of American politics (1992–2012). As we will see, a clear and consistent pattern emerges across diverse settings.

Our empirical strategy makes extensive use of regression analysis. Since almost all the regression models we will report in this chapter follow a similar form, we briefly describe this common model before delving into our findings. As shown in equation (1), in each dataset we model economic preferences as a function of dispositional openness and its interaction with political engagement. The interaction term allows the influence of openness to vary across citizens depending on how politically engaged they are. The reversal hypothesis posits that the coefficient for openness ($\beta 1$) will be opposite in sign to the coefficient for the interaction of openness and engagement ($\beta 3$), and that the absolute value of the latter will be larger than the former.

$$\hat{y} = \beta_0 + \beta_1(openness) + \beta_2(engagement) + \beta_3(openness \times engagement)$$
$$+ \sum_{k=1}^{K} \gamma_k \, control \, variable_k \tag{1}$$

This is because the former tells us how openness influences opinion when political engagement is at its minimum value (i.e., zero), while the latter tells us how the influence of openness changes as engagement increases from minimum to maximum. For example, if we are predicting support for social welfare spending, and β_1 is estimated to be -0.50 and β_3 is estimated to be 1.00, then openness decreases support for social welfare by 50 percentage points among the unengaged, but increases support for social welfare by 50 points among the highly engaged (i.e., $-50 + 100 = 50$). That is, as engagement increases from low to high, the effect of openness increases from -50 to 50, an overall change of 100 points. This basic pattern will be replicated many times in the coming analyses, and can be seen in the regression tables reported in the appendix to this chapter.

In each analysis, our dependent variable is an indicator of preferences for more or less government intervention in economic matters. In some cases, we rely on general values concerning the proper role of government versus markets. In other cases, we use specific policy items such as taxes and spending or government versus private health insurance. As is typical in this literature, we will often average over policy-specific heterogeneity by creating scales from the highly correlated individual policy items. These scales represent a more general, latent policy orientation toward redistribution, social insurance, and market regulation (e.g., Ansolabehere, Rodden, and Snyder 2008; Feldman and Johnston 2014). To keep things simple, we always code the dependent variable so that higher scores indicate a preference for a *larger* government role (i.e., "liberalism") and lower scores indicate a preference for *limiting* the role of government (i.e., "conservatism"). For ease of discussion, we will occasionally refer to the dependent variable as "economic liberalism."

We operationalize political engagement as interest in and knowledge about American politics. In most cases, our measure of engagement consists of a scale created from responses to standard political knowledge questions and subjective questions about the respondent's interest in politics (these two variables are, as one might expect, highly correlated).[1] We also include in our models a set of standard control variables, including age, gender, race and ethnicity, education, income, employment status,

---

[1] This construction also implies that a strong interest in politics can partially offset a lack of factual knowledge, and vice versa. Such "mixed" individuals will occupy middle values of the engagement scale. We think this is a reasonable way to think about engagement. For example, many people may be unable to identify the Chief Justice of the U.S. Supreme Court, but may nonetheless care enough about contemporary policy debates to assimilate some of the positions of their favored elites. Similarly, some people who claim to be uninterested may nonetheless know a good deal about American politics. Still, the *most* engaged citizens will have both a great deal of interest and knowledge. An alternative

union membership, and Southern residency. The controls occasionally vary due to data limitations; we indicate when this is so. We do not control for partisanship and ideological identification (as some readers might expect) because these are *mediators* of the effects of personality. For example, the impact of personality on economic opinion may be channeled by the initial effect of the former on party identification, with economic opinions being subsequently driven by partisan cue-taking (see Chapters 5 and 6; see also Johnston and Wronski 2015). Therefore, controlling for these political predispositions would obscure any impact of personality that operates through them. One need only control for party identification and political ideology if one posits that they cause both personality and economic attitudes. Ultimately, we assume – along with the vast majority of scholars in this literature (e.g., Gerber et al. 2010; Jost et al. 2003; Mondak 2010) – that our indicators of personality are exogenous to political identity.[2]

Our key independent variable is dispositional openness, as defined in previous chapters. Given that scholars have used a wide array of indicators to distinguish between open and closed personality orientations, we tap this general dimension in various ways throughout this chapter. These variables are available in a number of public datasets and in nationally representative datasets we have collected ourselves. Some of these indicators are "naturally" coded so that higher values imply closed personalities. For example, high levels of authoritarianism, need for closure, and conscientiousness correspond to a closed personality orientation. Other indicators are either naturally coded so that high values indicate openness (i.e., openness to experience) or can be coded in either direction without loss of intuition (e.g., openness to change versus conservation values). Thus, in some cases, high scores on our key independent variable correspond to dispositionally open citizens, and, in other cases, they correspond to dispositionally closed citizens. This should be clear in

---

modeling strategy would include interactions of openness with both knowledge and interest separately. We choose the more parsimonious approach of a single engagement scale. Again, these two variables are correlated.

[2] It is, of course, always possible that this assumption is incorrect, and that personality is shaped extensively by political identity. If true, this would force a major paradigm shift in the study of personality and politics. For better or worse, our study operates within the current paradigm. As we will see, however, most items used to measure openness in this literature appear face-valid as exogenous indicators. Indeed, in at least one case, exogeneity to political identity and values was the very impetus for the creation of the items (Feldman and Stenner 1997; Stenner 2005). We will provide more discussion of these issues in the concluding chapter when we turn a critical eye to our theory and results.

each case simply given the name of the variable (e.g., need for *closure* or *openness* to experience), but we will be explicit about how to interpret each analysis.

A final modeling consideration concerns race and ethnicity. As discussed in Chapter 3, there is good reason to expect that the influence of openness will vary across racial and ethnic groups. However, data availability often limits our ability to examine such variation. In most nationally representative surveys, the sample size is between 1,000–2,000 individuals, which leaves only small samples of minority group members, and thus low power for detecting conditional effects like the one we have proposed. Our strategy for examining racial and ethnic heterogeneity is thus as follows. We first examine the reversal effect for all respondents, and simply control for race and ethnicity in our regression models. In the last empirical section of this chapter, we turn to an examination of racial and ethnic heterogeneity in the effects of openness. Specifically, we draw on representative data where we have sufficient minority group observations to reliably estimate the reversal effect, and we estimate separate models for self-identified African Americans and Latinos (these are the only two minority groups for whom we have sufficient observations). We do not report separate models for non-Latino whites, but we discuss the patterns we have observed in our examinations of this group. As a general matter, the pattern for whites is largely identical to what we observe in the first sections of this chapter using the full samples, albeit effect sizes for openness are typically larger in magnitude. As we will see, however, there is heterogeneity when we examine minority group members separately. Specifically, personality matters little for black Americans, while Latinos look more similar to the full sample and to whites in terms of the influence of openness on economic opinion. This is consistent with our discussion in Chapter 3.

Regression estimates for all models and groups are presented in the chapter appendix. In the body of this chapter, we report key findings for the joint impact of openness and engagement in a more readily interpretable graphical format. In all figures, except where indicated, the y-axis represents our estimate of the quantity of interest: the difference between open and closed citizens in terms of average economic liberalism.[3] The y-axis thus represents the estimated *relationship* between openness and

[3] For nonlinear models (e.g., ordered probit for ordinal dependent variables), we estimate the average effect of openness on the predicted probabilities of category membership using the observed value approach. That is, we calculate the effect for all observations in the data, and then average over the data to obtain the overall estimate. This accounts for

economic preferences. The x-axis represents increasing levels of political engagement, ranging from the lowest sample values at the origin to the highest sample values at the upper end.[4] Taken as a whole, each plot shows how the relationship between openness and economic preferences changes as political engagement varies over its entire range. Consistent with our theory, we expect this relationship to reverse in sign as engagement changes from low to high. We make this reversal easier to see by placing a horizontal dashed line at the zero value of the y-axis.

We plot two sets of estimates for each model, one representing the difference in economic attitudes between citizens at the 5th and the 95th percentiles of a given measure of openness, and one representing the difference between those at the 25th and 75th percentiles. These estimates are placed side by side at each level of engagement, with filled circles representing the 5–95 percent effect and open circles representing the 25–75 percent effect. The former shows the practical maximum effect of each personality trait at a given level of engagement, while the latter shows the expected change in economic attitudes as the trait varies from moderately low to moderately high. Extended vertical lines from point estimates represent 95 percent confidence intervals.[5] These intervals indicate the range of values within which we are reasonably confident that the true value of the parameter rests given the assumptions of the statistical model. The 95 percent intervals, in conjunction with the horizontal dashed line at y = 0 can be used to conduct standard significance tests for the effect of openness at each level of engagement.

We begin by examining five widely used indicators of the open-closed personality dimension: *authoritarianism, need for closure, openness to experience, conscientiousness*, and Schwartz's (1992) *openness to change versus conservation* value dimension. In a final set of analyses, we rely on *dispositional risk aversion* as our measure of openness, and we switch out political engagement with a measure of whether individuals rely on personal (i.e., self-interested) or impersonal (i.e., other-interested) criteria in making judgments about economic matters. We then turn to our results for blacks and Latinos.

the fact that the effect is conditional on the value of all other variables in the model (see Hanmer and Kalkan 2013).

4 Rather than crowd the x-axis with labels, we simply label the origin, the midpoint, and the endpoint of the engagement scale as "Low," "Medium," and "High," respectively. In most cases, we will estimate the effect of openness at five values of engagement to cover the range of this variable: 0, 0.25, 0.5, 0.75, and 1. As the equation for the conditional effect of openness is a linear function of engagement in the case of OLS, and typically close to linear (at least locally) in the case of nonlinear models, visual interpolation can be used to obtain rough estimates at values of engagement in between those we report.

5 We use simulation from the joint posterior distribution of the model parameters to obtain confidence bounds for all quantities reported in figures (see Gelman and Hill 2007, Chapter 7).

Authoritarianism and Economic Preferences

We begin our analysis of the reversal hypothesis by examining the trait of authoritarianism. Defined as a preference for social conformity over individual autonomy (Feldman 2003), authoritarianism is perhaps the most intensively studied dispositional construct in political psychology. Contemporary scholars view its manifestations as a functional response to chronic feelings of threat and an aversion to disorder and uncertainty. As Hetherington and Weiler explain, "the reason people at opposite ends of the authoritarianism distribution differ in their feelings about a range of issues under most circumstances is because those scoring high tend to perceive threats fairly constantly in their battle to achieve clarity and impose order" (2009: 34). Numerous studies have shown that authoritarians are highly sensitive to threat in the environment. Experimental work indicates that high (but not low) authoritarians respond to threat by expressing heightened political intolerance (Feldman 2003; Stenner 2005), by avoiding information that runs counter to their political preferences (Feldman and Stenner 1997; Lavine et al. 2005), and by denigrating members of out-groups (Greenberg et al. 1990). Authoritarians are also more persuaded by messages when they are framed as threats or potential losses rather than as opportunities or potential gains (Lavine et al. 1999).

Observational studies indicate that authoritarianism is linked to a fear of falling prey to a variety of societal ills (e.g., Duckitt 2001), prompting Altemeyer (1996) to write that authoritarians "stand about ten steps closer to the panic button than the rest of the population." As evidence of authoritarianism's deep-seated nature, authoritarians appear to be more sensitive to threatening concepts even when they are presented below the level of conscious awareness. For example, Lavine and colleagues (2002) found that high (vs. low) authoritarians responded more quickly to threatening but not non-threatening words (e.g., "war" vs. "sunshine") on an automatic word recognition task. They also found that authoritarians responded more quickly to target words that are semantically related to threatening connotations of a dual meaning prime (e.g., the target word "weapons" when following the prime word "arms") but *not* to target words that are semantically related to nonthreatening connotations of the prime (e.g., the target word "legs" when following the prime word "arms"). Hetherington and Weiler (2009) also present evidence from survey data that authoritarianism is linked to other traits related to uncertainty aversion, such as the need for cognition and closure (see also Jost et al. 2003 for a review of earlier research). Taken together, this work suggests that authoritarianism captures an absence of dispositional openness: high levels of the trait stand in opposition to tolerance for threat and uncertainty, the appreciation of difference and complexity, and a preference for a diverse range of life experiences.

However, measurement problems have plagued research on authoritarianism ever since Adorno and colleagues (1950) introduced their original F-scale to tap the construct. As Altemeyer (1981) and others have detailed, the F-scale suffers from several deficiencies, including a reliance on positively worded items (inviting acquiescence bias) and poor internal consistency. Altemeyer (1981, 1988) successfully tackled the response bias and reliability problems with a reconceptualized and updated version of the measure that he referred to as Right-Wing Authoritarianism (RWA). Unfortunately, the RWA scale – as political scientists have pointed out – suffers from the inclusion of explicitly *political* content (e.g., "gays and lesbians are just as healthy and moral as anyone else," reverse scored). As Stenner argues, "the scale is tainted throughout by specific references to what ought to be done with minorities, dissidents, and deviants; it essentially sums the very attitudes we are endeavoring to explain" (2005: 22–33). To avoid the obvious problem of tautological relationships, measures of personality should capture relevant motivational and cognitive proclivities without referencing specific political objects, actors, or events.

With these considerations in mind, we follow other political scientists in relying on a four-item battery of childrearing values to tap a predisposition to authoritarianism (e.g., Feldman and Stenner 1997; Hetherington and Weiler 2009; Stenner 2005). The items are presented to respondents with the following instruction: "Although there are a number of qualities that people feel that children should have, every person thinks that some are more important than others. I am going to read you pairs of desirable qualities. Please tell me which one you think is more important for a child to have." The four dichotomous forced-choice items are independence versus respect for elders, obedience versus self-reliance, curiosity versus good manners, and being considerate versus being well behaved. High authoritarianism is indicated by a preference for "obedience," "respect for elders," "good manners," and "well-behaved," whereas low authoritarianism is indicated by a preference for "self-reliance," "independence," "curiosity," and "considerate."[6] These items are designed to create a trade-off between a promotive and self-directed personality type and a preventive one that requires adherence to established norms, authorities, rules, and institutions.

---

[6] These items have also been utilized to measure Lakoff's (2002) "strict father" and "nurturing parent" moralities (Barker and Tinnick 2006). These two moral schemas map closely to the closed and open personality types, respectively. They also overlap substantially with openness to experience from the Big Five and various values from the openness versus conservation dimension in Schwartz's (1992) value theory.

Cross-sectional Tests in the 2000–2012 American National Election Studies

Our first empirical tests utilize data from the 2000, 2004, 2008, and 2012 American National Election Studies (ANES).[7] The ANES is the premier survey of American public opinion and political behavior during election years, and includes nationally representative samples of the American public. These four studies contain both a broad set of economic preference measures as well as the childrearing values (see Table 4.1). We constructed a scale for each ANES year by summing the responses to the four childrearing items, with higher values reflecting high authoritarianism (i.e., a closed personality) and lower values reflecting low authoritarianism (i.e., an open personality). Our first dependent variable – operationalized identically in all four ANES years – taps broad values related to the role of government in economic matters. Each of the three items asks respondents to choose between two statements: one that expresses skepticism of markets and a preference for more government involvement in economic matters, and one that expresses skepticism about the role of government and a preference for free markets and individual responsibility. These items are commonly used in political science as a measure of support for the value of *limited government*. We created a scale by summing responses to the three items, with higher values reflecting greater *support* for government intervention in the economy. That is, our dependent variable is coded so that higher values indicate economic liberalism.

Our second dependent variable utilizes several policy preference items related to social welfare and redistribution, operationalized similarly in each ANES survey. In 2000 and 2004, we rely on three items: preferences for (1) more or less government spending and services; (2) government-guaranteed jobs and income; and (3) government or private provision of health insurance.[8] The same three items were available in 2008; however, we excluded the guaranteed jobs question as only half of the sample received it.[9] In 2012, we rely on these same

---

[7] Extensive information regarding the ANES generally and these specific studies can be found here: www.electionstudies.org/.

[8] In 2000, respondents were randomly assigned to receive one of two item formats. The first utilized the typical ANES seven-point scale format, while the second utilized a branching format resulting in a five-point scale. The three middle options of the former were combined to form a five-point scale, and the two samples were combined to maximize sample size. In 2004, 2008, and 2012, all respondents received the seven-point format.

[9] In addition, half of the sample was randomly assigned to receive new versions of the health insurance and spending items. Both of the new versions of these items utilized slightly different wordings and a branching format. We combine the two subsamples to maximize sample size.

TABLE 4.1. *Measurement of key variables in the American*
National Election Studies

___

Authoritarianism (all years)

Although there are a number of qualities that people feel that children should have, every person thinks that some are more important than others. I am going to read you pairs of desirable qualities. Please tell me which one you think is more important for a child to have ("open" values are on the left and "closed" values are on the right):

(1) Self-Reliance or Obedience
(2) Independent or Respect for Elders
(3) Curiosity or Good Manners
(4) Considerate or Well-Behaved

Economic Values (all years)

Next, I am going to ask you to choose which of two statements I read comes closer to your own opinion. You might agree to some extent with both, but we want to know which one is closer to your own views.

(1) "The main reason government has become bigger over the years is because it has gotten involved in things that people should do for themselves," or "Government has become bigger because the problems we face have become bigger."
(2) "We need a strong government to handle today's complex economic problems," or "The free market can handle these problems without government being involved."
(3) "The less government, the better," or "There are more things the government should be doing."

Economic Policy Attitudes

2000, 2004, and half of sample in 2008:

(1) Some people think the government should provide fewer services even in areas such as health and education in order to reduce spending. Other people feel it is important for the government to provide many more services even if it means an increase in spending.
(2) Some people feel there should be a government insurance plan which would cover all medical and hospital expenses for everyone. Others feel that all medical expenses should be paid by individuals through private insurance plans like Blue Cross or other company-paid plans.
(3) Some people feel the government in Washington should see to it that every person has a job and a good standard of living. Others think the government should just let each person get ahead on their own.

2008 (half of sample):

(1) Do you think the government should provide MORE services than it does now, FEWER services than it does now, or ABOUT THE SAME NUMBER of services as it does now?
(2) Do you FAVOR, OPPOSE, or NEITHER FAVOR NOR OPPOSE the U.S. government paying for all necessary medical care for all Americans?

2012:

(1) Same as 2000 and 2004

(2) Same as 2000 and 2004

(3) Same as 2000 and 2004

(4) Do you favor, oppose, or neither favor nor oppose the health care reform law passed in 2010? This law requires all Americans to buy health insurance and requires health insurance companies to accept everyone.

(5) A proposal has been made that would allow people to put a portion of their Social Security payroll taxes into personal retirement accounts that would be invested in stocks and bonds. Do you FAVOR this idea, OPPOSE it, or NEITHER FAVOR NOR OPPOSE IT?

---

three items, along with two additional ones that were only included in this study: opposition to the new "health care law" (i.e., the Affordable Care Act) and support for the partial privatization of Social Security. Higher values on each scale represent support for greater government intervention.[10] Finally, political engagement was operationalized similarly in each year as the average of two measures of political interest and one of political knowledge.[11]

The results are displayed in Figures 4.1 (for economic values) and 4.2 (for economic policy preferences).[12] Panels A through D of Figure 4.1

---

[10] The reliability of the three-item scales in 2000 and 2004 were 0.59 and 0.71, respectively. In 2008, the correlation between the spending and insurance items was 0.42. The reliability of the five-item scale in 2012 was 0.74. An exploratory factor analysis of the latter items strongly indicates a single-factor solution. The reader might also wonder about the relationship between authoritarianism and more straightforward questions of redistribution from rich to poor. We also replicated the reversal pattern for the classic ANES items asking whether we should increase or decrease federal spending on "welfare programs" and "the poor." Given that welfare has strong racial associations and the spending on the poor item has limited variance (most people think we should spend more), we choose to focus on the standard ANES seven-point policy scales that use a more balanced presentation and more concrete policy content. It is notable, given the limitations of the poor and welfare spending items, that the reversal effect still holds.

[11] In each year, political interest is measured with two items: self-reported interest in political campaigns and the extent to which the respondent generally follows government and public affairs. In 2000 and 2004, political knowledge was measured with six factual questions. In 2008, we rely on the interviewer's subjective rating of the respondent's political knowledge. In 2012, we use nine factual items to measure knowledge. The alpha coefficients for the overall engagement scales in the 2000–2012 studies are, respectively, 0.73, 0.72, 0.67, and 0.71.

[12] Regression models for economic values were estimated via maximum likelihood with an ordered probit link, while models for policy preferences were estimated via ordinary least squares. Replication code and data for all analyses in this book are available at the first author's website.

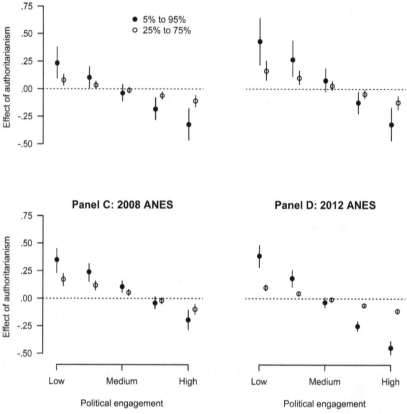

FIGURE 4.1. The relationship between authoritarianism and liberal economic values across political engagement, 2000–2012 ANES

show the relationship between authoritarianism and economic values at varying levels of political engagement in 2000, 2004, 2008, and 2012, respectively. Recall that the y-axis represents the estimated difference between high and low authoritarians in support for government over markets.[13] The x-axis represents increasing levels of political engagement. As can be seen in the figure, the pattern strongly conforms to the reversal hypothesis.

[13] For the economic values models, we report the change in the predicted probability that a respondent with a given level of engagement provides two or more responses supportive of a greater government role in economic matters. In other words, we report the change in probability of scoring 2 or 3 (versus 0 or 1) on the values dependent variable.

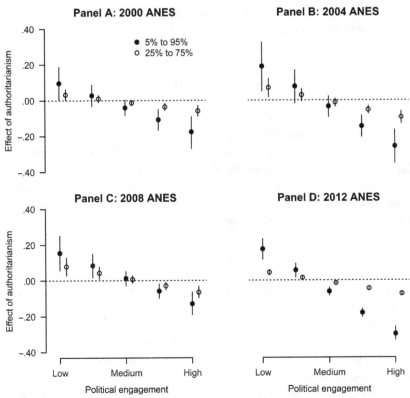

FIGURE 4.2. The relationship between authoritarianism and economic policy liberalism across political engagement, 2000–2012 ANES

The positive estimates at low and medium-low levels of political engagement indicate that authoritarianism is associated with skepticism about the sufficiency of markets, and with support for a greater government role in the economy. In other words, unengaged citizens who score high on authoritarianism are significantly more economically *liberal* than those who score low on authoritarianism. High authoritarians, for example, are more likely than low authoritarians to believe that "we need a strong government to handle today's complex economic problems," while low authoritarians are more likely to believe that "the free market can handle these problems without the government being involved."

Moreover, these relationships are of substantial magnitude. The y-axis can be interpreted as the shift in economic liberalism associated with a particular change in authoritarianism. Thus, unengaged citizens at moderately high (75%) levels of authoritarianism are between five and fifteen percentage points more economically liberal than their counterparts at moderately low (25%) levels of authoritarianism.[14] Comparing citizens at the upper (95%) and lower (5%) ends of authoritarianism, the differences are particularly stark. Across the four election years, high authoritarians at low levels of engagement are between ten and forty percentage points more liberal than unengaged low authoritarians. In all four years, the results strongly confirm our expectations for instrumentally motivated citizens: those with a closed personality prefer a stronger government hand in the economy than comparatively open citizens.

When we turn to engaged citizens, the relationship between authoritarianism and economic values is strikingly different. Among those who know and care about politics, authoritarianism is associated with greater *opposition* to government involvement in the economy, as indicated by the negative, statistically significant estimates in Panels A–D of Figure 4.1. At high levels of engagement, it is low authoritarians (i.e., open citizens) who prefer government intervention and high authoritarians (i.e., closed citizens) who support a greater role for markets. These effect sizes are also substantial, essentially mirroring those for the unengaged.[15] This pattern is consistent with our expectations for expressively motivated citizens, who bring their economic preferences into line with their cultural orientations and with those of co-partisan elites.

Figure 4.2 presents the results for our second dependent variable: support for social welfare and redistribution, including taxes and spending on social services, employment and unemployment protection, health insurance, and the privatization of Social Security. The overall pattern is essentially identical to what we observe for economic values. At low and moderately low levels of political engagement, high authoritarians are more likely to support increases in government spending and services than low authoritarians. This pattern holds in all four election years. In line with the reversal hypothesis, at high and moderately high levels of engagement, it is just the opposite: those *low* in authoritarianism are more likely to prefer a strong government role in the provision of economic security. And again, the effect sizes are substantial. Large changes in authoritarianism correspond to ten to thirty percentage point shifts in economic policy preferences, with the largest effects in 2012

---

[14] The effect varies a bit from year to year, and is smaller as engagement increases. We report ranges of effect sizes throughout this chapter to capture this variation.

[15] The estimate for engaged citizens in 2008 is somewhat smaller, however. This may reflect the substantial economic uncertainty present during this time period.

among engaged citizens. In sum, using two distinct operationalizations of economic opinion (i.e., economic values and economic policy attitudes), and across four election studies, we find that authoritarianism is a strong and significant predictor of economic preferences, but that the qualitative nature of the relationship is diametrically opposite across levels of political engagement.

Authoritarianism and Health Insurance Reform: The 1992–1994 ANES Panel Study

The foregoing analyses relied on cross-sectional data to examine the conditional relationship between authoritarianism and economic opinion. Our assumption is that personality is causally prior to economic preferences. Although we find the reverse causal sequence unlikely, it is worthwhile to consider the impact of authoritarianism using a model that offers stronger leverage on causal direction. Fortunately, the ANES conducted a panel study in 1992 and 1994 that is well suited to our purposes. First, the 1992 wave contains the same four authoritarianism items used in our cross-sectional models. Second, the two waves straddle a significant national debate over health insurance reform, and they each contain an identical measure of attitudes toward government involvement in the provision of health insurance.

As Lenz (2012) explains, panel data are useful for disentangling the direction of causality between two constructs, but they present unique problems of their own. In cross-sectional data, the estimate of the causal effect of X on Y may be inflated if Y also causes X. With panel data, this problem may be overcome by measuring X at a time point prior to Y and controlling for prior values of Y, effectively examining changes in Y over time as a function of initial values of X. The difficulty is that this approach may underestimate the effect of X on Y, as any preexisting association between X and Y due to the causal effect of X on Y at the first time point is captured by the lagged dependent variable included as a control. Thus, only increases above and beyond this initial association are included in the estimate of the effect of X at time one on Y at time two. In this way, if no association is found between X and Y using the panel approach, despite finding a large cross-sectional relationship, this could be because: (1) the entire relationship is accounted for by the causal effect of Y on X, or (2) no *changes* in the association between X and Y occurred over the period from time one to time two. Therefore, the optimal use of panel data involves waves that straddle a period in which the dependent variable rises in salience, prompting citizens to consider it more carefully

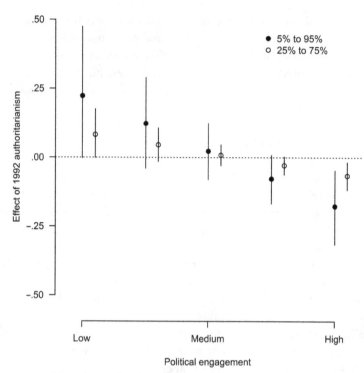

FIGURE 4.3. The relationship between authoritarianism and changes in support for government health insurance from 1992–1994 across political engagement, ANES

and to (perhaps) change their attitudes in the process (Lenz 2012). Health care reform between 1992 and 1994 is just such a period (Dancey and Goren 2010; Winter 2008), thus allowing a strong test of the reversal hypothesis.

We rely on support for a greater government role in health insurance in 1994 as our dependent variable. The wording of this item is identical to that in the 2000 and 2004 ANES (see Table 4.1). To test the reversal hypothesis, we estimated a model identical to the cross-sectional models discussed earlier, but with an added control for health insurance preferences in 1992. Authoritarianism, engagement, and all controls are also measured in 1992. As Figure 4.3 indicates, we find strong support for the reversal hypothesis. Among unengaged individuals, the coefficient for authoritarianism is positive and substantively meaningful, indicating that support for government-provided health insurance increases more between 1992 and 1994 among those high (vs. low) in authoritarianism.

A moderate difference in authoritarianism (25th to 75th percentile) is associated with an increase in support for government insurance of five to ten percentage points, while a large difference (5th to 95th percentile) is associated with a substantial increase of thirteen to twenty-three points. Further, the interaction between authoritarianism and political engagement is negative, statistically significant, and large. At the highest levels of engagement, the relationship is fully reversed with large changes in authoritarianism linked to an increase in opposition to government health insurance of seven to seventeen points.

Summary

Taken together, these cross-sectional and panel analyses provide compelling evidence that authoritarianism – one of the most commonly used indicators of the open-closed dimension of personality – is strongly related to economic values and policy attitudes, though in distinct ways across levels of political engagement. Among unengaged citizens, authoritarianism predicts support for expansive government intervention in the economy, while among engaged citizens, it predicts support for a limited government approach. This suggests that authoritarianism may have political consequences quite different from those assumed in past work. In previous studies, authoritarianism was linked to conservative values, policy attitudes, and political identities.[16] Most of this work has examined the impact of authoritarianism on ideological self-placement, ethnocentrism, and preferences in the cultural domain – issues such as gay marriage, immigration, and the like. As our analyses indicate, this simple model does not extend to preferences in the economic domain. In fact, for a large subgroup of the population – that is, politically unengaged individuals – authoritarianism is linked to stereotypically *left-wing* economic preferences. That is, among those who are unlikely to view economic issues through the prism of cultural and identity politics, authoritarianism promotes support for government-provided social welfare and restrictions on the free market. By contrast, among the engaged – who are likely to view economic debates in the symbolic terms provided by partisan elites – our results confirm what the literature has often predicted, but rarely found: open citizens support a strong government role in the economy while closed citizens support more limited government.

---

[16] E.g., Feldman and Stenner (1997); Hetherington and Suhay (2011); Hetherington and Weiler (2009); Peterson, Doty, and Winter (1993); Stenner (2005); Van Hiel, Mervielde, and Fruyt (2004).

The Need for Closure and Economic Policy Preferences

Thus far we have focused on authoritarianism as an indicator of the open-closed personality dimension. Another variable closely related to this general dimension of personality is the need for closure. As we noted in Chapter 2, people who are high in need for closure dislike uncertainty and ambiguity; consequently, they attempt to reach conclusions quickly and decisively. This tendency leads them to "seize" quickly on available information and to "freeze" on conclusions once they are reached. Consistent with this description, the need for closure is associated with greater reliance on stereotypes, greater reluctance to change or incorporate new information into existing attitudes, and a desire for uniformity within groups (Kruglanski et al. 2006; Webster and Kruglanski 1994). More relevant to our purposes, individuals high (vs. low) in the need for closure identify as conservatives, align themselves with the Republican Party, express hostility toward cultural outsiders, and adopt conservative preferences on cultural issues like gay rights (Jost et al. 2003, 2009; see also Chirumbolo 2002; Federico, Golec, and Dial 2005, Federico et al. 2012; Golec 2002; Kemmelmeier 1997, 2007; Kossowska and Van Hiel 2003; Van Hiel, Pandelaere, and Duriez 2004). Given the definition of the construct, this is to be expected: perhaps more so than any other personality dimension examined by political psychologists, the need for closure directly and unambiguously taps an aversion to uncertainty and a preference for the familiar (Kruglanski 2004), making it an ideal measure of the closed personality orientation. Indeed, one of the animating concepts behind the recent renaissance of interest in personality and politics – the notion of ideology as a form of "motivated social cognition" that allows people to meet underlying psychological needs for certainty and security – derives from the broader line of work on "lay epistemics" in social psychology that originally introduced the need for closure concept (Jost et al. 2003; Kruglanski and Webster 1996).

Individual differences in the need for closure are typically measured using self-report items. The full, original version of the Need for Closure Scale consists of forty-two items that cover multiple facets of the motivation to obtain closure, including preference for order and structure, desire for predictability, decisiveness, discomfort with ambiguity, and close-mindedness (Webster and Kruglanski, 1994). Although this measure has the virtue of conceptual breadth, its length makes it impractical to use in representative surveys of adults. As a result, most research on the political correlates of the need for closure has relied on student samples, limiting its generalizability. Moreover, the full version of the Need for Closure Scale has been plagued by low correlations between some of the subscales aimed at measuring its facets (Roets and Van Hiel 2007). Thus, recent work has focused on the development of shorter, more internally consistent measures (Pierro and Kruglanski 2006; Roets and Van Hiel 2011).

Given these measurement considerations, we rely on one of these short measures – a fourteen-item version of the Need for Closure Scale developed by Pierro and Kruglanski (2006).[17] This measure was included in the 2008 Knowledge Networks survey discussed briefly in Chapter 3, which we use here to test the reversal hypothesis.[18] The items for this scale are listed in Table 4.2. High need for closure – corresponding to a closed personality orientation – is indicated by strong agreement with statements like, "I prefer to be with people who have the same ideas and tastes as myself." Low need for closure – which represents an open orientation – is indicated by *disagreement* with statements like, "I prefer things to which I am used to those I do not know, and cannot predict."

As before, political engagement was measured using items tapping political knowledge and interest.[19] Economic policy attitudes were assessed with two items, one tapping general preferences about levels of government spending and services and the second tapping preferences about government-guaranteed jobs and income. The wording and seven-point response scales for these two items are virtually identical to those employed in the ANES surveys (see Table 4.2).[20] Each scale was recoded to range from zero to one, and then averaged such that higher scores indicate greater support for social welfare. As with authoritarianism, the

[17] All items used a six-point response scale ranging from 1 (*strongly disagree*) to 6 (*strongly agree*). Responses to the fourteen items were averaged and recoded to run from zero to one. Higher scores indicate a higher need for closure ($\alpha = 0.81$).

[18] The 2008 survey interviewed a nationally representative sample of $N = 1,511$ Americans. To obtain a nationally representative sample, Knowledge Networks (now GfK) chooses potential panel respondents through a scientific probability sample initially contacted via random-digit dialing telephone interviews. Adults successfully contacted are invited to participate in the web panel. If they agree, panel members are provided with a WebTV interface and free internet access in return for completing a weekly survey (for representativeness evidence, see Krosnick and Chang 2001). Our 2008 survey used a probability sample of all panel members eighteen years of age or older. Among panel members randomly selected for the 2008 survey, 65.7 percent completed the survey. Considering the rate at which households were recruited for the web panel (20%) and the rate at which at least one individual in each household completed an overall profile survey (54.5%), the final cumulative response rate (RR1) for our 2008 survey was 7.2 percent.

[19] Specifically, we used a composite of eight multiple-choice items tapping political knowledge and one item measuring interest in politics ($\alpha = 0.69$).

[20] The correlation between the spending and jobs items was 0.46.

TABLE 4.2. *Measurement of key variables in the 2008 Knowledge Networks Study*

Need for Cognitive Closure

Read each of the following statements and decide how much you would agree with each according to your attitudes, beliefs, and experiences. Please respond according to the following scale, using only one number for each statement.

(1) In case of uncertainty, I prefer to make an immediate decision, whatever it may be.

(2) When I find myself facing various, potentially valid alternatives, I decide in favor of one of them quickly and without hesitation.

(3) I prefer to decide on the first available solution rather than to ponder at length what decision I should make.

(4) I get very upset when things around me aren't in their place.

(5) Generally, I avoid participating in discussions on ambiguous and controversial problems.

(6) When I need to confront a problem, I do not think about it too much and I decide without hesitation.

(7) When I need to solve a problem, I generally do not waste time in considering diverse points of view about it.

(8) I prefer to be with people who have the same ideas and tastes as myself.

(9) Generally, I do not search for alternative solutions to problems for which I already have a solution available.

(10) I feel uncomfortable when I do not manage to give a quick response to problems that I face.

(11) Any solution to a problem is better than remaining in a state of uncertainty.

(12) I prefer activities where it is always clear what is to be done and how it needs to be done.

(13) After having found a solution to a problem, I believe that it is a useless waste of time to take into account diverse possible solutions.

(14) I prefer things to which I am used to those I do not know, and cannot predict.

Economic Policy Attitudes

(1) Some people think the government should provide fewer services even in areas such as health and education in order to reduce spending. Other people feel it is important for the government to provide many more services even if it means an increase in spending.

(2) Some people feel the government in Washington should see to it that every person has a job and a good standard of living. Others think the government should just let each person get ahead on their own.

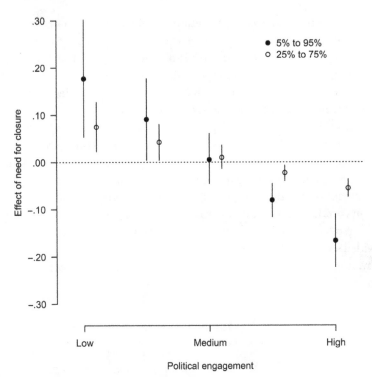

FIGURE 4.4. The relationship between need for cognitive closure and economic policy liberalism across political engagement, 2008 KN

y-axis represents the percentage point change in support for social welfare as a function of changes in the need for closure from low to high.[21]

As can be seen in Figure 4.4, the reversal effect is clearly evident in the data: the effect of the need for closure on support for social welfare is statistically significant and *positive* among citizens low in engagement, and statistically significant and *negative* among those high in engagement. For less engaged individuals, a moderate change in need for closure corresponds to an increase in support for greater government spending and economic protection of five to ten percentage points, and a large change in need for closure corresponds to a ten- to twenty-point increase. In other words, among the unengaged, people who are averse to uncertainty and ambiguity are between five and twenty points more supportive

---

[21] This model was estimated via OLS. Unfortunately, the 2008 survey did not include measures of support for limited government (on the dependent variable side) or a measure of union membership (on the independent variable side).

of spending on social welfare programs than citizens who are relatively comfortable with uncertainty. The pattern is the opposite for the politically engaged. Here, need for closure promotes opposition to a larger government role in the economy. At upper levels of engagement, those high in need for closure are between five and fifteen points less supportive of social welfare than those who score low on the trait.

Thus, as in prior research (e.g., Federico et al. 2012; Jost et al. 2003), we find that individual differences in the need for closure are linked to right-wing attitudes.[22] However, for economic issues, this obtains only among the politically engaged (see also Federico and Goren 2009). When engagement is low, those high in need for closure are more left-wing than their uncertainty-tolerant counterparts. This seems intuitive: citizens who are averse to uncertainty should be more likely to prefer a government-provided social safety net than those who are more comfortable with uncertainty. It is only via the conditioning effects of symbolic party politics that need for closure becomes strongly linked to free market economic views.

Openness to Experience, Conscientiousness, and Economic Preferences

As we described in Chapter 2, the openness to experience and conscientiousness dimensions of the Big Five model of personality also tap into the open-closed personality dimension. Openness to experience connotes a tolerance of uncertainty and a preference for novel and diverse experiences and ideas (signifying an open personality), whereas conscientiousness is associated with a preference for restraint and discipline aimed at warding off insecurity and social disorder (signifying a closed personality). As we reviewed in Chapter 2, these two dimensions are also consistently the most ideologically relevant of the Big Five: high levels of openness are associated with identifications, attitudes, and voting patterns that tilt to the left, whereas high levels of conscientiousness are associated with responses that tilt to the right (Mondak 2010; see also Jost et al. 2003).

Evidence for the political centrality of openness to experience and conscientiousness comes from a number of sources. However, much of the earliest work is based on student data (e.g., Carney et al. 2008; Gosling, Rentfrow, and Swann 2003; McCrae 1996; Riemann et al. 1993; Trapnell and Wiggins

---

[22] Importantly, our sample is also more representative of the general population than most psychological studies that typically draw on relatively small convenience samples, such as undergraduates.

1990). In many respects, this is to be expected given the origins of research on personality and politics in psychology, which has historically relied on convenience samples of college students. However, given the limitations of student data, researchers in a variety of disciplines have subsequently made an effort to reach broader community samples via snowball sampling techniques, opt-in internet surveys, and surveys of political elites both in the United States (e.g., Carney et al. 2008; Mehrabian 1996) and in other nations (e.g., Italy; see Barbaranelli et al. 2007; Caprara 2006; Caprara, Barbaranelli, and Zimbardo 1999). Only very recently have researchers taken steps to examine the relationships between the Big Five and political attitudes in nationally representative samples of adults or surveys approximating representative samples (e.g., via sampling and matching techniques; see Gerber et al. 2010). In this regard, a major obstacle has been the length of the instruments originally developed to measure the Big Five traits, with some batteries having hundreds of items (Costa and MaCrae 1992; see also Mondak 2010).

Fortunately, psychometric work has led to the development of shorter Big Five scales, and research using them with representative samples has produced results remarkably similar to those obtained in convenience samples: openness to experience consistently emerges as the most powerful Big Five predictor of political preferences, with those high on the trait showing more liberal preferences, while conscientiousness is the runner-up, with the most conscientious being more conservative (e.g., Gerber et al. 2010; Mondak 2010; Mondak and Halperin 2008; Schoen and Schumann 2007). These are precisely the two Big Five traits that correspond most closely to the open-closed dimension (Carney et al. 2008).

To test the reversal hypothesis with openness to experience and conscientiousness, we use the short Ten-Item Personality Inventory (or TIPI; Gosling et al. 2003), which has become a mainstay of political science research on the five-factor model of personality. This instrument presents respondents with a sequence of ten trait pairs, and asks them to indicate the extent to which each trait within each pair applies to themselves (there are two pairs per dimension, as shown in Table 4.3). For example, openness to experience is assessed using the trait pairs "open to new experiences, complex" and "conventional, uncreative" (reverse coded).

We should note that the TIPI has weaker psychometric properties than longer measures, particularly with respect to the internal consistency of each two-item composite (Credé et al. 2012). This is an inevitable consequence of the desire to cover each trait as broadly as possible with a small number of items (Gosling et al. 2003). Nevertheless, this limitation

TABLE 4.3. *Measurement of key variables in the 2008 CCAP,*
2009 CCES, and 2012 ANES

The Big Five (Gosling et al. 2003)

Here are a number of personality traits that may or may not apply to you. Indicate the extent to which you agree or disagree with each statement. You should rate the extent to which the pair of traits applies to you, even if one characteristic applies more strongly than the other.

    (1) Extraverted, enthusiastic (Extraversion)
    (2) Reserved, quiet (Extraversion; reverse-coded)
    (3) Sympathetic, warm (Agreeableness)
    (4) Critical, quarrelsome (Agreeableness; reverse-coded)
    (5) Dependable, self-disciplined (Conscientiousness)
    (6) Disorganized, careless (Conscientiousness; reverse-coded)
    (7) Calm, emotionally stable (Emotional Stability)
    (8) Anxious, easily upset (Emotional Stability; reverse-coded)
    (9) Open to new experiences, complex (Openness to Experience)
  (10) Conventional, uncreative (Openness to Experience; reverse-coded)

CCAP: Economic Policy Attitudes

    (1) Which comes closest to your view about providing health care in the United States? (a) The government should provide everyone with health care and pay for it with tax dollars; (b) Companies should be required to provide health insurance for their employees and the government should provide subsidies for those who are not working or retired; (c) Health insurance should be voluntary. Individuals should either buy insurance or obtain it through their employers as they do currently. The elderly and the very poor should be covered by Medicare and Medicaid as they are currently.
    (2) Do you favor raising federal taxes on families earning more than $200,000 per year? (a) strongly favor; (b) somewhat favor; (c) somewhat oppose; (d) strongly oppose.

CCES: Economic Policy Attitudes

    (1) The first item asked the respondents to indicate the percentage of their state's budget deficit that should be offset with spending cuts versus tax increases. 100% indicates all spending cuts, and 0% indicates all tax increases.
    (2) The second item was a similar format to (1), but asked the respondents to indicate the percentage of any tax increases that should be consumption based rather than income based.
    The next four items were all dichotomous "roll call votes" on issues considered in the U.S. Congress:
    (3) Support for the Recovery and Reinvestment Act
    (4) Support for the SCHIP bill for spending on children's health insurance
    (5) Support for health insurance reform
    (6) Support for universal health insurance

is partially offset by the fact that surveys relying on it are able to reach large adult samples in which longer instruments would be difficult to administer. Moreover, the TIPI – despite its brevity – shows a high level of predictive validity. Scores on the five dimensions are stable over time and strongly correlated with those obtained using longer, more extensive Big Five instruments (Gosling et al. 2003). Moreover, they show associations with political attitudes that closely match those reported in research in which longer measures are used (e.g., Barbaranelli et al. 2007; Gerber et al. 2011; Mondak and Halperin, 2008). Taken together, these considerations converge in suggesting that the TIPI is a valid and appropriate measure of the Big Five traits in the context of mass surveys (McCrae 2015: 106).

The TIPI was included in three datasets that contain measures of other constructs relevant to our theory: the 2008 Cooperative Campaign Analysis Project (CCAP), the 2009 Cooperative Congressional Election Study (CCES), and the 2012 ANES.[23] In all three surveys, responses to the TIPI items were recoded to zero to one, reversed when necessary, and then averaged to form one scale for each trait. In the CCAP, engagement was measured with twelve factual knowledge items and one item measuring interest in politics. Economic opinion was captured by attitudes toward the government's role in health insurance and attitudes toward increasing taxes on the wealthy.[24] In the CCES, engagement was measured with a single item asking respondents how often they follow politics (no knowledge items were available). The economic items included beliefs about whether state budget deficits should be addressed through tax increases or spending cuts, the percentage of any tax increases that should be income rather than consumption based, support for the Recovery and Reinvestment Act of 2009 (i.e., the 2009 fiscal stimulus bill), support for the SCHIP bill regarding government spending on children's health insurance, support for health insurance reform, and support for universal government-guaranteed health insurance.[25] These CCAP and CCES

---

[23] The 2008 CCAP is a six-wave panel study administered by YouGov/Polimetrix, Inc., conducted through the internet. The first of the six waves was collected in December 2007 and the last wave was collected in November 2008; five waves were fielded before the 2008 election, and one was fielded after. The survey employed a mix of sampling and matching techniques to approximate a random digit dialing sample (see Vavreck and Rivers 2008). The 2009 CCES was also administered by YouGov/Polimetrix, Inc., via the internet in the fall of 2009, and contained approximately 13,000 respondents.

[24] The correlation between the two economic items was 0.59. The reliability of the resulting engagement scale in the 2008 CCAP was $\alpha = 0.86$.

[25] The reliability of the resulting scale in the 2009 CCES was high, again suggesting that a variety of economic policy items strongly tap a single underlying dimension ($\alpha = 0.85$).

measures are summarized in Table 4.3. In the 2012 ANES, we examine the economic values and policy attitudes reported in the authoritarianism analyses (see Table 4.1).[26] In all cases except values in the 2012 ANES, we averaged responses to these items, and rescaled the range from zero to one such that higher values indicate greater support for government involvement in economic matters. Our models include each of the Big Five traits (as suggested by previous work, e.g., Mondak 2010), political engagement, and the five interactions between each personality trait and engagement.[27]

We discuss the results from these three datasets by trait, beginning with openness to experience. The estimates are shown in Panels A–D of Figure 4.5. Looking first at the results in the CCAP, we find strong support for the reversal hypothesis. At low levels of engagement, openness to experience promotes opposition to government intervention in the economy. Individuals high in openness are about seven percentage points less economically liberal than individuals low in openness, and this effect is statistically significant. As engagement rises, the impact of openness turns positive. At high levels of engagement, openness to experience is strongly associated with economic liberalism, with the most open citizens about thirty percentage points more liberal than the least open citizens. The results for the 2009 CCES and the 2012 ANES are similar, but mixed at low engagement. In the 2009 CCES, we find no evidence of a reversal effect: at low levels of engagement, openness to experience is entirely unrelated to economic policy liberalism. In the 2012 ANES, the effect of openness on economic values and policy preferences is in the expected, negative direction, but is only significant for policy preferences. Overall, the results for openness to experience strongly support the expected positive relationship among engaged citizens, but provide only mixed support for the expected negative relationship among the unengaged.

The estimates for conscientiousness are shown in Panels A–D of Figure 4.6. Recall that conscientiousness is an indicator of a closed personality orientation; the pattern of effects should therefore be opposite to that of openness to experience. Looking first at the 2008 CCAP, we find strong support for the reversal effect. At low levels of engagement, conscientiousness is associated with economic liberalism, while at high levels of engagement, it is associated with economic conservatism. At low levels of engagement, those high in conscientiousness are about seven

---

[26] The CCAP and CCES do not include measures of economic values.

[27] All models, with the exception of values in the 2012 ANES, were estimated via OLS.

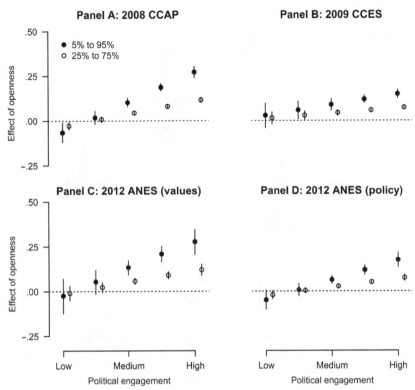

FIGURE 4.5. The relationship between openness to experience and liberal economic values and policies across political engagement, 2008 CCAP, 2009 CCES, and 2012 ANES

points more liberal than those low in conscientiousness. At high levels of engagement, the conscientious are about ten points more conservative. This pattern is nearly identical in the 2009 CCES. However, the 2012 ANES provides mixed results. As expected, conscientiousness strongly and significantly promotes conservatism in both economic values and policy preferences when engagement is high. When engagement is low, we find a meaningful, marginally significant relationship for values, but we find no relationship at all for policy.

In sum, our examination of the Big Five in three national surveys provides additional – though not uniform – support for the reversal hypothesis.[28] For engaged respondents in all three studies, openness to experience

---

[28] We also find differences in effect size for the Big Five compared to our previous dispositional indicators. Specifically, while openness to experience strongly promotes liberalism among the engaged – rivaling in effect size all of our other indicators – conscientiousness

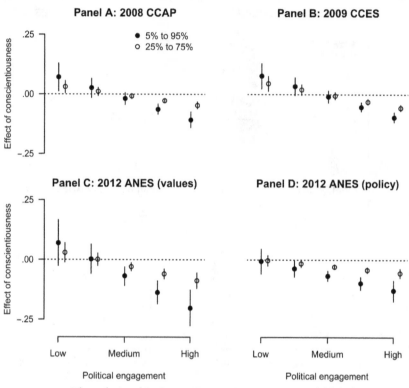

FIGURE 4.6. The relationship between conscientiousness and liberal economic values and policies across political engagement, 2008 CCAP, 2009 CCES, and 2012 ANES

promotes economic liberalism and conscientiousness promotes economic conservatism. However, among unengaged respondents, the findings are mixed: In eight total tests, we find strong support for the reversal hypothesis in four cases, weak support in one case, and no support in three cases. We can only speculate about why the effects are more fragile among the unengaged. It may be that when these traits are measured with just two items, there is simply too much noise to detect reliable effects among politically inattentive individuals (for whom such relationships are notoriously noisy). Whatever the reason, our results suggest that the effects of

is more weakly related to economic preferences for both the engaged and the unengaged. This is consistent with much previous research that finds openness to be the most important trait predictor of political ideology (e.g., Carney et al. 2008; Gerber et al. 2010; McCrae 1996).

openness to experience and conscientiousness on economic preferences are more reliable among the engaged than the unengaged.[29]

Openness to Change versus Conservation and Economic Values

As described in detail in Chapter 2, the open-closed dimension of personality is also reflected in the relative emphasis a person places on different types of core human values. Accordingly, we should expect to observe the reversal effect in the context of the relationship between personal values and economic preferences. Fortunately, the U.S. sample from the 2011 wave of the World Values Survey[30] included several items measuring Schwartz's (1992) *openness to change versus conservation* value dimension. In Schwartz's theory, core human values are conceptualized as enduring goals that are limited in number, similar in content and structure across human societies (having their roots in universal biological and social needs), transcend specific situations, and are ordered by individuals in terms of importance. An individual's ranking of core values defines the way that person copes with choices that involve multiple competing goals. For example, is it better to pursue new and diverse experiences – with the possible risks that such behavior entails – or play it safe and pursue known ends? The relative ranking of values such as "security" and "excitement" will play an important role in determining how an individual behaves across situations. While both values represent desirable ends, they often have conflicting behavioral implications, creating a tension that is resolved through the elevation of one value at the expense of the other (Tetlock 1986). The *conservation* end of this dimension is defined by the broad values of "security," "conformity," and "tradition," while the *openness* end is defined by "self-direction," "stimulation," and to a lesser extent, "hedonism." Prototypical indicators for the conservation end include "family security," "social order," "obedient," and "discipline." Prototypical indicators for the openness end include "creativity," "curious," "an exciting life,"

---

[29] There is reason to believe this may be true more generally – that is, for all indicators of the open-closed dimension. We return to this issue in the conclusion. As a preview, we suggest that the reversal for unengaged citizens may be fragile for at least two reasons. First, unengaged citizens may show less stability and reliability in their economic attitudes because they generally spend less time thinking about politics. Second, the amount of exposure to politics required to reverse the effect of openness on economic liberalism from negative to positive may be quite low.

[30] www.worldvaluessurvey.org/WVSDocumentationWV6.jsp

and "daring." As Schwartz argues, openness "arrays values in terms of the extent to which they motivate people to follow their own intellectual and emotional interests in unpredictable and uncertain directions versus to preserve the status quo and the certainty it provides in relationships with close others, institutions, and traditions" (1992: 43).

Clearly, the openness to change versus conservation value dimension is conceptually close to the open-closed personality dimension, and it overlaps strongly with other indicators of openness such as authoritarianism, need for closure, and the endorsement of binding moral foundations (Feldman 2003; Haidt 2012).[31] For each of six indicators of the openness to change versus conservation dimension in the 2011 WVS (see Table 4.4), respondents were asked to place themselves on a six-point scale ranging from "not at all like me" to "very much like me." We created a single scale from these items with higher scores reflecting greater openness.[32] We measured *liberal economic values* with two correlated ten-point items tapping general orientations toward government involvement in the economy. The first item was anchored by "incomes should be made more equal" and "we need larger income differences as incentives for individual effort." The second item was anchored by "government should take more responsibility to ensure that everyone is provided for" and "people should take more responsibility for themselves" ($r = 0.44$).[33]

---

[31] Empirically, as we detail in the appendix to Chapter 6, openness to change is strongly (negatively) correlated with both authoritarianism and the need for closure. Further, as we would expect, the Big Five trait of openness to experience is strongly and positively associated with the openness to change values of stimulation and self-direction, and strongly and negatively associated with the conservation values of conformity, tradition, and security (Parks-Leduc, Feldman, and Bardi 2015; Roccas et al. 2002). There is thus a tight connection between this dimension and the other primary trait constructs utilized in the study of mass ideology. Indeed, research suggests that conservation versus openness is a strong predictor of left-right identifications in both the United States and in Europe (Caprara et al. 2006; Caprara and Zimbardo 2004), and serves as a foundation for several important values related to cultural orientations in American politics, such as moral traditionalism and concern with law and order (Goren 2013; Schwartz, Caprara, and Vecchione 2010).

[32] Specifically, we calculated the respondent-specific mean for all ten value items and subtracted this mean from the values for each individual item for each respondent. We then averaged these mean-deviated scores for the six items measuring openness versus conservation. Schwartz (1992) recommended this procedure to extract individual differences in the use of the value-importance rating scale. In practical terms, it does not actually make any difference whether we mean-deviate the items or use raw scores; the results are nearly identical.

[33] A third item was arguably worthy of inclusion in this scale: "Private ownership of business and industry should be increased" versus "Government ownership of business and industry should be increased." However, this item substantially reduced the reliability of

TABLE 4.4. *Measurement of key variables in the 2011 WVS*

Openness to Change versus Conservation

(1) It is important to this person to think up new ideas and be creative; to do things one's own way

(2) Living in secure surroundings is important to this person; to avoid anything that might be dangerous

(3) Adventure and taking risks are important to this person; to have an exciting life

(4) It is important to this person to always behave properly; to avoid doing anything people would say is wrong

(5) Tradition is important to this person; to follow the customs handed down by one's religion or family

(6) It is important to this person to have a good time; to "spoil oneself"

Economic Values

(1) "Incomes should be made more equal" or "We need larger income differences as incentives for individual effort."

(2) "Government should take more responsibility to ensure that everyone is provided for" or "People should take more responsibility for themselves."

These items were recoded to a 0 to 1 scale and averaged so that higher values indicate support for a stronger government role. Finally, as knowledge items were unavailable in the WVS, we measured political engagement with a single, four-category item asking respondents, "How interested would you say you are in politics?" We controlled for our standard set of demographics.[34]

The results, shown in Figure 4.7, strongly support the reversal hypothesis. At the lowest level of political interest, an increase in openness is associated with a decrease in broad liberal values related to the redistribution of income and the provision of social welfare. As in previous analyses, among those most likely to think in instrumental terms (i.e., the unengaged), those with open personalities wish to limit the role of government while closed citizens prefer to expand it. Conversely, among those most likely to think in expressive terms (i.e., the engaged), openness

the overall scale, and was uncorrelated with the responsibility item. This is likely due to the fact that, in the U.S. case, though not worldwide, more than 80 percent of respondents place themselves on the first five points of the response scale, indicating substantial aversion to the nationalization of industry. A few other items were also a part of this section of the WVS survey, but each represented a belief about the world and/or economics rather than a preference regarding government's role in the economy.

[34] The union membership item was unavailable, however, and thus was not included as a control in this analysis.

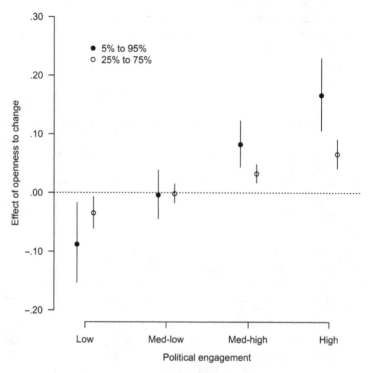

FIGURE 4.7. The relationship between openness to change vs. conservation and liberal economic values across political engagement, 2011 WVS

is associated with a preference for a more active government role in the economy while conservation is associated with a preference for limited government. The effects range from about five to ten percentage points among the unengaged, and from about five to fifteen points among the engaged. In sum, even with a rather crude measure of political engagement, we obtain clear support for the reversal hypothesis.[35]

Risk Aversion, Self-Interest, and Social Welfare Preferences

Dispositional risk aversion comprises a less commonly examined, but nonetheless conceptually integral measure of the open-closed personality dimension (Kam 2012; Kam and Simas 2010). As we noted in previous chapters, open individuals tend to be tolerant of risk and perhaps even

---

[35] See also Malka and colleagues (2014) for similar analyses using the World Values Survey in a comparative context. We discuss this study in greater detail in the concluding chapter.

risk-seeking, while closed individuals tend to be risk-averse. This is likely due to the tendency of closed individuals to focus more on potential losses than gains (Luttig and Lavine 2015; Oxley et al. 2008; Shook and Fazio 2009), leading to a preference for sure things over mixed gambles (Kahneman and Tversky 1979). Given these tendencies, we should also find evidence for the reversal hypothesis in the relationship between general risk preferences and economic opinion.

To explore this possibility, we turn to data from Wave 22 of the 2008–9 ANES panel study,[36] which included a seven-item measure of risk aversion developed by Kam (see Kam 2012; Kam and Simas 2010). These items, shown in Table 4.5, were averaged to form a scale in which higher values indicate greater risk aversion (reflecting a closed orientation) and lower values indicate greater risk acceptance (reflecting an open orientation).[37] Wave 22 of the ANES survey also included our standard measure of authoritarianism, providing us with an additional opportunity to replicate our findings for this trait.

To this point, we have used standard measures of political engagement as the moderator of the relationship between personality and economic opinion. This survey did not include such measures. It did, however, include four items that asked respondents to rate the extent to which they rely on *personal* versus *impersonal* considerations in making political judgments. Specifically, respondents used a ten-point agree/disagree scale to respond to the following statements: "I make political decisions based on what is in my best interest," "I make political decisions in the interest of my family and friends," "I make political decisions in the interest of others in society (in the interest of other Americans)," and "I make political decisions based in the interest of others in the world at large." We constructed a scale such that higher scores indicate greater use of impersonal relative to personal considerations.[38] As a general

---

[36] The 22nd Wave was collected in October 2009, and included 2,175 respondents. Of these, 1,244 were originally recruited for the first cohort of the panel study in late 2007, and 931 were recruited for the second cohort in the summer of 2008. All surveys were conducted through the internet by Knowledge Networks, and participants were offered $10 per month to complete one approximately thirty-minute survey.

[37] Several of the items are modified versions of items contained in openness to experience and need for cognitive closure scales, which again suggests the deep connections between the openness concept and risk and uncertainty (e.g., "I like new and exciting experiences." "I prefer friends who are exciting and unpredictable.").

[38] Since we are interested in the relative use of each possible judgment strategy, and the fact that citizens may use the common item format in distinct ways (i.e., anchor on different points of the ten-point scale), we first calculated the respondent-specific mean for all four items, and then subtracted their responses to each item from that mean. We then

TABLE 4.5. *Measurement of key variables in the 22nd Wave*
of 2008–2009 ANES Panel

Risk Aversion

(1) "You should be cautious about making major changes in life" versus "You will never achieve much in life unless you act boldly" (seven-point scale)

(2) "Suppose you were betting on horses and were a big winner in the third or fourth race. Would you be more likely to continue playing or take your winnings?" (five-point scale, ranging from "definitely continue playing" to "definitely take my winnings")

(3) "I would like to explore strange places" (five-point agree/disagree scale)

(4) "I like to do frightening things" (five-point agree/disagree scale)

(5) "I like new and exciting experiences" (five-point agree/disagree scale)

(6) "I prefer friends who are exciting and unpredictable" (five-point agree/disagree scale)

(7) "In general, how easy or difficult is it for you to accept taking risks?" (four-point scale, ranging from "very difficult" to "very easy"

Personal versus Impersonal Political Decision Making

(1) "I make political decisions based on what is in my best interest"

(2) "I make political decisions in the interest of my family and friends"

(3) "I make political decisions in the interest of others in society (in the interest of other Americans)"

(4) "I make political decisions based in the interest of others in the world at large"

Economic Policy Attitudes

"Some people think the government should provide fewer services, even in areas such as health and education, in order to reduce spending. Others feel it is important for the government to provide many services, even if it means an increase in spending. Where would you place yourself on this scale?"

matter, we expect that citizens who think about politics in personal (*qua* self-interested) terms will resemble the unengaged in viewing economic policy through the lens of desired levels of social protection, whereas citizens who think in impersonal (more abstract, other-directed) terms will be less instrumental in their economic policy judgments. The latter is, of course, a somewhat weak expectation, as there is nothing

averaged these mean-deviated responses into a single scale ranging from "predominantly personal considerations" to "predominantly impersonal considerations." The reliability of this four-item scale was quite good ($\alpha = 0.79$), the two "personal" items were strongly negatively related to the overall scale, and the two "impersonal" items were strongly positively related to the overall scale, as expected. That is, the more someone utilizes self- or familial-interested considerations to form judgments, the less likely they are to use other-interested or world-interested considerations.

intrinsically *expressive* about being other- or world-interested in one's political judgments (e.g., one might desire social protection in a universal sense). Our expectations are therefore asymmetric: we have strong reason to believe that self-interested individuals will look more like the unengaged than other-interested individuals, but it is unclear whether we will observe the reversal effect so that dispositional risk aversion will be associated with economic conservatism among other-interested individuals.

Social welfare preferences were assessed using a single, five-point item capturing support for government spending and services. Among those who profess to rely on self-interested considerations in forming political judgments, we expect risk-averse individuals to be more supportive of social welfare than risk-tolerant individuals. By contrast, among those who claim to think about politics in more impersonal terms, we explore whether risk-tolerant citizens are *more* supportive of social welfare than risk-averse citizens (similar to the engaged). For authoritarianism, we expect high scorers to be more supportive of social welfare when thinking about politics in self-interested terms, and we explore whether low scorers are more supportive of social welfare when thinking about politics in more impersonal terms.

The results of these analyses, shown in Figure 4.8, support the reversal hypothesis. Among those who rely predominantly on self-interested considerations, both authoritarianism and risk aversion are associated with greater support for government spending and services. Those who score high on the authoritarianism scale are about twenty percentage points more likely to support government spending and services than those who score low on the scale. Similarly, those who indicate greater risk aversion are about fifteen percentage points more likely to support government spending and services than those who are risk-tolerant. In line with the reversal hypothesis, these relationships change dramatically as reliance on impersonal considerations rises. Among those who report a mix of personal and impersonal considerations, authoritarians are ten points more likely to *oppose* government spending and services than non-authoritarians. Similarly, risk-averse individuals are slightly more likely to oppose a greater government role in the economy than those who are comparatively risk-tolerant. Finally, among those who use predominantly impersonal considerations, high authoritarians and the risk-averse are about forty and twenty percentage points more likely to oppose social welfare than low authoritarians and the risk acceptant, respectively.

The empirical tests in this section extend our analysis in two ways. First, we use a different but theoretically relevant moderator variable: whether

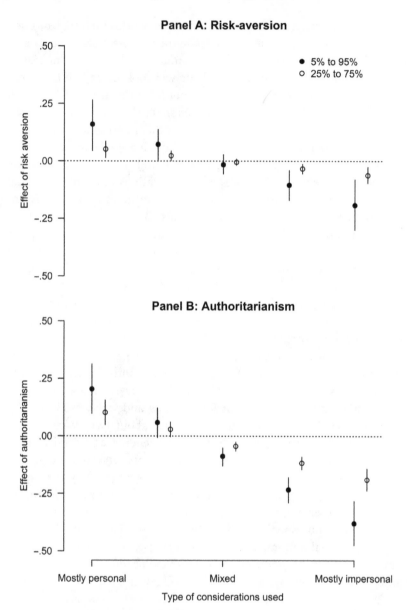

FIGURE 4.8. The relationship between risk preferences and authoritarianism and support for government spending and services across use of impersonal vs. personal considerations, 2009 ANES

respondents focus on personal, relatively self-interested concerns when making policy judgments, or whether they focus on more impersonal considerations. Substituting this measure for the standard engagement variable, we replicate the reversal hypothesis. Second, we provide evidence for the reversal hypothesis using a direct measure of dispositional risk aversion (Kam 2010). This finding may be of particular relevance to the political economy literature, which almost universally (to our knowledge) predicts that risk aversion will promote support for redistribution and social welfare. Here, we show that the opposite relationship is often observed. It is only among the subset of citizens who think predominantly in self-interested terms that risk aversion promotes a pro-government orientation on economic policy. Contrary to traditional rational choice approaches, but in line with an expressive perspective on the roots of economic preferences, risk aversion often promotes opposition to social welfare.

Openness and Economic Preferences among Blacks and Latinos

To this point, we have ignored the potential for racial and ethnic heterogeneity in the relationship between openness and economic preferences. However, our discussion in Chapter 3 suggests that personality may not have uniform effects across ethnic and racial groups (see also Gerber et al. 2010). In this final section, we consider potential variation among self-identified non-Latino whites, Latinos (or Hispanics), and blacks (or African Americans). We choose these three groups because we have sufficient sample sizes available in certain representative datasets to generate reliable estimates of the quantities of interest for blacks and Latinos. Our study is merely an initial foray into systematically addressing the potential for group-based heterogeneity in personality effects. We leave additional explorations of these and other subgroups to future research.

We begin by noting that the results presented in the previous sections are very similar to those for non-Latino whites considered alone. Specifically, the pattern of estimates for each analysis is typically the same, though the effect sizes tend to be larger when whites are considered independently. That is, indicators of openness have their strongest influence on economic opinion for whites. Indeed, of the three subgroups we have examined, the reversal effect is most consistent, and largest in substantive size, for whites. Since the findings for whites look quite similar to what we have already presented, we focus here on blacks and Latinos.

As discussed in Chapter 3, there are at least two reasons to expect variation in the relationship between openness and economic opinion when comparing these groups to whites (and to the full sample results). First, whites' economic preferences are more variable than those of Latinos and especially those of blacks, and the same holds for partisan affiliation (both groups, and blacks in particular, skew heavily toward the Democratic Party). Second, if the effects of personality are mediated by partisan identification and elite cue-taking among engaged citizens (as our theory specifies), the strong partisan skew among blacks and Latinos should constrain the operation of this pathway. For these reasons, we expect openness to be largely unrelated to economic opinion among black Americans, for whom the skew in economic opinion and party identification is particularly severe (see also Gerber et al. 2010[39]). We expect Latinos to fall somewhere in the middle (between blacks and whites).

Unfortunately, most of the datasets at our disposal have too few minority respondents to conduct sufficiently powered tests of the reversal hypothesis. This is the case for need for closure, openness to change versus conservation, and dispositional risk aversion. However, we have large, high-quality samples of blacks and Latinos (Ns > 1,000) in the American National Election Studies. First, as the ANES includes identical (or very similar) indicators across election years, we can combine the 2000, 2004, 2008, and 2012 ANES to increase our sample size for each group. Second, the 2008 and 2012 ANES include oversamples of both blacks and Latinos. This allows us to test the reversal hypothesis using three indicators of the open-closed dimension. We look first at authoritarianism by combining the 2000–12 studies. We then turn to openness to experience and conscientiousness in the 2012 ANES.

The estimates for authoritarianism are shown in Figure 4.9. Panels A and B examine the relationship between authoritarianism and economic values (i.e., support for limited government) for blacks and Latinos, respectively. Panels C and D do the same for economic policy preferences. These variables are defined as they were for the full samples in Figures 4.1 and 4.2 (see also Table 4.1). The pattern is consistent with our tentative hypotheses. First, we find no evidence that authoritarianism is related to economic preferences among blacks at *any* level of political

---

[39] Though Gerber and colleagues (2010) do not emphasize the importance of engagement or political identity to personality effects.

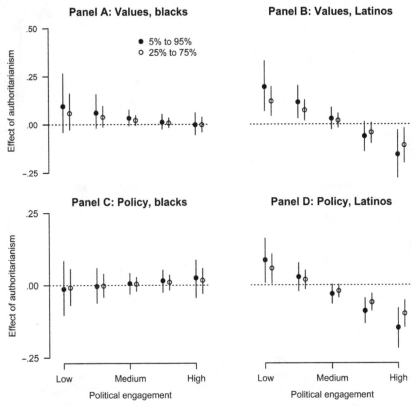

FIGURE 4.9. The relationship between authoritarianism and liberal economic values and policies across political engagement for African Americans and Latinos, 2000–2012 ANES

engagement. By contrast, the estimates for Latinos nicely fit the reversal hypothesis and are similar to those for the full sample and for non-Latino whites. For both values and policy preferences, authoritarianism is associated with economic liberalism among politically unengaged Latinos, and economic conservatism among politically engaged Latinos. Thus, the reversal pattern holds for both Latinos and whites, though with stronger effect sizes for whites.

Figure 4.10 considers the political impact of openness to experience. The pattern here is similar to authoritarianism, such that there are no effects for blacks, but effects for Latinos that are similar to those for the full sample and for whites. When engagement is low, openness to experience is associated with conservative economic values and policy preferences among Latinos. As engagement rises, the relationship reverses

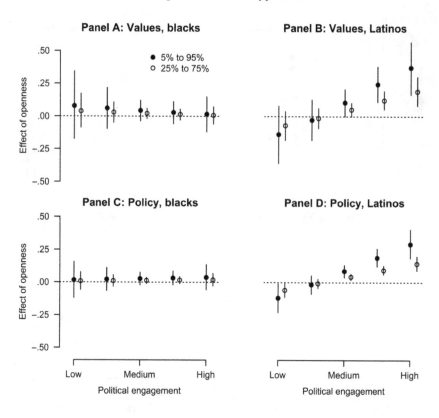

FIGURE 4.10. The relationship between openness to experience and liberal economic values and policies across political engagement for African Americans and Latinos, 2012 ANES

such that at high engagement openness promotes economic liberalism.[40] Finally, in Figure 4.11 we present the results for conscientiousness. Here, the results are a bit more mixed. For blacks, there is a hint of a positive effect of conscientiousness on economic values at moderate and low levels of engagement (though inefficiently estimated), which declines to zero at high levels of engagement. This pattern does not replicate for economic policy. For Latinos, the pattern is consistent with the reversal

---

[40] The reversal at low levels of engagement is significant for economic policy, but only approaches significance for economic values. Thus, as in the full sample analyses, the reversal effect at low engagement is less robust for openness to experience than for authoritarianism.

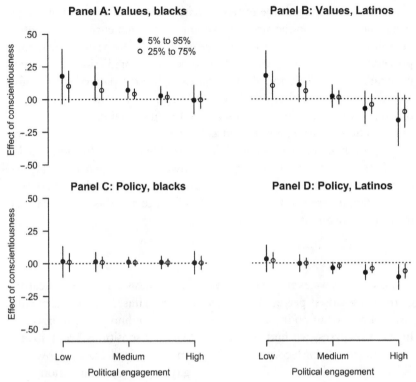

FIGURE 4.11. The relationship between conscientiousness and liberal economic values and policies across political engagement for African Americans and Latinos, 2012 ANES

hypothesis in both cases, but here too the estimates are inefficiently estimated. Nonetheless, at high levels of engagement, conscientiousness predicts economic conservatism, and at low levels of engagement – for economic values at least – conscientiousness predicts economic liberalism. This is the same pattern observed for the full sample and for whites.[41]

In sum, we have examined the reversal hypothesis among blacks and Latinos for three indicators of the open-closed dimension of personality: authoritarianism, openness to experience, and conscientiousness. Among blacks, we find little evidence that personality shapes economic opinion. For Latinos, however, the results are similar to those for whites,

---

[41] These results also reflect the stronger influence of openness to experience than conscientiousness, a pattern observed for whites and consistently obtained in the literature (e.g., Carney et al. 2008).

though smaller in magnitude and less precisely estimated. To our knowledge, this is the first systematic attempt to compare the influence of personality on political attitudes across these three groups. On the basis of the theory presented in Chapter 3, we made two tentative predictions: personality would matter little for black Americans, but the pattern for Latinos would be similar to that of whites. Although the analyses presented in this section provide provisional support for these claims, we stress that our conclusions are tentative and subject to revision. Data availability issues prevent extensive testing of the reversal hypothesis for both blacks and Latinos. We would be surprised, however, if the general contours of our findings were completely overturned in future work, as they rest on a strong theoretical foundation.[42] Needless to say, this is an area that deserves more attention in the literature.

Conclusion

In this chapter, we examined the reversal hypothesis across six indicators of the open-closed personality dimension, ten datasets spanning twenty years of American politics, and three prominent ethno-racial subgroups. In these analyses, we find that psychological dispositions are a strong force in structuring economic opinion in the United States. However, unlike the case for cultural issues (e.g., gay marriage, immigration), the effects of personality on economic opinion do not flow from the straightforward logic of elective affinity. It is simply not the case that the standard personality variables we examined are uniformly associated with either economic liberalism or conservatism. Rather, the effects of personality depend on the way in which citizens construe economic policy debates. Among the politically unengaged – who we argue view politics from an instrumental point of view – a closed personality orientation was consistently linked to support for redistribution and social welfare. That is, among those who are attuned to the consequences of economic policies, a closed personality orientation was linked to a preference for government-provided economic protection from the vagaries of the free market. Among the engaged, however – who we argue construe politics through a more expressive lens – a closed personality orientation was consistently linked to opposition to social welfare.

It is striking how robust this reversal pattern appears to be. It holds in at least some cases for every one of the personality variables we examined,

---

[42] We will provide additional evidence for racial and ethnic heterogeneity consistent with our theory in Chapter 5.

including authoritarianism, the need for closure, openness to experience, conscientiousness, openness to change versus conservation, and dispositional risk aversion. Our results are all the more striking given the inconclusive nature of the relationship between personality and economic preferences in past research (e.g., Hibbing et al. 2014b). However, our findings were not entirely symmetrical. The relationship between openness and economic preferences was stronger among politically engaged citizens. Here, the positive link between openness and support for government intervention was statistically significant in twenty-one out of twenty-one tests in full samples. Moreover, the effects were often quite large in magnitude. For the unengaged, the predicted reversal obtained in seventeen of twenty-one tests, and the magnitude of the effect was often smaller. This should come as little surprise, as preferences among the unengaged are notoriously "noisier" and less stable than among better-informed citizens. Nevertheless, the signal was far from faint among the unengaged, and our findings indicate that the reversal effect is a robust phenomenon.

In additional analyses, we find notable differences in this pattern across racial and ethnic groups. Specifically, the reversal effect extends to whites and Latinos, but not to blacks. We believe this latter null result is consistent with the relative lack of diversity in economic opinion and the overwhelming tendency of African Americans to identify with the Democratic Party. The latter observation effectively closes off the political impact of openness among engaged blacks, as the effect operates largely through political identification and elite cue-taking (processes we explore further in Chapters 5 and 6).

In sum, this chapter established the reversal effect as an important phenomenon in American mass politics. The work of the next three chapters is to empirically explore the *mechanisms* by which it is produced.

Appendix

TABLE A4.1. *Estimates for authoritarianism in cross-sectional data*

	Economic Values				Economic Policy			
	2000	2004	2008	2012	2000	2004	2008	2012
Authoritarianism	0.92 (0.29)	1.33 (0.35)	1.57 (0.27)	1.10 (0.15)	0.13 (0.06)	0.19 (0.07)	0.20 (0.07)	0.17 (0.03)
Engagement	0.97 (0.36)	0.88 (0.35)	0.96 (0.28)	0.97 (0.16)	0.12 (0.08)	0.18 (0.07)	0.17 (0.07)	0.22 (0.03)
Auth X Engage	-2.12 (0.51)	-2.23 (0.51)	-2.31 (0.39)	-2.40 (0.23)	-0.36 (0.11)	-0.45 (0.10)	-0.38 (0.10)	-0.48 (0.04)
Age	0.06 (0.15)	-0.44 (0.16)	-0.54 (0.11)	-0.06 (0.06)	-0.01 (0.03)	-0.06 (0.03)	-0.13 (0.03)	0.04 (0.01)
Male	-0.38 (0.07)	-0.24 (0.07)	-0.32 (0.05)	-0.26 (0.03)	-0.02 (0.01)	-0.03 (0.01)	-0.08 (0.01)	-0.02 (0.01)
Black	0.83 (0.11)	0.68 (0.11)	0.81 (0.09)	1.03 (0.05)	0.17 (0.02)	0.12 (0.02)	0.15 (0.02)	0.19 (0.01)
Hispanic	0.39 (0.15)	0.22 (0.17)	0.57 (0.09)	0.47 (0.05)	0.06 (0.03)	0.05 (0.03)	0.11 (0.02)	0.10 (0.01)
Education	-0.03 (0.12)	-0.05 (0.14)	-0.30 (0.10)	-0.21 (0.06)	-0.04 (0.03)	0.01 (0.03)	-0.02 (0.02)	0.00 (0.01)
Income	-0.96 (0.25)	-0.44 (0.16)	-0.38 (0.12)	-0.28 (0.06)	-0.19 (0.05)	-0.20 (0.03)	-0.21 (0.03)	-0.13 (0.01)
Unemployed	0.07 (0.16)	0.09 (0.19)	0.13 (0.11)	0.07 (0.06)	0.07 (0.03)	0.07 (0.04)	-0.02 (0.03)	0.05 (0.01)
Union	0.17 (0.09)	0.30 (0.10)	-0.04 (0.08)	0.08 (0.04)	0.03 (0.02)	0.05 (0.02)	0.00 (0.02)	0.05 (0.01)
South	-0.14 (0.06)	0.08 (0.08)	-0.31 (0.05)	-0.06 (0.03)	-0.04 (0.01)	-0.02 (0.02)	-0.05 (0.01)	-0.01 (0.01)
Intercept					0.51 (0.05)	0.60 (0.05)	0.69 (0.05)	0.40 (0.02)
PRE / R^2	0.09	0.09	0.07	0.17	0.11	0.15	0.14	0.16
N	1,425	980	1,963	5,160	1,477	1,011	1,976	5,329

Notes: Data are from the 2000–12 American National Election Studies. Entries for economic values are ordered probit coefficients and standard errors (in parentheses). Entries for policy are ordinary least squares estimates and standard errors. All dependent variables are coded so that higher values indicate more liberal preferences. "PRE" is the proportionate reduction in error for the values models.

TABLE A4.2. *Estimates for authoritarianism in panel data*

Authoritarianism	0.22 (0.12)
Engagement	0.08 (0.12)
Auth X Engage	−0.40 (0.17)
Age	0.01 (0.06)
Male	−0.01 (0.03)
Black	0.11 (0.04)
Education	0.04 (0.05)
Income	−0.10 (0.05)
Unemployed	0.08 (0.05)
Union	0.03 (0.03)
South	0.01 (0.03)
Lagged Preferences	0.41 (0.04)
Intercept	0.22 (0.09)
R^2	0.25
N	598

Notes: Data are from the 1992–4 American National Election Studies panel. The dependent variable is support for government guaranteed health insurance, and is measured in 1994. Entries are ordinary least squares estimates and standard errors (in parentheses). All independent variables are measured in 1992.

TABLE A4.3. *Estimates for need for closure*

Need for Closure	0.39 (0.14)
Engagement	0.19 (0.09)
NFC X Engage	−0.76 (0.18)
Age	−0.03 (0.03)
Male	−0.05 (0.01)
Black	0.18 (0.03)
Hispanic	0.07 (0.02)
Education	0.05 (0.02)
Income	−0.14 (0.03)
Unemployed	0.03 (0.03)
South	−0.05 (0.01)
Intercept	0.43 (0.07)
R^2	0.12
N	1,511

Notes: Data are from a 2008 Knowledge Networks national survey commissioned by Christopher Federico. The dependent variable is economic policy liberalism. Entries are ordinary least squares estimates and standard errors (in parentheses).

TABLE A4.4. *Estimates for the Big Five*

	CCAP	CCES	2012 ANES	
			Values	Policy
Openness to Experience	−0.12 (0.05)	0.04 (0.05)	−0.12 (0.25)	−0.08 (0.05)
Conscientiousness	0.12 (0.05)	0.13 (0.05)	0.34 (0.24)	−0.01 (0.04)
Extraversion	0.03 (0.04)	0.05 (0.04)	0.35 (0.21)	0.01 (0.04)
Agreeableness	0.04 (0.05)	0.06 (0.05)	−0.13 (0.25)	−0.07 (0.05)
Emotional Stability	−0.03 (0.04)	−0.02 (0.04)	−0.13 (0.23)	0.01 (0.04)
Political Engagement	−0.17 (0.07)	0.05 (0.05)	−0.20 (0.38)	−0.14 (0.07)
Openness X Engage	0.58 (0.07)	0.18 (0.06)	1.48 (0.39)	0.38 (0.07)
Conscientiousness X Engage	−0.31 (0.07)	−0.30 (0.05)	−1.33 (0.39)	−0.21 (0.07)
Extraversion X Engage	−0.11 (0.05)	−0.10 (0.05)	−0.69 (0.33)	−0.10 (0.06)
Agreeableness X Engage	0.08 (0.07)	0.09 (0.06)	0.54 (0.39)	0.17 (0.07)
Emotional Stability X Engage	−0.25 (0.06)	−0.16 (0.05)	−0.31 (0.36)	−0.09 (0.07)
Age	−0.09 (0.02)	−0.05 (0.02)	−0.02 (0.06)	0.04 (0.01)
Male	−0.07 (0.01)	−0.07 (0.01)	−0.23 (0.03)	−0.02 (0.01)
Black	0.12 (0.01)	0.23 (0.01)	0.96 (0.05)	0.18 (0.01)
Hispanic	0.05 (0.01)	0.07 (0.01)	0.43 (0.05)	0.09 (0.01)
Education	0.11 (0.01)	0.08 (0.01)	−0.08 (0.06)	0.04 (0.01)
Income	−0.22 (0.01)	−0.15 (0.01)	−0.18 (0.06)	−0.10 (0.01)
Unemployed	0.05 (0.01)	0.01 (0.01)	0.04 (0.06)	0.04 (0.01)
Union	0.08 (0.01)	0.07 (0.01)	0.06 (0.04)	0.04 (0.01)
South	−0.04 (0.01)	−0.04 (0.01)	−0.08 (0.03)	−0.02 (0.01)
Intercept	0.75 (0.05)	0.52 (0.05)		0.57 (0.04)
PRE / R²	0.14	0.15	0.17	0.14
N	12,744	12,634	5,154	5,325

Notes: Data are from the 2008 Cooperative Campaign Analysis Project (CCAP), the 2009 Cooperative Congressional Election Study (CCES), and the 2012 American National Election Study (ANES). The dependent variable for the CCAP, CCES, and ANES policy columns is economic policy liberalism, and entries are ordinary least squares estimates and standard errors (in parentheses). The dependent variable for the ANES values column is liberal economic values, and entries are ordered probit estimates and standard errors. "PRE" is the proportionate reduction in error for the values model.

TABLE A4.5. *Estimates for openness to change versus conservation*

Openness to Change	−0.18 (0.08)
Engagement	−0.29 (0.06)
Openness X Engage	0.53 (0.12)
Age	−0.01 (0.03)
Male	−0.03 (0.01)
Black	0.09 (0.02)
Hispanic	0.06 (0.02)
Education	0.02 (0.02)
Income	−0.23 (0.03)
Unemployed	0.02 (0.02)
South	−0.02 (0.01)

Intercept	0.66 (0.04)
R^2	0.08
N	2,105

Notes: Data are from the 2011 U.S. wave of the World Values Survey. The dependent variable is liberal economic values. Entries are ordinary least squares estimates and standard errors (in parentheses).

TABLE A4.6. *Estimates for risk aversion and authoritarianism*

	Risk Aversion	Authoritarianism
Trait	0.29 (0.11)	0.21 (0.05)
Impersonal	0.71 (0.14)	0.61 (0.07)
Trait X Impersonal	−0.82 (0.24)	−0.73 (0.12)
Age	−0.05 (0.03)	−0.07 (0.03)
Male	−0.05 (0.01)	−0.04 (0.01)
Black	0.18 (0.02)	0.20 (0.02)
Hispanic	0.07 (0.03)	0.07 (0.03)
Education	0.21 (0.06)	0.15 (0.06)
Income	−0.24 (0.04)	−0.27 (0.04)
South	−0.04 (0.01)	−0.04 (0.01)
	0.22 (0.08)	0.35 (0.06)
R^2	0.10	0.12
N	2,214	2,165

Notes: Data are from the 22nd Wave of the 2008–9 ANES panel study. The dependent variable is support for government spending and services. The left column measures "openness" via risk aversion, and the right column measures it via authoritarianism. The moderating variable is use of impersonal (versus self-interested) considerations in thinking about politics. Entries are ordinary least squares estimates and standard errors (in parentheses).

TABLE A4.7. *Estimates for authoritarianism among blacks and Latinos*

	Blacks		Latinos	
	Values	Policy	Values	Policy
Authoritarianism	0.46 (0.36)	−0.02 (0.06)	0.88 (0.29)	0.11 (0.05)
Engagement	0.90 (0.46)	0.02 (0.08)	0.77 (0.37)	0.19 (0.07)
Auth X Engage	−0.50 (0.57)	0.05 (0.10)	−1.53 (0.48)	−0.31 (0.09)
Age	0.04 (0.13)	0.00 (0.02)	−0.33 (0.12)	0.00 (0.02)
Male	−0.26 (0.06)	−0.02 (0.01)	−0.22 (0.06)	−0.02 (0.01)
Education	−0.17 (0.12)	−0.01 (0.02)	−0.29 (0.12)	−0.05 (0.02)
Income	−0.14 (0.13)	−0.03 (0.02)	−0.47 (0.13)	−0.15 (0.03)
Unemployed	0.06 (0.10)	0.02 (0.02)	0.09 (0.11)	0.00 (0.02)
Union	0.03 (0.09)	0.03 (0.02)	−0.05 (0.09)	0.01 (0.02)

(*continued*)

	Blacks		Latinos	
	Values	Policy	Values	Policy
South	−0.02 (0.06)	−0.01 (0.01)	−0.16 (0.06)	−0.02 (0.01)
2004 dummy	−0.04 (0.15)	0.01 (0.03)	0.19 (0.22)	0.10 (0.04)
2008 dummy	−0.12 (0.12)	0.05 (0.02)	0.54 (0.16)	0.18 (0.03)
2012 dummy	−0.09 (0.11)	−0.01 (0.02)	0.04 (0.15)	0.03 (0.03)
Intercept		0.66 (0.05)		0.54 (0.05)
PRE / R^2	0.00	0.03	0.00	0.12
N	1,668	1,692	1,375	1,419

Notes: Data are from the 2000–12 American National Election Studies (ANES). Entries for economic values are ordered probit coefficients and standard errors (in parentheses). Entries for policy are ordinary least squares estimates and standard errors. "PRE" is the proportionate reduction in error for the values models.

TABLE A4.8. *Estimates for Big Five among blacks and Latinos*

	Blacks		Latinos	
	Values	Policy	Values	Policy
Openness to Experience	0.43 (0.79)	0.02 (0.10)	−0.71 (0.56)	−0.18 (0.09)
Conscientiousness	1.19 (0.73)	0.03 (0.10)	1.05 (0.058)	0.05 (0.09)
Extraversion	−0.39 (0.66)	−0.06 (0.09)	0.55 (0.54)	0.03 (0.09)
Agreeableness	1.19 (0.81)	0.12 (0.11)	−0.11 (0.59)	−0.02 (0.10)
Emotional Stability	−1.71 (0.81)	−0.08 (0.11)	−0.33 (0.55)	−0.11 (0.09)
Political Engagement	0.14 (1.09)	0.00 (0.14)	−0.77 (0.96)	−0.35 (0.15)
Openness X Engage	−0.27 (1.28)	0.04 (0.17)	2.34 (0.96)	0.61 (0.16)
Conscientiousness X Engage	−1.29 (1.20)	−0.02 (0.16)	−1.92 (0.99)	−0.25 (0.16)
Extraversion X Engage	1.01 (1.04)	0.20 (0.14)	−0.132 (0.87)	−0.15 (0.14)
Agreeableness X Engage	−1.28 (1.30)	−0.10 (0.17)	0.59 (1.01)	0.01 (0.17)
Emotional Stability X Engage	2.59 (1.33)	0.05 (0.17)	0.74 (0.96)	0.28 (0.16)
Age	0.36 (0.17)	0.06 (0.02)	−0.22 (0.15)	−0.02 (0.02)
Male	−0.15 (0.09)	−0.01 (0.01)	−0.12 (0.08)	−0.03 (0.01)
Education	−0.40 (0.17)	−0.02 (0.02)	−0.21 (0.16)	−0.03 (0.03)
Income	−0.31 (0.17)	−0.04 (0.02)	−0.57 (0.16)	−0.12 (0.03)
Unemployed	−0.03 (0.13)	−0.01 (0.02)	0.10 (0.13)	0.00 (0.02)
Union	0.00 (0.12)	0.01 (0.02)	0.01 (0.11)	0.01 (0.02)
South	−0.03 (0.09)	0.02 (0.01)	−0.20 (0.08)	−0.02 (0.01)
Intercept		0.54 (0.09)		0.79 (0.09)
PRE / R^2	0.00	0.05	0.06	0.09
N	885	917	850	

Notes: Data are from the 2012 American National Election Studies (ANES). Entries for economic values are ordered probit coefficients and standard errors (in parentheses). Entries for policy are ordinary least squares estimates and standard errors. "PRE" is the proportionate reduction in error for the values models.

5

Openness and Partisan-Ideological Sorting

In the previous chapter, we presented extensive evidence that dispositional openness structures economic preferences, but in diametrically opposite ways for politically engaged and unengaged citizens. Among those who know and care about politics, openness promotes an expansive orientation toward government reflected in support for redistribution, social insurance, and market regulation. Among unengaged citizens, however, openness is associated with a limited government orientation reflected in an opposing set of policy preferences. We believe this reversal reflects the fact that engaged and unengaged citizens think about economic issues in different ways. For the engaged, debates about the role of government are seen through the prism of competing identity groups: open citizens support redistribution because they identify with the cultural liberalism of the Democratic Party, and closed citizens oppose it because they identify with the cultural conservatism of the Republicans. Thus, for people whose political identities are part and parcel of their self-concept, the impact of personality on social welfare preferences is mediated by team loyalty. However, the "us versus them" cultural animus roiling political discourse is of less import to politically unengaged citizens. Instead, we argue, they construe economic policy debates primarily in terms of instrumental consequences for the self. Therefore, unengaged citizens with closed personalities resonate with the security and certainty of an expanded social safety net, while open types prefer the individualism and self-direction of a restrained government.

The goal of Chapters 5–7 is to empirically examine the mechanisms underlying the reversal effect. To do so, we unpack it into its primary components. In this chapter, we focus on the concept of *conditional dispositional sorting*: the hypothesis that politically engaged – but not unengaged – citizens form their political identities by latching onto prominent symbols of American politics as a function of personality, including "Democrat," "Republican," "liberal," and "conservative," among others. As we argued in Chapter 3, engaged citizens form an affinity with these symbols on the basis of cultural resonance (e.g., God, guns, gays). Then, through partisan cue-taking and elite signaling – which we examine in Chapter 6 – engaged citizens figure out what economic positions "fit" with their broader identities.

In this chapter, we provide evidence that the link between openness and political identity is strongly conditional on political engagement. Engagement is likely to strengthen the relationship between personality and political sorting in two key ways. First, engagement should provide citizens with a clearer awareness of the differences between ideologies, parties, and information sources, particularly with respect to the cultural differences central to dispositional sorting in the present era (Hetherington and Weiler 2009). As scholars have long argued, the engaged simply know more about the defining attributes of the two major parties in American politics. Second, and more important from our perspective, engagement should also reflect a heightened concern with the expressive implications of ideological and partisan affiliation. That is, people who know and care about politics should be especially attuned to how partisan and ideological groups reflect their personalities and broader cultural commitments.

Although our framework follows from a long line of work on the implications of political engagement (or "sophistication") for the structure of belief systems (e.g., Converse 1964; Zaller 1992), this research has received little attention in the literature on personality. Rather, as we noted in Chapter 2, most studies in this literature focus on the direct effects of personality, often assuming unconditional relationships between particular psychological dispositions and "matching" political orientations (Jost 2006; Jost et al. 2003). This approach leaves little room for the relevance of political engagement as a moderator in the construction of political identity (but see Jost et al. 2009).

However, if our argument is correct, psychological dispositions should structure attachment to political groups only among engaged citizens. If this turns out to be true, it would imply that personality does not invariably express itself in terms of standing decisions to identify with a particular ideology or party, contrary to the typical assumption in the literature. Consistent with these claims, a few recent studies suggest that engagement strengthens the relationship between indicators of the open-closed personality dimension on one hand and left-right self-placement and partisanship on the other (Federico et al. 2011; Federico and Goren 2009; Federico and Tagar 2014; see also Osborne and Sibley 2012). In this chapter, we expand on these findings. As in the previous chapter, we draw on a wide array of popular indicators of openness, and test our hypothesis with data that is more representative than the norm for the literature. We find that engagement not only moderates the relationship between openness and political identification; it also moderates the relationship between openness and citizens' media preferences and who they opt to discuss politics with at an interpersonal level. Overall, this chapter provides the most extensive evidence to date that dispositional openness strongly shapes broad political orientations and information acquisition in representative samples of the population, but only for those who know and care about American politics. Among the politically unengaged, personality matters very little.

We also extend our examination of racial and ethnic heterogeneity. In the previous chapter, we demonstrated that the reversal effect holds for Latinos, but not African Americans. As we argued in Chapters 3 and 4, one reason for this is the strong tendency among self-identified black citizens to identify with the Democratic Party. This means that the primary mechanism linking openness to economic preferences among engaged citizens is inoperative for this group. In the present chapter, we provide more direct evidence for this claim. We show that openness-related traits strongly predict political identification among engaged citizens in general, and to a somewhat lesser extent, among engaged Latinos, but only weakly or not at all among African Americans. This chapter reinforces our claim that scholars of personality and politics must take race and ethnicity seriously in theorizing the dispositional roots of partisanship and ideology.

The remainder of this chapter proceeds in a similar fashion to Chapter 4. We begin by examining the relationship between various indicators of dispositional openness and political identification and information seeking in the population as a whole, taking advantage of all relevant data at our disposal. In particular, we provide evidence for an interaction between engagement and dispositional openness using a wide array of trait indicators, measures of political identity and information seeking, and datasets spanning more than twenty years of American politics. We then estimate identical models for blacks and Latinos where we have data sufficient to the task.

Authoritarianism and Political Identity

As described in Chapters 2 and 4, studies of mass political behavior have often relied on authoritarianism as a primary (negative) indicator of openness. Hetherington and Weiler (2009) show that as a result of rising cultural divisions between Democrats and Republicans over the past two decades, authoritarianism is now a key basis of partisan and ideological sorting (see also Cizmar et al. 2014; Feldman 2003; Stenner 2005). In this chapter, we extend their work by demonstrating the *conditional* nature of the relationship between authoritarianism and political identity. In contrast to past work, we predict minimal authoritarianism-based sorting among unengaged citizens. At high levels of engagement, however, we expect authoritarianism to be among the most important bases of political identification.

Ideological Self-Labeling

During the 2012 presidential election, the survey firm YouGov conducted a series of surveys as part of its Model Politics initiative.[1] These data provide a unique opportunity to examine the factors that determine why citizens choose to identify with some ideological labels over others. In one wave of the panel, respondents were presented with a variety of labels associated with the left and right in contemporary American politics, including environmentalist, feminist, green, liberal, progressive, and socialist on the left, and conservative, Tea Party, and traditional on the right. We created two new count variables from these responses, one for left-wing labels (ranging from zero to six) and one for right-wing labels (ranging from zero to three). These variables indicate the number of left-wing and right-wing labels with which survey respondents identified. The survey also administered a five-item measure of authoritarianism similar to that used in Chapter 4.[2] To measure political engagement, we rely on items averaging political knowledge and interest.[3] We expect that authoritarianism will be associated with fewer liberal identifications and more

---

[1] See http://today.yougov.com/news/categories/model-politics/. Respondents were selected from YouGov's PollingPoint panel, an opt-in Internet panel, and then matched on a set of demographic and political characteristics to a random sample (stratified by age, gender, race, education, and region) from the 2005–7 American Community Survey. We thank Sunshine Hillygus for help with these data.

[2] The only difference is the inclusion of one additional value trade-off: "Is it more important for a child to be creative or disciplined?" See Table 4.1 for the other items.

[3] The former consisted of ten factual questions, and the latter was a standard self-report on a three-point scale, similar to the ANES.

conservative identifications. Moreover, we expect these relationships to hold principally – and perhaps *only* – among politically engaged citizens.[4]

We estimated two models of ideological self-labeling – one for liberal labels and one for conservative labels.[5] The results are shown in Figure 5.1. As in Chapter 4, the y-axis in each plot represents the effect of personality (i.e., the difference between high and low authoritarians in the predicted number of liberal or conservative labels with which respondents identify). The x-axis represents increasing levels of political engagement. Panel A depicts the estimates for liberal labels, and Panel B does so for conservative labels. As the figure indicates, there is strong evidence of conditional dispositional sorting. When engagement is low, there is only a small sorting effect: a moderate increase in authoritarianism (moving from the 25th to the 75th percentile) is associated with about 0.20 fewer liberal labels applied to the self, and a large increase in authoritarianism (moving from the 5th to the 95th percentile) is associated with about 0.50–0.75 fewer liberal labels. Put another way, at low levels of engagement, high and low authoritarians differ in ideological identification by less than one liberal label, on average. Moreover, there is no statistically significant association between authoritarianism and conservative identification at the lowest level of engagement, and only a weak relationship at moderately low levels of engagement. Overall, then, authoritarianism is only weakly associated with ideological self-labeling among politically unengaged citizens.

As expected, the association between authoritarianism and ideological self-labeling increases rapidly as engagement increases. Among the highly engaged, a moderate change in authoritarianism is associated with 0.50–0.65 fewer liberal identifications and 0.30–0.50 additional conservative identifications, and a large change in authoritarianism is associated with 1.5–2.0 fewer liberal labels and 0.85–1.25 more conservative labels. Thus, the net gap in left-right self-identification as a function of

---

[4] In contrast to Chapter 4, note that we have no expectations for a "reversal" in the context of political identification. We simply expect an enhancement of the influence of personality for the engaged relative to the unengaged.

[5] We modeled each as a poisson process. Specifically, we estimated a quasipoisson model to account for overdispersion in the dependent variables. The poisson distribution has only one parameter, and thus forces the mean and variance to be equal. This is rarely the case in practice. The quasipoisson model allows for overdispersion, which is simply an estimate of how much larger the variance is than the mean. The coefficients of the quasipoisson model can be interpreted identically to those of the poisson model, as changes in the log of the expected count. As in the previous chapter, all regression estimates are contained in the appendix to this chapter.

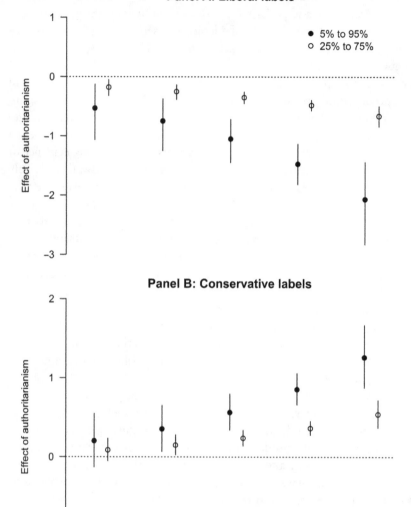

FIGURE 5.1. The relationship between authoritarianism and ideological self-labeling across political engagement, 2012 Model Politics

authoritarianism increases drastically as engagement moves from low to high. Among the politically engaged, high authoritarians are much more likely to identify with right-wing labels than left-wing labels, and vice-versa.

Partisan and Ideological Identification

The YouGov survey is appealing for its inclusion of a variety of ideological labels. However, the American National Election Studies (ANES) contain more representative samples of the American public, and we turn to these to conduct additional tests of the dispositional sorting hypothesis. As in Chapter 4, we draw on the 2000, 2004, 2008, and 2012 ANES studies. Each of these surveys contains traditional measures of partisan and ideological identification. The former asks respondents to indicate whether they identify as a Democrat, a Republican, an Independent, or "something else altogether." Respondents who identify as a Democrat or a Republican are then asked whether they identify "strongly" or "not strongly" with their party. Respondents who indicate Independent or something else are asked whether they feel closer to one party or the other. This branching method produces a seven-point scale ranging from "strong Democrat" to "strong Republican," including a middle "true Independent" category. Ideological identification is also measured on a seven-point scale, ranging from "extremely liberal" to "extremely conservative," but without the branching format. For both partisanship and ideology, we combined the three categories on the political left (e.g., leaning, weak, and strong Democrats) and the three on the political right (e.g., leaning, weak, and strong Republicans), and treated the "true Independent" and "moderate" categories as midpoints. This gave us two three-point scales measuring partisan and ideological identification, respectively.[6] We measured political engagement using the same items as Chapter 4, along with the same set of controls.

We estimated eight regression models,[7] one for partisanship and one for ideological self-identification in each election year. The relevant plots are shown in Figure 5.2. The y-axis in each panel shows the difference between high and low authoritarians in the probability of Republican (A–D) or conservative (E–H) identification. In other words, each figure shows how the propensity to identify with right-wing partisan and ideological groups changes as a function of authoritarianism at each level of

---

[6] The seven-point scales often demonstrate nonlinearity such that "leaners" are equally or more partisan than "weak" identifiers. Thus, we simply examine *identification*: citizens' willingness to place themselves in one category or the other.

[7] We treat each three-category dependent variable as ordinal, and use a probit link function.

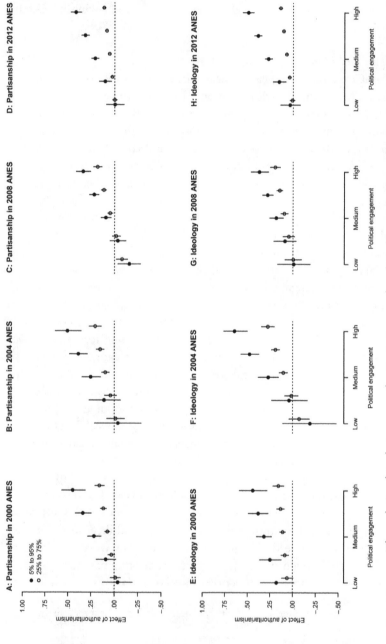

FIGURE 5.2. The relationship between authoritarianism and political partisanship and ideology across political engagement, 2000–2012 ANES

political engagement.[8] The estimates indicate that there is little connection between personality and political identity among unengaged citizens. With two exceptions – one in 2008 for partisanship (see later in this chapter) and one in 2000 for ideology – unengaged citizens who score low in authoritarianism are just as likely to identify as Republicans and conservatives as those who score high in authoritarianism. This is a critical finding. It is simply not true that authoritarianism is universally influential in shaping political orientations in the contemporary U.S. public. Among the broad swath of citizens who pay minimal attention to politics, authoritarianism is mostly unrelated to political identity.

As engagement increases, however, these relationships strengthen dramatically. At middling levels of engagement, a moderate change in authoritarianism is associated with a five to ten percentage point increase in the likelihood of identifying as a Republican or a conservative, and a large change in authoritarianism is associated with a ten to thirty percentage point increase. At the highest levels of engagement, citizens are quite strongly sorted by authoritarianism: moderate differences entail identification gaps of ten to thirty percentage points, and large differences in authoritarianism are associated with very large gaps. In 2004, for instance, highly engaged, high authoritarians are sixty-five percentage points more likely to identify as conservative than their engaged but low authoritarian counterparts. In 2012, engaged high authoritarians are forty-two points more likely to identify as Republican than engaged low authoritarians. These are strikingly large effect sizes.

Taken together, these findings provide support for – but also an important caveat to – Hetherington and Weiler's (2009) findings: the impact of authoritarianism on political identity depends critically on political engagement. Put another way, by averaging over engagement-based heterogeneity, previous work both overstates and understates the impact of authoritarianism on political orientation. It overstates its importance for unengaged citizens, but understates its importance for the engaged, for whom authoritarianism is more influential in shaping identity than previous research suggests. Among citizens who know and care about American politics, simple choices over childrearing values are among the best, if not the best, predictor of how citizens sort into partisan and ideological groups. Indeed, with the possible exception of race, no

---

[8] The results would look similar, but reversed in sign, for the probabilities of left-wing identification.

other predictor in our regression models reliably exceeds the influence of authoritarianism among the engaged (including income).

Finally, it is worth pointing out that the partisanship results for 2008 come with a twist (see Panel C). Here, in the midst of a financial crisis, an unanticipated reversal occurs such that at low levels of political engagement, high authoritarians are actually *less* likely to identify as Republicans and conservatives than low authoritarians. Although unexpected, it is intriguing that this reversal emerges only in 2008, during an economic meltdown presided over by a Republican president. If, as we have claimed, unengaged citizens are less concerned with the cultural aspects of party politics, it is possible that this reversal reflects a tendency among unengaged authoritarian individuals – that is, those who prioritize order, certainty, and security – to prefer the economic interventionism of the Democrats in a time of great economic uncertainty. It is impossible to test this hypothesis directly, but, as we will see, it replicates in other data during the same time period using a distinct measure of openness.

A Test with Panel Data

As in Chapter 4, the 1992–4 ANES panel study provides an opportunity to replicate our findings in a context with stronger claims on causal direction. Given that this period also corresponds with a sharp rise in cultural polarization between the parties (see Figure 3.2), there is reason to expect that many citizens may have reconsidered their partisan identities.[9] If so, then authoritarianism should, all else equal, promote movement toward the Republican Party from 1992 to 1994, and this should be particularly likely among the politically engaged. To test this idea, we estimated models similar to those described earlier, with partisanship measured in 1994 as the dependent variable and with initial partisanship in 1992 included as a control.

The results of this analysis are shown in Figure 5.3. The estimates are rather imprecise; this is due to both the relatively small sample size (about 550 respondents) and the fact that changes in partisanship are rather rare over short periods of time. Nonetheless, the pattern is similar to that from the cross-sectional data. At low levels of engagement, we find no tendency for authoritarianism to promote movement toward Republican identification from 1992 to 1994. At moderate and high levels of engagement, however, there is a significant increase. In particular,

---

[9] Recall from the discussion in Chapter 4 that it is important to examine periods where there is a strong expectation for a reconsideration of previous opinions.

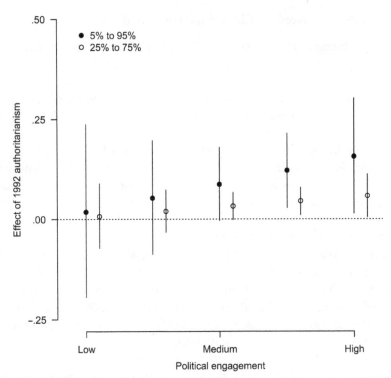

FIGURE 5.3. The relationship between authoritarianism and changes in partisanship from 1992–1994 across political engagement, ANES

engaged citizens high in authoritarianism were more likely than their low authoritarianism counterparts to shift in a Republican direction between 1992 and 1994. This is consistent both with our general theory, and with the claim that this period coincided with an acceleration in the polarization of party imagery along cultural lines.

Summary

In sum, our investigation of the relationship between authoritarianism and political identification strongly supports the conditional dispositional sorting hypothesis. Past work has considered this relationship in unconditional terms. In contrast, we have argued that openness influences political identity only among citizens who know and care about politics. The results of this first set of empirical tests could not be clearer. Authoritarianism is among the best predictors of political identity in American politics, but only for politically engaged citizens. Among the unengaged, we find little to no relationship at all.

Need for Closure and Political Identity

As in the previous chapter, our strategy is to look for consistent patterns across a range of indicators of openness utilized in the literature, and the need for closure is one of the most commonly used. Our 2008 Knowledge Networks survey contains a reliable fourteen-item measure of the need for closure that was utilized in Chapter 4 to test the reversal hypothesis (see Table 4.2). We estimated the same models as for authoritarianism – predicting partisan and ideological identification – but substituted the need for closure as our key independent variable. The results – depicted in Figure 5.4 – indicate that while there is little evidence of dispositional sorting among unengaged citizens, it is clearly evident among the engaged. For the latter, a moderate change in need for closure is associated with a ten to fifteen percentage point increase in the likelihood of identifying as a Republican and a conservative, whereas a large change in the trait is associated with a twenty to thirty percentage point increase. As with authoritarianism, then, sorting on the basis of need for closure depends strongly on political engagement, and among the engaged, need for closure is among the best predictors of partisan and ideological identification. Indeed, it is worth emphasizing once again the substantive magnitude of these personality effects. There are few other variables in American politics that predict thirty or more percentage point gaps in political identification. Citizens' general taste for certainty over uncertainty and ambiguity appears to be one of those few.

We again find an unanticipated reversal of the relationship between a measure of openness and partisan identification among the least engaged citizens in the 2008 data. At the lowest levels of engagement, citizens high in need for closure are about twenty-five points *less* likely to identify as Republicans in 2008 than their low need for closure counterparts. This mirrors our findings for authoritarianism in the 2008 ANES. The replication of this effect across two measures of a similar personality construct suggests that the authoritarianism pattern is not a fluke, but that a common underlying concern is driving unengaged, dispositionally closed citizens toward the Democratic Party during the 2008 election. Again, given that this occurred during the heart of the financial crisis, it is not unreasonable to read this pattern in a similar way to our results in the previous chapter; that is, as a flight to a party that represents government-provided economic security in a time period of substantial economic *un*certainty. This is more plausible given that unengaged citizens also show higher levels of volatility in partisanship itself over time (e.g., Lavine et al. 2012).

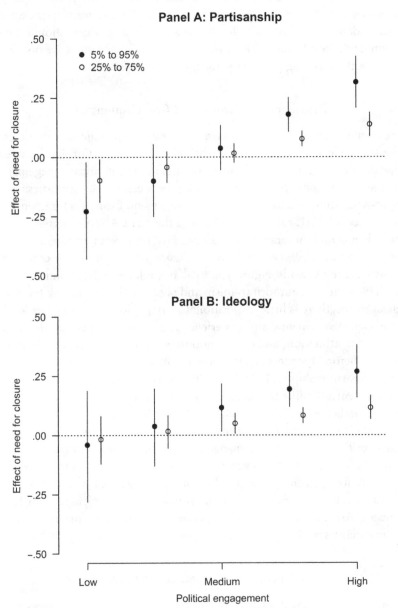

FIGURE 5.4. The relationship between need for cognitive closure and political partisanship and ideology across political engagement, 2008 KN

As with authoritarianism, however, this is an unanticipated finding. Moreover, we do not find this pattern with the Big Five traits in the 2008 CCAP data examined later in this chapter. Future work should thus examine the conditions under which personality might influence political identification among politically unengaged citizens as well.

The Big Five: Openness and Conscientiousness

We turn now to the Big Five traits of openness to experience and conscientiousness. Here, we expect an increasingly negative relationship between openness and right-wing affiliation as a function of political engagement, and an increasingly positive relationship between conscientiousness and right-wing affiliation as a function of engagement. Estimates for openness in the 2008 CCAP, the 2009 CCES, and the 2012 ANES – derived from models including interactions of all Big Five traits with engagement (see the chapter appendix) – are shown in Figure 5.5, and those for conscientiousness are shown in Figure 5.6.[10] All around, these data confirm what we have seen with authoritarianism and need for closure: at low levels of engagement, there is little dispositional sorting. However, at higher levels of engagement, openness to experience is a strong negative predictor of right-wing affiliation, and conscientiousness is a moderately strong positive predictor. Openness is a stronger predictor of both forms of identification (partisanship and ideology) than conscientiousness at all levels of engagement, a finding that is consistent with past work (e.g., Carney et al. 2008; Gerber et al. 2010; McCrae 1996; Mondak 2010). Further, the magnitude of the relationship between openness to experience and political identification among the engaged is quite impressive. For engaged citizens, the identification gap across levels of openness ranges from twenty to thirty-five percentage points. In sum, these two Big Five personality traits most strongly translate into political identity among highly engaged citizens. Among the unengaged, openness and conscientiousness play a substantially smaller role in shaping political orientation.

Values: Openness to Change versus Conservation

Our next set of analyses focuses on a key dimension of openness that Schwartz (1992) identified in his influential model of human values. As described in Chapter 4, the U.S. national sample from the 2011 wave of the

---

[10] See Chapter 4 for a description of these data.

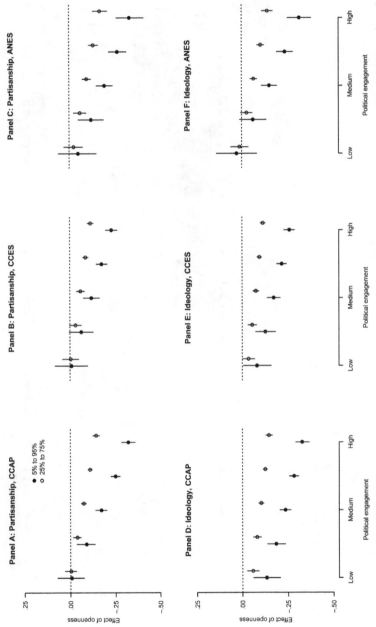

FIGURE 5.5. The relationship between openness to experience and political partisanship and ideology across political engagement, 2008 CCAP, 2009 CCES, and 2012 ANES

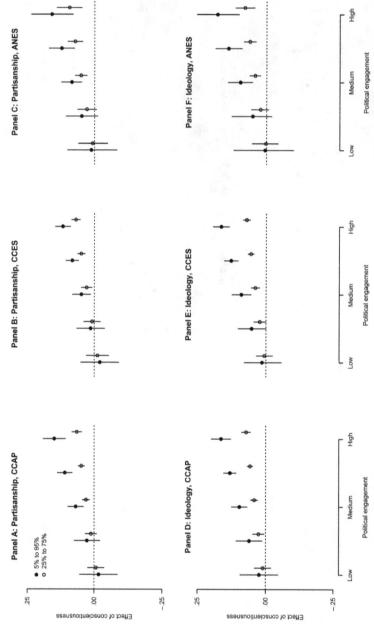

FIGURE 5.6. The relationship between conscientiousness and political partisanship and ideology across political engagement, 2008 CCAP, 2009 CCES, and 2012 ANES

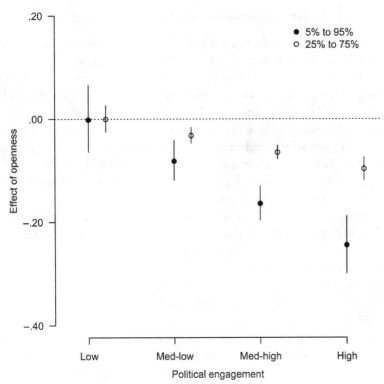

FIGURE 5.7. The relationship between openness to change vs. conservation and left-right identification across political engagement, 2011 WVS

World Values Survey contains six items operationalizing openness to change versus conservation. It also asks respondents to place themselves on a ten-point scale anchored on one end by "left" and on the other end by "right." We regressed this measure of ideological identification on the openness to change versus conservation scale, its interaction with political interest,[11] and our standard set of controls. The estimates, shown in Figure 5.7, support the dispositional sorting hypothesis: engaged – but not unengaged – respondents connect the political terms "left" and "right" to the value dimension of openness to change versus conservation. Engaged respondents moderately high in openness are about ten percentage points less right-wing than similarly engaged respondents moderately low in openness. The difference between engaged citizens high and low in openness is about one-quarter of the scale. Among citizens low in engagement, by contrast, this relationship drops significantly, and among the truly uninterested it is zero.

[11] Recall from Chapter 4 that political knowledge was not available in the 2011 WVS.

Moral Foundations and Political Identity

We now consider a set of variables associated with moral foundations theory (MFT; Graham et al. 2009; Haidt 2012). As we discussed in Chapter 2, MFT posits five primary foundations of moral judgment and decision making – harm, fairness, loyalty, authority, and sanctity – which can be grouped into individualizing (i.e., harm and fairness) and binding (i.e., loyalty, authority, and sanctity) categories. According to Haidt (2012), the primary line of left–right conflict in contemporary American politics is reflected in the subjective importance and perceived legitimacy of the binding foundations. Indeed, the latter are conceptually related to the other personality constructs examined in this chapter and previous ones; in particular, they overlap strongly with the construct of authoritarianism as defined in the recent literature (e.g., Feldman 2003; Hetherington and Weiler 2009), and with Schwartz's (1992) conservation versus openness to change value dimension.

In 2012, we conducted an online survey experiment as part of Duke University's module of the Cooperative Congressional Election Study (CCES). Prior to the experimental portion of the study (described further in Chapter 6), respondents completed a shortened version of the Moral Foundations Questionnaire, which measured the subjective importance that respondents place on the five foundations (see Table 6.3).[12] Consistent with previous work, we expect that individuals who rate the binding moral foundations as particularly important will be more likely to hold right-wing identities than those who place less value on them. Moreover, we expect these effects to be stronger among the politically engaged. Unfortunately, the 2012 CCES contained a relatively weak measure of engagement – it included an interest in politics item, but only two political knowledge items. These were skewed such that 45 percent of the sample attained the *highest* level of engagement and very few respondents scored low on the measure. We thus divided the sample into two groups: relatively low (bottom 55%) and relatively high (top 45%). Given this rather coarse distinction, we expect our results to be less differentiated by engagement than in previous analyses. In particular, we are limited in what we can say about the lowest levels of engagement.

Estimates of the impact of binding moral foundations on partisan and ideological identification, reported in Panels A and B of Figure 5.8, are consistent with those presented earlier: the more importance respondents

[12] We describe this survey instrument in detail in Chapter 6. See also www.yourmorals.org/explore.php.

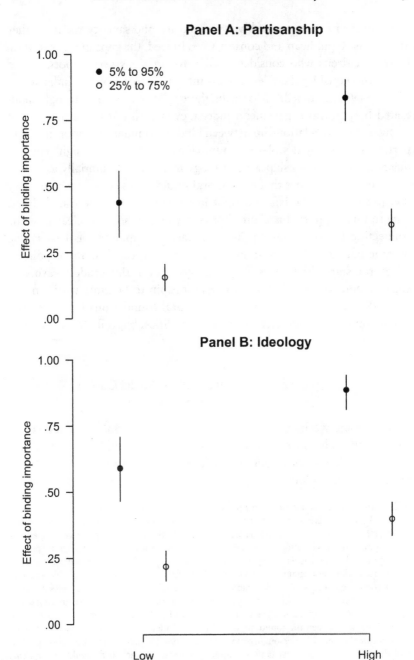

FIGURE 5.8. The relationship between binding moral foundation importance and political partisanship and ideology across political engagement, 2012 CCES

place on the foundations of loyalty, authority, and sanctity, the more they identify as Republican and conservative. Indeed, the gaps in identification between citizens who consider binding foundations very important and those who consider them less important is the largest of any indicator of openness yet examined.[13] Moreover, these relationships are strongly moderated by political engagement. Indeed, even with our crude measure of engagement, the relationship between binding foundation importance and partisanship nearly doubles when moving from "low" to "high" engagement, and the relationship with ideology increases substantially as well.

Recent work argues that these moral foundations constitute a primary division between the left and right in contemporary American politics. Our results support this claim, but conditionally so. It is clear that the connection between moral principles, partisanship, and ideology is due in large part to citizens who know and care a great deal about politics. Given the stark differences observed across even this crude measure of engagement, we would expect the relationship to be quite weak among the *truly* unengaged. In sum, binding moral foundations have a strong impact on political identity in American politics, but only for a subset of citizens.

Sources of Political Information: Media Choice and Social Networks

To this point we have examined dispositional sorting with respect to core political identifications. This is an important task, because partisanship and ideology are among the strongest inputs to a variety of political preferences, including those pertaining to social welfare and economic

---

[13] The strength of the relationship relative to other indicators of openness, however, is also likely a reflection of the fact that these moral foundations are conceptually much closer to the cultural orientations we believe drive the relationship between openness and political identification in the first place, and are thus more proximate to politics than our other indicators of personality. For example, two of the items measuring binding foundations ask about the importance of the following considerations: "Whether or not someone conformed to the traditions of society," and "Whether or not someone's action showed love for his or her country." While many items are close in content to standard personality scales, the more cultural and political items may strengthen the relationship between the foundations and political identification. This general problem of political content in personality measures has long plagued political psychology, and is the impetus for the construction of apolitical measures, such as the childrearing items measuring authoritarianism. We nonetheless consider the role of moral foundations here, because moral foundations theory has been influential in the recent literature in psychology. However, the reader should keep these caveats in mind when interpreting the effect sizes relative to other measures of openness.

redistribution (e.g., Cohen 2003). We now examine the impact of openness on two additional influences on political perception and judgment: media choice and political discussion partners.

Political Media Choice

Media outlets such as newspapers, online magazines, and cable news are primary sources of political information for citizens who follow politics. Importantly, however, citizens often seek out congenial media sources – that is, sources that share important identity attributes (Bennett and Manheim 2006; Iyengar and Hahn 2009; Iyengar et al. 2008; Lavine et al. 2005; Stroud 2008; Sunstein 2009). For example, Democrats may disproportionately watch MSNBC, because this network often reports news in a way that is congenial to Democrats and antagonistic to Republicans. This process of *selective exposure* is abetted by the increasing ideological fragmentation of the news media, which "allows people to construct their own personal information environment in which they only receive news from sources that share their ideological frame of reference" (Arceneaux and Johnson 2013). Research indicates that partisan biases in exposure to political information may be especially common among engaged citizens. For example, Iyengar and Hahn (2009) randomly attributed political news stories on a variety of topics to one of four media sources: Fox News, NPR, CNN, or the BBC. Participants in the study were provided with a brief headline of each story along with the news organization's logo, and were then asked to indicate which of the four reports on each issue they would most like to read. The authors found that Republicans preferred to read a story when it was attributed to Fox News, whereas Democrats preferred to read the same story when it was attributed to NPR, CNN, or the BBC (i.e., any outlet but Fox).[14] Importantly, they found that this selection bias was substantially enhanced – and to an equal extent among Republicans and Democrats – for those high in political engagement (see also Jacobson 2010; Taber and Lodge 2006).

In addition to items concerning ideological self-labeling, the 2012 YouGov Model Politics survey included a host of items asking about political media choice. We divided these into outlets that can be readily categorized as left- or right-leaning. Three sources were stereotypically right-leaning: *Fox News Sunday*, *Fox and Friends*, and *Fox Special Report*

---

[14] They also included a control condition in which a story was not attributed to any news source and found that partisans of both stripes expressed greater interest in reading a story when it was attributed to a desired source than when it contained no attribution.

with Bret Baier; and three sources were stereotypically left-leaning: *The Daily Show, The Colbert Report,* and *MSNBC Politics Nation.* We estimated models of media exposure similar to those for ideological self-labeling in Figure 5.1, with separate models for left- and right-leaning sources.[15] The expected count for each type of outlet was modeled as a function of authoritarianism and its interaction with engagement, as well as our standard set of controls.

The results, shown in Figure 5.9, are similar to those reported for political identification. The y-axis in Figure 5.9 represents the change in the expected count of regularly consumed media outlets as a function of moderate and large changes in authoritarianism, and the x-axis represents increasing levels of political engagement. Panels A and B indicate strong dispositional sorting into congenial media environments, but only among engaged citizens. At low and moderate levels of political engagement, authoritarianism bears little relationship to media choice. At high levels of engagement, however, there is a fairly strong relationship between authoritarianism and informational sorting. Here, highly authoritarian citizens consume more than one additional conservative outlet and about one fewer liberal outlet than citizens low in authoritarianism, producing an overall gap of about two outlets on average; moderate changes in authoritarianism correspond to a gap of a bit less than one outlet on average. These results suggest a tendency for engaged – but not unengaged – citizens to consume political media that "fit" their deep-seated personality orientations.

Political Discussion Partners

Given that people often prefer to discuss politics with like-minded individuals, informational sorting may also occur through the composition of one's social network (Mutz 2006; Pentland 2014). The people with whom we choose to discuss politics shape our understanding of the political world in a variety of ways: by providing information and opinions, by legitimizing or delegitimizing other information sources, by providing signals about what types of opinions are acceptable and unacceptable within a given social group, or simply by relaying information about partisan and ideological conflict at the elite level that would otherwise go unnoticed (e.g., Huckfeldt 2014; Huckfeldt, Johnson, and Sprague 2004; Sinclair 2012). Here, we examine whether dispositional openness shapes the partisan character of one's social network, and whether this relationship is more pronounced among politically engaged citizens.

---

[15] We again estimate quasipoisson models for the counts of liberal and conservative media outlets.

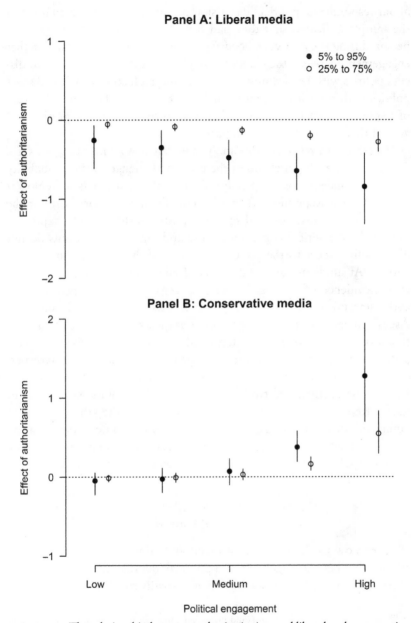

FIGURE 5.9. The relationship between authoritarianism and liberal and conservative media choices across political engagement, 2012 Model Politics

The 2000 American National Election Study included several questions about respondents' political discussion partners. About three quarters of the sample indicated that they had discussed politics with at least one person during the past year. Focusing on this subsample, we ask whether engagement increases the extent to which low authoritarians tend to discuss politics with left-leaning individuals and high authoritarians discuss politics with right-leaning individuals. To determine the political nature of respondents' social networks, they were asked to recall the presidential vote of their primary discussion partner.[16]

We report the results of this analysis in Panels A and B of Figure 5.10. The y-axis in each panel shows the estimated change in the probability that a respondent's primary political discussion partner is a Democrat (Panel A) or a Republican (Panel B). Our findings mirror those for the other aspects of dispositional sorting reported earlier in this chapter. At low levels of political engagement, low and high authoritarians do not differ with respect to the political leanings of their primary discussion partner. At moderate and high levels of engagement, however, we find strong evidence of sorting. Engaged citizens at the 75th percentile of authoritarianism are five to ten points less likely to have a Democratic discussion partner than engaged citizens at the 25th percentile of authoritarianism, and the former are ten to fifteen points more likely to have a Republican discussion partner. Engaged respondents at the 95th percentile of authoritarianism are ten to twenty points less likely to have a Democratic partner, and twenty-five to thirty-five points more likely to have a Republican discussion partner than those at the 5th percentile of authoritarianism. In sum, as we have seen with political identification and news media exposure, the impact of personality on political sorting within social networks is strongly moderated by engagement.

Openness and Political Identity among Blacks and Latinos

We turn now to the question of racial and ethnic heterogeneity in the relationship between openness and political identification. Does the role of personality in political sorting extend broadly to all racial subgroups?

[16] While a substantial proportion could not recall this information (~40%), the majority offered a response. We trichotomized the dependent variable such that two categories corresponded with partner votes for Gore or Bush, and individuals who responded "don't know," "other," or "ineligible to vote" were placed in a distinct category. The model was estimated as a multinomial logit to preserve the nominal character of the variable.

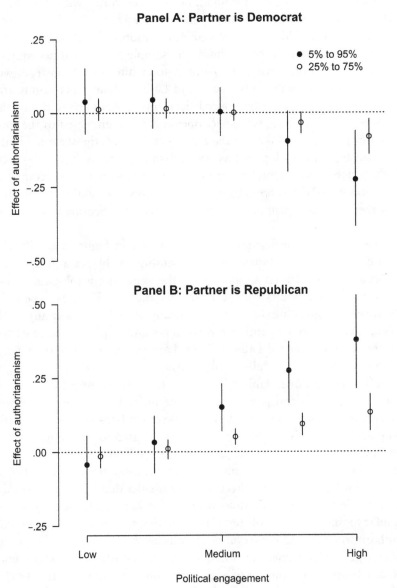

FIGURE 5.10. The relationship between authoritarianism and the partisanship of primary political discussion partners across political engagement, 2000 ANES

As in Chapter 4, we find that the patterns observed in the full-sample analyses reported previously hold for non-Latino whites, with effect sizes that are a bit larger than for the population as a whole. That is, openness influences political identification and information seeking more strongly among the engaged when we limit our sample to non-Latino whites. As such, we do not review the findings for whites in full; instead, we focus our attention here on blacks and Latinos. Our expectations are mixed. For blacks, the skew on partisanship is more severe than it is for ideology. Therefore, we expect openness to be unrelated to the former, but potentially linked to the latter. For Latinos, the skew for both partisanship and ideology is less severe than for blacks; thus, we expect both variables to respond to openness. As in Chapter 4, we combine the 2000–12 ANES surveys to examine the impact of authoritarianism, and then turn to openness to experience and conscientiousness in the 2012 ANES.

The results for authoritarianism are shown in Figure 5.11. Panels A and B report the estimates for partisanship for blacks and Latinos, respectively, and Panels C and D do the same for ideological identification. A few points emerge from this analysis. First, as expected, authoritarianism is unrelated to partisanship among blacks at any level of engagement. Second, authoritarianism is significantly related to partisanship among engaged Latinos. Thus, Latinos evince a pattern similar to that observed in the full-sample analyses and among whites, though the effect of authoritarianism is weaker. Even at the upper reaches of engagement, high and low authoritarians differ by only ten to fifteen percentage points. This weaker effect likely explains (at least in part) why authoritarianism is also more weakly related to economic preferences among engaged Latinos (see Chapter 4). Third, authoritarianism is significantly related to ideological identification among both blacks and Latinos, but again, the effect sizes are smaller than in the population as a whole (and for non-Latino whites). For Latinos, we see a pattern similar to that for the whole population, in that the relationship between authoritarianism and conservative identification increases as a function of engagement (for unengaged Latinos, the relationship is minimal). For blacks, however, the impact of authoritarianism is uniform across levels of engagement. Thus, overall, authoritarianism predicts party identification among engaged Latinos, as well as ideological identification among both minority groups. In all cases, however, the effects are smaller than for the population considered as a whole and for non-Latino whites considered separately.

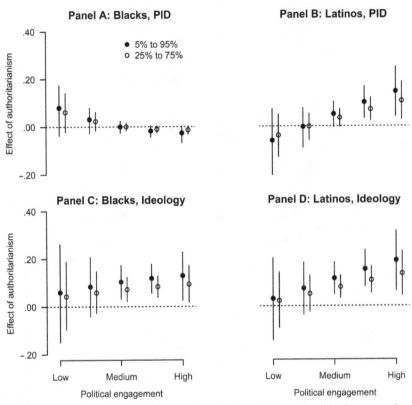

FIGURE 5.11. The relationship between authoritarianism and political partisanship and ideology across political engagement for African Americans and Latinos, 2000–2012 ANES

Figure 5.12 graphically displays the estimates for the Big Five traits of openness to experience and conscientiousness from the 2012 ANES. In this case, the results for blacks are consistent and clear: neither trait shows any link to either form of political identity (partisanship or ideological identification). Among Latinos, by contrast, the pattern looks very similar to the full sample analyses and those for whites. Indeed, openness to experience has a large, negative influence on both Republican and conservative identification for Latinos. At the upper reaches of engagement, Latinos differ by more than thirty-five percentage points in Republican affiliation across the range of openness. For ideological identification, the effect of openness exceeds twenty-five points among Latinos. This dovetails with what we found in Chapter 4: openness to experience had a meaningful impact on economic preferences among engaged Latinos.

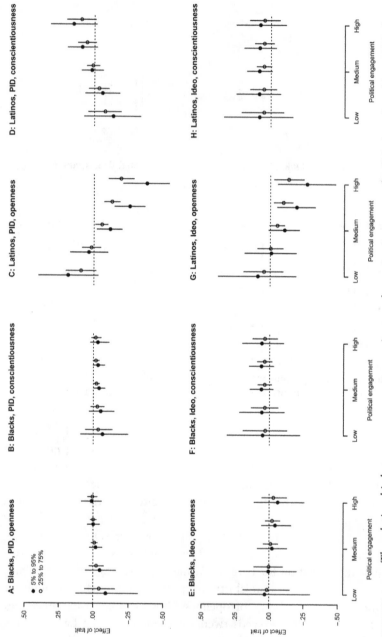

FIGURE 5.12. The relationship between openness to experience and conscientiousness and political partisanship and ideology across political engagement for African Americans and Latinos, 2012 ANES

At low levels of engagement, however, the relationship between openness and identity is nonsignificant.[17] Finally, there is a marginally significant – if weak – relationship between conscientiousness and political identification among Latinos. The effect of conscientiousness on partisanship is marginally significant at the highest levels of engagement, and falls to non-significance as engagement declines, but there is no significant relationship with ideological identification at any level of engagement. We conclude that openness exerts a strong impact on Latino political identification among engaged citizens, but that conscientiousness plays a more muted role. This is consistent with patterns in prior research. For blacks, neither openness nor conscientiousness is relevant to political identity at any level of engagement.

In sum, traits related to the open-closed personality dimension show substantial heterogeneity in their influence on political identification across major subgroups of the American electorate. For the population considered as a whole, and for whites (in analyses not shown here), there is a highly robust tendency for traits related to openness to inhibit (promote) right-wing (left-wing) identity and information seeking among politically engaged, but not unengaged, citizens. For blacks, however, this is rarely true. For engaged Latinos, openness influences political identity, just as it does for the broader population considered as a whole. The magnitude of these relationships is smaller for authoritarianism and conscientiousness, but of similar size for the trait of openness to experience. Thus, for both economic preferences (Chapter 4) and political identity (Chapter 5), Latinos fall between our full sample estimates (and those for whites) and those for blacks.

Conclusion

Using a variety of indicators of dispositional openness and multiple sources of data, we uncover a highly robust pattern for a large portion of the citizenry: closed citizens are attracted to right-wing labels, groups, media sources, and discussion partners, whereas open citizens are attracted to labels and sources on the political left. Importantly, however, we find strong and consistent evidence that these relationships are conditional on political engagement. Among politically inattentive individuals, there is scant association between personality and political sorting,

---

[17] There is also some suggestion that openness might promote Republican identification among unengaged Latinos, but the effect is inefficiently estimated.

while at high levels of engagement the impact of personality generally matches or exceeds that of standard demographic variables such as race and income (see Chapter 5 appendix). For example, the largest effect of income on partisanship in the American National Election Studies occurs in 2008. A change from the 5th percentile to the 95th percentile of income corresponds with a twenty-eight-percentage point change in the probability of Republican identification. An equivalent change in authoritarianism at high levels of engagement corresponds with a thirty-point change. In other years, and for ideological identification generally, the differences in effect sizes are quite a bit larger. The only other variable in our models that consistently rivals the effect of personality on political identification is race, with black identifiers much less likely to identify as Republican than non-blacks. Age, gender, employment status, union membership, Latino identification, Southern residency, and education[18] all fall well short in their influence. Personality is clearly not all that matters when it comes to political identity, but it is consistently among the most important factors in shaping how engaged citizens orient themselves in contemporary American politics. Using several representative surveys and a wide range of indicators of dispositional openness, this chapter provides the most extensive evidence to date that this is so.

Conditional dispositional sorting constitutes the first mechanistic claim in our theory. In American politics, openness is a powerful determinant of how politically engaged citizens group themselves in political space. While this is an important contribution to the literature in its own right, it also has implications for the formation and meaning of economic preferences. As we have argued, political identity serves as an anchor by which citizens orient themselves when it comes to judgments about complex public policy disputes. In this view, understanding the bases of political affiliation and information seeking is the key to understanding the roots of economic opinion among politically engaged citizens. It is the task of the next chapter to explore these implications directly.

---

[18] However, education does have an additional effect on identity *through* personality traits, especially authoritarianism.

Appendix

TABLE A5.1. *Estimates for authoritarianism and ideological labels*

	Liberal Labels	Conservative Labels
Authoritarianism	−1.08 (0.46)	0.45 (0.39)
Engagement	1.22 (0.33)	0.47 (0.35)
Auth X Engage	−0.34 (0.59)	0.72 (0.50)
Age	−0.61 (0.21)	0.29 (0.18)
Male	−0.37 (0.09)	0.16 (0.07)
Black	0.26 (0.16)	−0.42 (0.14)
Latino	0.40 (0.17)	−0.27 (0.16)
Education	0.57 (0.17)	−0.26 (0.14)
Income	−0.48 (0.22)	0.16 (0.18)
Unemployed	0.07 (0.17)	−0.04 (0.14)
Union	0.06 (0.11)	−0.11 (0.09)
South	−0.14 (0.10)	0.12 (0.07)
N	965	975

Notes: Data are from the 2012 YouGov Model Politics survey. The dependent variables are counts of liberal and conservative labels, respectively. Entries are poisson coefficients and standard errors corrected for over-dispersion (in parentheses).

TABLE A5.2. *Estimates for authoritarianism, partisanship, and ideology*

	Partisanship				Ideological Identification			
	2000	2004	2008	2012	2000	2004	2008	2012
Authoritarianism	−0.13 (0.31)	−0.11 (0.37)	−0.70 (0.29)	−0.01 (0.16)	0.60 (0.34)	−0.53 (0.42)	−0.04 (0.34)	0.10 (0.16)
Engagement	−1.12 (0.39)	−0.89 (0.37)	−1.34 (0.31)	−0.39 (0.17)	−0.64 (0.42)	−1.33 (0.39)	−0.76 (0.33)	−0.57 (0.17)
Auth X Engage	1.93 (0.55)	1.68 (0.55)	2.22 (0.42)	1.35 (0.24)	1.06 (0.60)	2.54 (0.61)	1.44 (0.49)	1.36 (0.24)
Age	−0.37 (0.16)	−0.19 (0.18)	0.12 (0.12)	−0.11 (0.06)	0.51 (0.17)	0.40 (0.19)	0.58 (0.13)	0.32 (0.06)
Male	0.12 (0.07)	0.14 (0.08)	0.14 (0.06)	0.15 (0.03)	0.12 (0.07)	0.11 (0.09)	0.10 (0.06)	0.12 (0.03)
Black	−1.35 (0.14)	−1.28 (0.13)	−1.29 (0.11)	−1.57 (0.07)	−0.44 (0.12)	−0.22 (0.13)	−0.46 (0.11)	−0.61 (0.05)
Latino	−0.27 (0.16)	−0.46 (0.18)	−0.52 (0.10)	−0.64 (0.06)	.05 (.17)	−0.54 (0.19)	−0.32 (0.11)	−0.31 (0.05)
Education	0.24 (0.13)	0.00 (0.15)	0.08 (0.11)	0.07 (0.07)	−0.21 (0.13)	−0.22 (0.16)	−0.13 (0.11)	−0.02 (0.07)
Income	0.98 (0.27)	0.66 (0.18)	1.02 (0.13)	0.43 (0.07)	0.70 (0.28)	0.88 (0.19)	0.76 (0.14)	0.28 (0.07)
Unemployed	0.22 (0.16)	−0.21 (0.22)	−0.05 (0.12)	−0.01 (0.07)	0.15 (0.18)	−0.32 (0.23)	0.04 (0.14)	−0.08 (0.07)
Union	−0.43 (0.10)	−0.32 (0.11)	−0.30 (0.09)	−0.14 (0.05)	−0.14 (0.10)	−0.21 (0.11)	0.03 (0.09)	−0.15 (0.05)
South	0.17 (0.07)	0.06 (0.09)	0.29 (0.06)	0.16 (0.04)	0.15 (0.07)	0.19 (0.09)	0.34 (0.06)	0.11 (0.04)
PRE	0.17	0.25	0.23	0.22	0.06	0.09	0.05	0.09
N	1,478	1,009	2,010	5,315	1,363	794	1,536	4,884

Notes: Data are from the 2000–12 American National Election Studies. Entries are ordered probit coefficients and standard errors (in parentheses). "PRE" is the proportionate reduction in error.

TABLE A5.3. *Estimates for authoritarianism in panel data*

Authoritarianism	0.08 (0.50)
Engagement	0.13 (0.53)
Auth X Engage	0.67 (0.73)
Age	−0.22 (0.24)
Male	0.09 (0.12)
Black	−0.71 (0.19)
Education	−0.26 (0.23)
Income	0.56 (0.25)
Unemployed	−0.60 (0.23)
Union	−0.26 (0.16)
South	0.01 (0.12)
Lagged PID	1.11 (0.06)
PRE	0.60
N	701

Notes: Data are from the 1992–4 American National Election Studies panel. The dependent variable is partisanship, and is measured in 1994. Entries are ordered probit estimates and standard errors (in parentheses). All independent variables are measured in 1992. "PRE" is the proportionate reduction in error.

TABLE A5.4. *Estimates for need for closure*

	Partisanship	Ideology
Need for Closure	−1.51 (0.72)	−0.28 (0.72)
Engagement	−1.20 (0.46)	−0.80 (0.45)
NFC X Engage	3.47 (0.96)	1.91 (0.95)
Age	−0.03 (0.16)	0.45 (0.16)
Male	0.22 (0.06)	0.23 (0.06)
Black	−1.21 (0.16)	−0.72 (0.14)
Latino	−0.60 (0.12)	−0.48 (0.12)
Education	−0.35 (0.11)	−0.57 (0.11)
Income	0.52 (0.17)	0.22 (0.16)
Unemployed	−0.12 (0.15)	−0.28 (0.15)
South	0.39 (0.07)	0.35 (0.07)
PRE	0.21	0.11
N	1,487	1,511

Notes: Data are from a 2008 Knowledge Networks national survey commissioned by Christopher Federico. The dependent variables are partisanship (left column) and ideological identification (right column). Entries are ordered probit estimates and standard errors (in parentheses). "PRE" is the proportionate reduction in error.

TABLE A5.5. *Estimates for Big Five*

	Partisanship			Ideology		
	CCAP	CCES	ANES	CCAP	CCES	ANES
Openness to Experience	−0.03 (0.18)	−0.03 (0.20)	−0.23 (0.27)	−0.63 (0.17)	−0.38 (0.18)	0.14 (0.27)
Conscientiousness	−0.08 (0.18)	−0.10 (0.19)	0.06 (0.26)	0.11 (0.17)	0.07 (0.17)	0.01 (0.26)
Extraversion	−0.01 (0.14)	−0.02 (0.16)	0.03 (0.23)	−0.30 (0.14)	−0.15 (0.14)	0.13 (0.23)
Agreeableness	0.20 (0.19)	0.09 (0.20)	0.39 (0.27)	0.36 (0.18)	0.42 (0.18)	0.33 (0.27)
Emotional Stability	−0.01 (0.16)	0.10 (0.17)	−0.12 (0.24)	0.02 (0.16)	0.06 (0.15)	−0.27 (0.25)
Political Engagement	0.21 (0.24)	0.30 (0.21)	0.47 (0.41)	−0.21 (0.24)	0.27 (0.19)	0.56 (0.40)
Openness X Engage	−1.58 (0.25)	−0.96 (0.23)	−1.33 (0.42)	−1.00 (0.24)	−0.83 (0.21)	−1.71 (0.42)
Conscientiousness X Engage	0.82 (0.25)	0.68 (0.22)	0.80 (0.42)	0.71 (0.24)	0.71 (0.20)	0.89 (0.42)
Extraversion X Engage	0.28 (0.19)	0.20 (0.18)	0.50 (0.35)	0.59 (0.19)	0.25 (0.17)	0.06 (0.35)
Agreeableness X Engage	−0.60 (0.26)	−0.43 (0.23)	−0.99 (0.42)	−0.66 (0.25)	−0.74 (0.21)	−1.00 (0.42)
Emotional Stability X Engage	1.01 (0.22)	0.44 (0.20)	0.75 (0.37)	0.77 (0.22)	0.51 (0.18)	0.95 (0.39)
Age	0.15 (0.07)	0.41 (0.07)	−0.14 (0.06)	0.55 (0.07)	0.86 (0.07)	0.32 (0.06)
Male	0.28 (0.02)	0.23 (0.02)	0.16 (0.04)	0.30 (0.02)	0.19 (0.02)	0.11 (0.03)
Black	−1.08 (0.05)	−1.23 (0.04)	−1.46 (0.07)	−0.33 (0.04)	−0.33 (0.03)	−0.48 (0.05)
Latino	−0.42 (0.05)	−0.25 (0.04)	−0.58 (0.06)	−0.26 (0.04)	−0.07 (0.03)	−0.22 (0.05)
Education	−0.51 (0.05)	−0.39 (0.04)	−0.17 (0.07)	−0.69 (0.05)	−0.56 (0.04)	−0.28 (0.07)
Income	0.45 (0.05)	0.46 (0.05)	0.31 (0.07)	0.29 (0.05)	0.24 (0.04)	0.17 (0.07)
Unemployed	−0.25 (0.05)	−0.06 (0.04)	0.04 (0.07)	−0.18 (0.05)	−0.01 (0.04)	−0.04 (0.07)
Union	−0.30 (0.02)	−0.31 (0.04)	−0.12 (0.05)	−0.24 (0.02)	−0.20 (0.04)	−0.12 (0.04)
South	0.16 (0.02)	0.18 (0.02)	0.20 (0.04)	0.16 (0.02)	0.19 (0.02)	0.17 (0.03)
PRE	0.23	0.23	0.21	0.14	0.08	0.06
N	12,542	12,164	5,312	12,079	12,515	4,886

Notes: Data are from the 2008 Cooperative Campaign Analysis Project (CCAP), the 2009 Cooperative Congressional Election Study (CCES), and the 2012 American National Election Study (ANES). The dependent variables are partisanship and ideological identification, and entries are ordered probit estimates and standard errors (in parentheses). "PRE" is the proportionate reduction in error.

TABLE A5.6. *Estimates for openness to change and left-right orientation*

Openness to Change	0.00 (0.07)
Engagement	0.32 (0.05)
Openness X Engage	−0.51 (0.11)
Age	0.00 (0.02)
Male	0.03 (0.01)
Black	−0.04 (0.02)
Latino	0.02 (0.02)
Education	−0.07 (0.02)
Income	0.14 (0.02)
Unemployed	0.01 (0.02)
South	0.00 (0.01)
Intercept	0.45 (0.04)
R^2	0.08
N	2,110

Notes: Data are from the 2011 U.S. wave of the World Values Survey. The dependent variable is left-right placement. Entries are ordinary least squares estimates and standard errors (in parentheses).

TABLE A5.7. *Estimates for moral foundations, partisanship, and ideology*

	Partisanship	Ideology
Importance of Binding Foundations	3.32 (0.58)	4.25 (0.56)
Engagement	−1.44 (0.47)	−1.45 (0.45)
Binding X Engage	3.83 (0.88)	3.38 (0.85)
Age	−0.19 (0.24)	0.22 (0.22)
Male	0.03 (0.10)	0.04 (0.10)
Black	−1.49 (0.23)	−0.51 (0.17)
Latino	−0.13 (0.20)	0.07 (0.19)
Education	−0.10 (0.18)	−0.25 (0.17)
Income	0.55 (0.25)	0.27 (0.23)
Unemployed	−0.05 (0.17)	−0.28 (0.16)
Union	−0.47 (0.16)	−0.25 (0.15)
South	0.08 (0.10)	0.10 (0.10)
PRE	0.38	0.27
N	769	766

Notes: Data are from the 2012 Cooperative Congressional Election Study (CCES). The dependent variables are partisanship (left column) and ideological identification (right column). Entries are ordered probit estimates and standard errors (in parentheses). "PRE" is the proportionate reduction in error.

TABLE A5.8. *Estimates for authoritarianism and media consumption*

	Liberal Media	Conservative Media
Authoritarianism	−2.91 (0.88)	−0.63 (0.85)
Engagement	1.53 (0.54)	1.83 (0.71)
Auth X Engage	1.68 (1.05)	1.91 (1.02)
Age	−0.38 (0.31)	0.95 (0.29)
Male	−0.22 (0.14)	−0.07 (0.12)
Black	0.59 (0.23)	−0.15 (0.22)
Hispanic	0.51 (0.25)	−0.02 (0.26)
Education	0.25 (0.25)	−0.82 (0.24)
Income	0.06 (0.32)	−0.08 (0.30)
Unemployed	−0.03 (0.27)	−0.23 (0.25)
Union	−0.04 (0.16)	−0.21 (0.16)
South	−0.26 (0.15)	0.15 (0.12)
N	975	975

Notes: Data are from the 2012 YouGov Model Politics survey. The dependent variables are counts of liberal and conservative media outlets, respectively. Entries are poisson coefficients and standard errors corrected for over-dispersion (in parentheses).

TABLE A5.9. *Estimates for authoritarianism and political discussion partners*

	Democrat Partner	Republican Partner
Authoritarianism	0.38 (0.67)	−0.42 (0.69)
Engagement	2.69 (0.85)	1.19 (0.87)
Auth X Engage	0.46 (1.22)	3.43 (1.25)
Age	−1.23 (0.35)	−1.90 (0.35)
Male	−0.29 (0.15)	−0.25 (0.15)
Black	0.53 (0.21)	−1.80 (0.36)
Hispanic	−0.08 (0.32)	−0.96 (0.38)
Education	0.65 (0.27)	0.35 (0.27)
Income	1.12 (0.62)	2.08 (0.60)
Unemployed	−0.36 (0.34)	−0.53 (0.38)
Union	0.36 (0.19)	0.03 (0.20)
South	−0.68 (0.15)	−0.29 (0.15)
Intercept	−1.74 (0.50)	−1.04 (0.50)

Notes: Data are from the 2000 American National Election Study. The dependent variable is the partisanship of the respondent's primary political discussion partner. The first column compares the outcome "Democratic partner" to a response of "don't know," and the second column compares the outcome "Republican partner" to "don't know." Entries are multinomial logistic regression coefficients and standard errors (in parentheses).

TABLE A5.10. *Estimates for authoritarianism, partisanship, and ideology, blacks and Latinos*

	Blacks		Latinos	
	PID	Ideo	PID	Ideo
Authoritarianism	0.65 (0.45)	0.22 (0.41)	−0.26 (0.31)	0.14 (0.34)
Engagement	0.04 (0.60)	−0.67 (0.50)	−0.79 (0.39)	−0.53 (0.42)
Auth X Engage	−1.30 (0.73)	0.43 (0.62)	1.00 (0.51)	0.64 (0.55)
Age	−0.42 (0.17)	0.13 (0.14)	−0.07 (0.14)	0.60 (0.14)
Male	0.16 (0.08)	0.09 (0.07)	0.12 (0.07)	−0.04 (0.07)
Education	0.15 (0.17)	−0.16 (0.13)	0.07 (0.14)	−0.20 (0.13)
Income	0.06 (0.18)	0.14 (0.14)	0.57 (0.15)	0.24 (0.15)
Unemployed	0.19 (0.12)	0.01 (0.10)	−0.12 (0.12)	−0.17 (0.12)
Union	−0.24 (0.13)	−0.10 (0.09)	−0.14 (0.10)	−0.09 (0.10)
South	−0.09 (0.08)	0.04 (0.07)	0.33 (0.07)	0.14 (0.07)
2004 Dummy	0.27 (0.19)	0.25 (0.17)	−0.28 (0.23)	−0.67 (0.24)
2008 Dummy	0.08 (0.16)	−0.04 (0.13)	−0.62 (0.17)	−0.54 (0.18)
2012 Dummy	0.07 (0.15)	−0.15 (0.12)	−0.44 (0.16)	−0.60 (0.17)
PRE	0.00	0.01	0.00	0.06
N	1,701	1,214	1,419	1,135

Notes: Data are from the 2000–12 American National Election Studies. The dependent variables are partisanship and ideological identification. Entries are ordered probit coefficients and standard errors (in parentheses). "PRE" is the proportionate reduction in error.

TABLE A5.11. *Estimates for Big Five, partisanship,*
and ideology, blacks and Latinos

	Blacks		Latinos	
	PID	Ideo	PID	Ideo
Openness to Experience	−0.85 (1.03)	0.12 (0.84)	1.00 (0.59)	0.40 (0.64)
Conscientiousness	−0.68 (0.93)	0.32 (0.78)	−0.81 (0.60)	0.44 (0.66)
Extraversion	1.41 (0.81)	0.55 (0.70)	−0.02 (0.55)	0.05 (0.58)
Agreeableness	−1.95 (1.06)	−0.21 (0.85)	0.04 (0.63)	−0.91 (0.67)
Emotional Stability	0.60 (1.06)	−0.90 (0.84)	−0.52 (0.58)	0.43 (0.65)
Political Engagement	−1.56 (1.35)	−0.48 (1.13)	−0.22 (1.00)	0.75 (1.01)
Openness X Engage	1.10 (1.71)	−0.50 (1.32)	−3.25 (1.03)	−1.75 (1.07)
Conscientiousness X Engage	−0.03 (1.56)	0.10 (1.25)	1.83 (1.07)	0.02 (1.10)
Extraversion X Engage	−2.71 (1.33)	−1.36 (1.05)	0.96 (0.92)	−0.19 (0.94)
Agreeableness X Engage	2.50 (1.71)	0.10 (1.32)	−0.19 (1.09)	0.94 (1.13)
Emotional Stability X Engage	−0.15 (1.74)	1.40 (1.35)	0.82 (1.03)	−0.60 (1.09)
Age	−0.47 (0.22)	0.15 (0.17)	0.04 (0.17)	0.76 (0.17)
Male	0.14 (0.11)	0.17 (0.09)	0.05 (0.09)	0.02 (0.08)
Education	0.65 (0.24)	−0.03 (0.17)	0.10 (0.17)	−0.11 (0.17)
Income	0.14 (0.23)	0.06 (0.17)	0.62 (0.18)	0.17 (0.17)
Unemployed	0.18 (0.16)	−0.05 (0.13)	−0.06 (0.14)	−0.21 (0.15)
Union	−0.21 (0.16)	−0.09 (0.12)	−0.18 (0.12)	−0.09 (0.12)
South	−0.16 (0.12)	−0.03 (0.09)	0.22 (0.09)	0.04 (0.09)
PRE	0.00	0.03	0.03	0.03
N	911	725	885	743

Notes: Data are from the 2012 American National Election Study. The dependent variables are partisanship and ideological identification. Entries are ordered probit coefficients and standard errors (in parentheses). "PRE" is the proportionate reduction in error.

6

Openness and Elite Influence

We have argued that economic preference formation among politically engaged citizens is motivated by expressive goals. However, the social meaning of a given policy position does not come ready-made; rather, it is constructed in the context of competition among elites. Parties package economic policies as part of a broader platform. As we argued in Chapter 3, in contemporary American politics, Democrats and Republicans bind cultural orientations to economic policies, and thus bind dispositional openness to economic preferences. This point is of theoretical interest to both political scientists and psychologists. For the former, it means that economic preferences cannot be treated as "givens." Rather, they are endogenous to the cultural conflict that has roiled American politics in the past few decades. In a sense, economic conflict among those who follow politics is cultural conflict in disguise. For the latter, our perspective suggests that the association between personality and political preferences is not simply a matter of unmediated elective affinity or natural resonance with the substantive content of policy. Rather, politics matters. The political impact of personality hinges on how the parties align on cultural and economic issues at a given point in time. The upshot is that a more complete understanding of American mass politics requires attention to both the psychology of individual differences and the role of elite actors in shaping how citizens make sense of the issues. The present chapter is an empirical investigation of this interaction.

To this point, we have provided only indirect evidence for the role of elites in shaping the political effects of personality. We have shown that political engagement "reverses" the relationship between openness and economic preferences (Chapter 4), and that engaged – but not unengaged – citizens translate their psychological dispositions into partisan and ideological identities, and into strategies for political information seeking (Chapter 5). In this chapter, we look for direct evidence of elite influence. In Chapter 3, we argued that elite influence operates through two related pathways. First, engaged citizens use partisan and ideological symbols as information regarding the alignment between cultural identities and economic positions. Simply by taking a stand on an economic issue, elite actors associate that stand with partisan and ideological symbols that are infused with cultural content. We refer to this process as *partisan cue-taking*. Second, elites may signal a cultural identity directly in the context of taking a position on an economic issue. For example, a member of Congress might express support for gay marriage in close proximity to expressing support for raising the minimum wage. In this example, the attraction that open citizens feel to the pro-marriage position will "spill over" to create a positive evaluation of raising the minimum wage (and vice versa for closed citizens; e.g., Tesler 2012). We refer to this pathway as *cultural signaling*. In both cases, elite position-taking creates an indirect link between dispositional openness and economic preferences.

In this chapter, we empirically examine these two mechanisms of elite influence, and demonstrate that they occur primarily among politically engaged citizens. To do so, we shift gears from observational analysis of surveys to controlled experiments. Experiments allow us to study contexts that might be difficult to observe in the real world; for example, a cultural conservative supporting a raise in the minimum wage. By creating this contextual variation artificially, we can see what happens in theoretically relevant, yet rarely observed situations. These experiments also help to clarify a causal ambiguity present in the reversal findings presented in Chapter 4. In particular, although we believe the impact of personality on economic opinion among the engaged is mediated by elite influence, it is possible that elites are simply following the lead of highly active citizens (Abramowitz 2010). That is, perhaps Republican elites align their economic positions with the bulk of politically active closed citizens, while Democratic elites do the same for open citizens. This reverses cause and effect; in this view, citizens lead elites.

Correlational evidence such as that presented in Chapter 4 cannot distinguish between these two possibilities. We need a way to compare the relationship between openness and economic opinion across contexts where the *only* change is the link between elite cues and policy stands.

Controlled experiments are ideally suited to this task. Using experiments, we construct the relevant contexts by varying the nature of elite cues (e.g., whether the Republicans are said to take a position to the right or left of the Democrats), and by randomly assigning citizens to these contexts. Random assignment ensures that the only difference between respondents across contexts is the elite cue. If the relationship between openness and economic liberalism among engaged citizens is due to a natural resonance with policy content, then we should observe little variation in this relationship across experimental conditions (because policy content is held constant). That is, if the relationship between openness and economic liberalism is direct rather than mediated by elite cue-taking, then it should hold regardless of how elites line up on the issue. If we are correct, however, engaged citizens should "follow culture," such that the influence of openness will be conditional on how elite actors align themselves on a given issue.

The bulk of this chapter will focus on four survey experiments dealing with domestic economic issues. Then we switch to observational data and issues of international trade, which allow us to consider an additional source of variation in the alignment between culture and economics. There are at least two reasons why closed (versus open) citizens may support protectionist policies in matters of trade. First, as we argued in Chapter 3, closed citizens may focus more on the potential economic downsides of trade (e.g., labor market insecurity), while open citizens may focus more on its upsides (e.g., lower prices). Second, closed citizens may be more likely to view international trade (and globalization more generally) as a cultural threat, while open citizens may be more likely to see trade and globalization as an opportunity for greater exposure to diverse cultures and experiences (Johnston et al. 2015; Mansfield and Mutz 2009). As the two parties are not sharply divided on trade, the alignment between personality, culture, and economics among engaged citizens should be opposite to that of domestic issues. That is, on domestic issues, engaged *closed* citizens prefer a free market approach (as we demonstrated in Chapter 4), whereas on international trade issues, we expect *open* citizens to prefer a free market approach. In essence, this set of analyses examines naturally occurring (rather than experimentally conceived) variation in issue context – one that we expect to reverse the sign on the relationship between openness and economic opinion among engaged citizens. Taken as a whole, this chapter suggests that the impact of personality on economic preferences among politically engaged citizens is highly malleable, reflecting the importance of parties and elite actors in determining how deep-seated psychological dispositions become linked to economics.

Unfortunately, our sample sizes for the four experiments are too small to examine racial and ethnic heterogeneity in cue-taking as a function of openness. While we have good reason to expect that personality-based cue-taking will be minimal among blacks but potentially significant among Latinos (see Chapters 4 and 5), we simply do not have the data to test these claims. We thus examine our hypotheses for the full samples, ignoring racial and ethnic differences. However, in the final sections of this chapter, where we examine trade preferences in large national datasets, we estimate our models separately for blacks and Latinos, as in previous chapters.

Experimental Evidence for Partisan Cue-Taking

In our first two experiments, we examine how partisan and ideological cues alter the relationship between personality and economic opinion. Our general expectation is that open and closed citizens will adopt the economic policy positions of their culturally favored elites, and will place less weight on the actual ideological content of the positions. Thus, we expect elites to shape the relationship between openness and support for expansive or limited government. Moreover, we expect this experimental effect to be limited to politically engaged citizens, that is, those whose partisan identities are tightly bound to personality. In sum, we expect that engaged citizens will follow their favored elites at the expense of economic policy content, which is consistent with an expressive motive for political engagement. In particular, we expect closed citizens to show greater support for free market policy options when linked to the Republican Party and open citizens to support government intervention when linked to the Democratic Party. However, we expect this relationship between personality and economic opinion to be sharply attenuated – or even reversed – when Republicans are linked to interventionist policies and Democrats are linked to free market policies.

We may only observe attenuation rather than a full reversal in such counter-stereotypical conditions because there are preexisting linkages between openness and economic liberalism, forged prior to our experiments (see Chapter 4). Consider, for example, a situation where, in the absence of party cues, 75 percent of open citizens express a liberal opinion on an issue and 75 percent of closed citizens express a conservative position. Then, we expose them to counter-stereotypical cues in which Republicans take the liberal position and Democrats take the conservative position. If one-third of these open citizens change their position from liberal to conservative and one-third of these closed citizens change their position from conservative to liberal, then 50 percent of each group will now be liberal and 50 percent will be conservative. This means that the correlation between openness and policy preferences will be zero in the counter-stereotypical condition. In this example, our experiment produced a large treatment effect. However, as a result of the preexisting relationship between openness and opinion, there was no reversal in the counter-stereotypical condition, only attenuation. Our point is that this pattern still indicates a strong effect of elite cues in a manner consistent with our theory.

Partisan and Ideological Cues I: The 2011 YouGov Experiment[1]

The data for this experiment come from a national sample of U.S. adults collected by the survey firm YouGov from March 4–9, 2011.[2] Respondents were presented with four economic policy items – government-provided health insurance, financial regulation, unemployment insurance, and Social Security privatization – each modeled on the seven-point ANES format. The wording for each issue is shown in Table 6.1.

Our key hypothesis concerns the change in the effect of personality on economic liberalism across the two experimental groups. In the *control* condition, opposing positions on each policy were attributed to "some people" and "others," while in two *elite cues* conditions these were replaced with either party or ideological labels corresponding to contemporary stereotypes of the American left and right (i.e., Democrats and liberals took interventionist positions on the issues, while Republicans and conservatives took limited government positions). Given our relatively small sample, we consider the partisan and ideological cue conditions together to maximize statistical power.[3] Respondents were randomly

---

[1] These data were also utilized in Johnston and Wronski (2015), but their paper did not consider the conditioning effect of political engagement.

[2] The sampling design utilized matched random sampling on the following variables: age, gender, race, education, party identification, political ideology, and political interest. Data collection was funded by the National Science Foundation via a dissertation improvement grant to Chris Johnston (Award #: 1023255).

[3] When we examine the two experimental conditions separately, we find a substantially larger treatment effect for partisan relative to ideological cues for engaged citizens. This is, we think, consistent with research that suggests that partisanship is more stable than, and indeed often shapes, ideological identification (e.g., Levendusky 2009). Given the small sample sizes in each condition at each level of engagement, however, we hesitate to draw firm conclusions about the relative importance of each type of cue in moderating the effect of openness.

TABLE 6.1. *Treatments in the 2011 YouGov experiment*

[In experimental conditions, "Some people" and "Others" are replaced with party or ideological labels]

Some people believe there should be a government insurance plan which would cover all medical expenses for everyone. Suppose these people are at one end of a scale, at point 1.
Others believe that all medical expenses should be paid by individuals through private insurance plans. Suppose these people are at the other end, at point 7.
And, of course, some other people have opinions somewhere in between, at points 2, 3, 4, 5, or 6.
Where would you place YOURSELF on this scale?
  (1) Government insurance plan
  (7) Private Insurance plan

Some people believe that we should get rid of government provided unemployment insurance altogether. Suppose these people are at one end of the scale at point 1.
Others believe that we should greatly increase unemployment insurance. Suppose these people are at the other end of the scale at point 7.
And, of course, some other people have opinions somewhere in between at points 2, 3, 4, 5, or 6.
Where would you place YOURSELF on this scale?
  (1) Get rid of unemployment insurance altogether
  (7) Greatly increase unemployment insurance

Some people believe that we should greatly increase government regulation of the financial industry. Suppose these people are at one end of the scale at point 1.
Others believe that we should get rid of financial regulations altogether. Suppose these people are at the other end of the scale at point 7.
And, of course, some other people have opinions somewhere in between at points 2, 3, 4, 5, or 6.
Where would you place YOURSELF on this scale?
  (1) Greatly increase financial regulations
  (7) Get rid of financial regulations altogether

Some people believe that we should allow people to invest all of their Social Security benefits in the private markets. Suppose these people are at one end of the scale at point 1.
Others believe that all Social Security benefits should be handled by the government. Suppose these people are at the other end of the scale at point 7.
And, of course, some other people have opinions somewhere in between at points 2, 3, 4, 5, or 6.
Where would you place YOURSELF on this scale?
  (1) Allow all benefits to be invested in private markets
  (7) All benefits handled by government

assigned to the same experimental condition for all four economic policy items, which were recoded so that higher values correspond to more interventionist (i.e., liberal) attitudes.[4] We thus created an overall scale by averaging responses to the four items ($\alpha = 0.79$).

Prior to the experimental portion of the study, respondents completed a short survey, including a series of items measuring three indicators of dispositional openness: authoritarianism (measured the same way as in the ANES studies in Chapters 4 and 5), the need for closure, and Schwartz's (1992) openness versus conservation value dimension. The items for the latter two scales are shown in Table 6.2. In the appendix to this chapter, we show that these three traits load strongly on a superordinate latent dimension that we label "openness."[5] These results provide further support for the idea that these variables are tapping a common latent dimension of personality. We use respondents' scores on this latent factor as our key independent variable. High values indicate an open personality orientation, and low values indicate a closed orientation.

We estimated two models to test our hypotheses – one for the control condition and one for the combined elite cues condition. Each model regressed economic policy attitudes on latent openness, political engagement, the interaction of openness with engagement, and our standard set of controls.[6] The estimates of primary interest are shown in Figure 6.1, while full regression tables can be found in the appendix to this chapter. The x-axis represents increasing levels of political engagement, and the y-axis represents the difference in average economic liberalism comparing citizens at the 95th percentile of openness and those at the 5th percentile. The filled circles are estimates for the control condition, and the empty circles are estimates for the elite cues condition.

The results strongly support our two primary claims: (1) the influence of openness on economic policy attitudes is conditional on elite cues, and (2) elite influence is largely restricted to politically engaged individuals. The conditioning effect of elite cues is most easily seen by comparing the

---

[4] For the four issues, interventionist attitudes correspond with pro-government insurance, anti-Social Security privatization, pro-financial regulation, and pro-unemployment insurance.

[5] Specifically, we estimated a confirmatory factor model in which authoritarianism, need for closure, and openness to change were assumed to be latent variables indicated by their respective survey items, and a superordinate latent variable ("openness") was indicated by these three latent traits. The standardized loadings of the three latent traits on superordinate openness are 0.79, 0.51, and 0.76 for authoritarianism, need for closure, and openness to change, respectively.

[6] Engagement was measured as the average of five objective political knowledge items and political interest. Union membership was not included in these data.

TABLE 6.2. *Items measuring openness in the 2011 YouGov experiment*

"How would you place your views on this scale? 1 means you agree completely with the statement on the left; 10 means you agree completely with the statement on the right; and if your views fall somewhere in between, you can choose any number in between."

Schwartz (1992) Conservation versus Openness to Change

[Left] To have a good life one must be willing to pursue adventures and take risks
[Right] A safe and secure environment is the best foundation for a good life

[Left] It is best for everyone if people try to fit in instead of acting in unusual ways
[Right] People should be encouraged to express themselves in unique and possibly unusual ways

[Left] People should not try to understand how society works but just accept the way it is
[Right] People should constantly try to question why things are the way they are

[Left] It is most important to give people the freedom they need to express themselves
[Right] Our society will break down if we allow people to do or say anything they want

[Left] We should admire people who go their own way without worrying what others think
[Right] People need to learn to fit in and get along with others

Need for Nonspecific Cognitive Closure

[Left] I don't like going into a situation without knowing what I can expect from it
[Right] I enjoy the uncertainty of going into a new situation without knowing what might happen

[Left] In most social conflicts, I can easily see which side is right and which is wrong
[Right] In most social conflicts, I can easily see how both sides could be right

[Left] I think it is fun to change my plans at the last moment
[Right] I hate to change my plans at the last moment

[Left] I like to have friends who are unpredictable
[Right] I don't like to be with people who are capable of unexpected actions

[Left] I tend to put off making important decisions until the last possible moment
[Right] I usually make important decisions quickly and confidently

estimates for the control condition to the cue condition within each level of political engagement – that is, comparing the paired filled and open circles at each level of engagement on the x-axis. Looking first at unengaged citizens, we see no significant effect of openness in the control condition, and no significant change in the effect of openness on economic

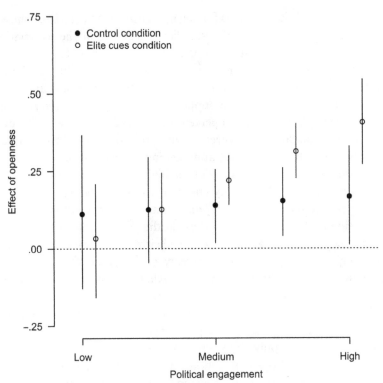

FIGURE 6.1. The moderating effect of partisan and ideological cues on the relationship between openness and economic policy liberalism across political engagement, 2011 YouGov experiment

opinion moving from the control condition to the partisan-ideological cues condition. In other words, there is no relationship between openness and economic policy preferences for unengaged citizens, and they are also entirely unresponsive to elite cues. However, this also means that we fail to replicate the *negative* relationship between openness and economic liberalism that we established as part of the reversal pattern in Chapter 4. Although we can only speculate about the reason for this null result, we note that our sample size is substantially smaller than for the data examined in Chapter 4, and it is less representative than data drawn from the ANES. Indeed, the confidence intervals for the unengaged estimates are very large. Regardless, this null finding should be considered a failure of the reversal hypothesis and added to the list of results from Chapter 4. As we noted in the conclusion to that chapter, it is quite possible that the negative impact of openness on economic liberalism among the unengaged is less reliable than the positive effect among the engaged.

We turn now to the estimates for engaged citizens. As Figure 6.1 shows, there is a large and statistically significant increase in the association between openness and economic liberalism when moving from the control condition to the partisan-ideological cues condition. In the control condition, engaged citizens at the 95th percentile of openness are about fifteen percentage points more supportive of government intervention than engaged citizens at the 5th percentile. This is comparable to the estimates seen in Chapter 4. However, moving from the control to the treatment condition, this gap doubles at moderately high levels of engagement, and is two and a half times larger at the highest levels of engagement. In the presence of elite cues, highly engaged citizens at the 95th percentile of openness are more than *forty points* more supportive of government intervention in the economy than those at the 5th percentile of openness. This finding indicates that among engaged citizens, the influence of openness is highly conditional on the presence of elite cues. When such cues are absent, we find a significant, yet somewhat modest effect of openness on economic liberalism. When they are present, however, openness is by far the best predictor of economic opinion in our model. Income is the second-best predictor of economic preferences, yet its maximum effect in the cues condition is only sixteen percentage points – which is less than half the effect size of openness among engaged citizens. The importance of elite cues in the formation of economic opinion is reinforced by the change in explained variance from the control condition to the combined treatment conditions. The R^2 in the control condition is 0.10, indicating that the model explains 10 percent of the variance in economic preferences. In the presence of elite cues, the explained variance nearly doubles to 19 percent.

This experiment provides initial support for a key theoretical claim: traits related to dispositional openness are associated with economic liberalism among the engaged, in large part due to the role elite actors play in packaging economics with other dimensions of political conflict within an overall party platform. In particular, engaged citizens use party cues to learn what "people like me" should believe, and adopt the preferences of partisans that fit their personality. The upshot is that the effect of openness on economic opinion increases substantially in the presence of partisan and ideological cues. Importantly, random assignment to treatment conditions allows us to isolate the mechanism of elite influence in a way that is not possible with observational studies, such as those in Chapter 4. The only characteristic that systematically varies across conditions is the presence of elite cues, and the presence of such cues is therefore the only explanation for the enhanced effect of openness observed among engaged citizens.

Partisan and Ideological Cues II: The 2012 CCES Experiment

Our second national survey experiment was embedded in Duke University's post-election module of the 2012 Cooperative Congressional Election Study (CCES). Approximately 820 respondents recruited for the 2012 CCES took part in this study, which was conducted by the survey firm YouGov. The experiment was designed to test the influence of elite cues, utilizing a distinct measure of openness and a larger set of cue manipulations, including *counter-stereotypical* cues. To measure openness, the study included a thirty-item instrument for measuring Haidt's five moral foundations (2012; Haidt and Joseph 2007). According to moral foundations theory (as described in previous chapters), moral judgment rests on five foundations thought to be universal across human cultures, which are care/harm, fairness/cheating, loyalty/betrayal, authority/subversion, and sanctity/degradation.[7] The first two are considered "individualizing" foundations, as their function is to protect individual rights. These foundations elevate the individual as the primary locus of moral concern. The latter three are "binding" moral foundations in that their function is to protect the in-group. Haidt and colleagues argue that the importance ascribed to the binding foundations represents the core division separating left from right in American politics. In Chapter 5, we demonstrated that the relative importance ascribed to these foundations – that is, loyalty, authority, and sanctity – is highly related to left-right orientations, but that the relationship is considerably stronger among engaged citizens. In this experiment, we show that the relationship between the rated importance of the binding foundations and economic opinion is simultaneously conditional on engagement and elite cues.

The thirty items used to measure moral foundations – shown in Table 6.3 – are divided into two sets. The first set asks respondents about the relevance of different inputs to moral judgment, and the second set asks respondents to agree or disagree with fifteen specific moral claims.[8] Space limitations on the CCES module necessitated randomly assigning

---

[7] Haidt and his colleagues have recently discussed a sixth possible foundation – liberty versus oppression (Iyer et al. 2012) – but we do not consider this foundation further here, as it remains a tentative proposal rather than an accepted part of the theory (see Graham et al. 2013).

[8] Within each set, the items cycle through the five moral foundations in the order listed previously, such that each set contains three items for each of the five foundations.

TABLE 6.3. Moral foundations items in the 2012 CCES experiment

---

"When you decide whether something is right or wrong, to what extent are the following considerations relevant to your thinking?" Six response options from "Not at all relevant" to "Extremely relevant."

> Whether or not someone suffered emotionally
> Whether or not some people were treated differently than others
> Whether or not someone's action showed love for his or her country
> Whether or not someone showed a lack of respect for authority
> Whether or not someone violated standards of purity and decency
> Whether or not someone cared for someone weak or vulnerable
> Whether or not someone acted unfairly
> Whether or not someone did something to betray his or her group
> Whether or not someone conformed to the traditions of society
> Whether or not someone did something disgusting
> Whether or not someone was cruel
> Whether or not someone was denied his or her rights
> Whether or not someone showed a lack of loyalty
> Whether or not an action caused chaos or disorder
> Whether or not someone acted in a way that God would approve of

"Please read the following sentences and indicate your agreement or disagreement." Six response options from "Strongly disagree" to "Strongly agree."

> Compassion for those who are suffering is the most crucial virtue.
> When the government makes laws, the number one principle should be ensuring that everyone is treated fairly.
> I am proud of my country's history.
> Respect for authority is something all children need to learn.
> People should not do things that are disgusting, even if no one is harmed.
> One of the worst things a person could do is hurt a defenseless animal.
> Justice is the most important requirement for a society.
> People should be loyal to their family members, even when they have done something wrong.
> Men and women each have different roles to play in society.
> I would call some acts wrong on the grounds that they are unnatural.
> It can never be right to kill a human being.
> I think it's morally wrong that rich children inherit a lot of money while poor children inherit nothing.
> It is more important to be a team player than to express oneself.
> If I were a soldier and disagreed with my commanding officer's orders, I would obey anyway because that is my duty.
> Chastity is an important and valuable virtue.

---

respondents to only fifteen of the thirty items. We thus utilize all available items for each respondent to construct our measure.[9] We calculated the average rated importance of the individualizing foundations, and subtracted this from the average rated importance of the binding foundations. This final measure can be conceptualized as the importance of binding foundations relative to individualizing foundations. Respondents who score high on this scale place greater weight on the binding moral foundations of authority, loyalty, and sanctity, relative to the individualizing foundations of harm and fairness. Thus, high values of this measure indicate *low* openness.

To validate this operationalization, consider the distributions in Figure 6.2. The top panel shows the overall distribution of the final measure for the entire CCES sample. As can be seen, the distribution is centered to the left of zero, indicating that the typical respondent considers individualizing foundations more important than binding foundations.[10] The bottom panel is a scatter plot of the measure against ideological self-identification. It shows that self-identified liberals place relatively less weight on binding foundations, while conservative identifiers tend to place relatively equal weight on the two types of foundations. This is consistent with moral foundations theory (see Haidt 2012) and our analyses in Chapter 5 using this measure.

The experimental portion of the survey was built into the text of three economic policy items: regulation of the financial industry, corporate tax rates, and partial privatization of Medicare. The design was similar to the 2011 YouGov experiment, with a few important differences. First, the experiment contained seven distinct conditions, which are listed in Table 6.4. The control condition attributed the two competing positions on each issue to "many people" and "many other people," while each of the treatment conditions attributed a given position to one left-leaning or right-leaning source (i.e., "Many Democrats believe" or "Many Republicans believe," "Many Liberal Democrats believe" or "Many Conservative Republicans believe," "Barack Obama believes" or

---

[9] We mean-deviated all responses within respondent and within each set of items to control for differential use of the common measurement instrument (e.g., individual differences in anchoring). This is the strategy Schwartz (1992) advocated for his value-importance ratings (see Chapter 4).

[10] This is consistent with moral foundations theory, which posits that the primary moral divide between the right and left is over the importance of *binding* not individualizing foundations. That is, most people accept the legitimacy of the harm and fairness foundations, but there is substantial heterogeneity in perceived importance of the binding foundations. This creates an overall distribution skewed toward the individualizing foundations.

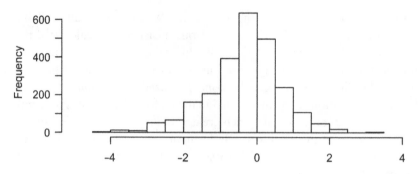

Importance of binding relative to individualizing moral foundations

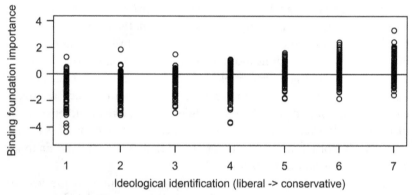

Ideological identification (liberal -> conservative)

FIGURE 6.2. Descriptive statistics for binding moral foundation importance in the 2012 CCES experiment

"Mitt Romney believes"). The six cue conditions varied such that they were either *stereotypical* or *counter-stereotypical* with respect to the positions typically taken by the parties. Thus, in the stereotypical conditions, right-leaning sources (Republicans, conservatives, Romney) took the limited government position (i.e., the conservative position) and left-leaning sources (Democrats, liberals, Obama) took the interventionist position (i.e., the liberal position). In the counter-stereotypical conditions, these positions were reversed so that right-leaning sources took the interventionist position and left-leaning sources took the limited government position. This stereotypicality manipulation allows us to examine whether the relationship between openness and economic opinion changes when the positions elites take are inconsistent with the stances typically taken in American politics.[11] Thus, the experiment is a 3 (cue source: party,

---

[11] Another difference from the 2011 study is that each respondent was randomly assigned to a condition separately for each issue. For example, a respondent might be assigned to

TABLE 6.4. *Treatments in the 2012 CCES experiment*

"[X] that current regulation of the financial industry does not go far enough toward preventing future economic crises and should be increased. [Y] that current regulation of the financial industry goes too far in restricting the ability of financial institutions to make loans and should be decreased."

"[X] that the United States should decrease its corporate tax rate in order to spur investment and job creation. [Y] that corporations do not pay their fair share in taxes and the corporate tax rate should be increased."

"[X] that sustaining Medicare requires partial privatization such that future beneficiaries receive government payments and purchase health care from private providers. [Y] that partial privatization would not keep up with rising health care costs and would force future Medicare beneficiaries to pay the bulk of their health care."

Treatment conditions

X = "Many people believe," Y = "Many others believe"

X = "Many Republicans believe," Y = "Many Democrats believe"

X = "Many Democrats believe," Y = "Many Republicans believe"

X = "Many Conservative Republicans believe," Y = "Many Liberal Democrats believe"

X = "Many Liberal Democrats believe," Y = "Many Conservative Republicans believe"

X = "Barack Obama believes," Y = "Mitt Romney believes"

X = "Mitt Romney believes," Y = "Barack Obama believes"

---

ideology and party, presidential candidate) x 2 (pairing: stereotypical cue vs. counter-stereotypical cue) design with a dangling control group. For our primary analysis, however, we collapse across the cue source factor to maximize sample size, and examine the influence of stereotypical versus counter-stereotypical cues.

Second, as we noted in Chapter 5, the 2012 CCES did not contain a strong measure of political engagement. We therefore built a measure from the three available items tapping political interest and knowledge: general interest in news and public affairs, and two knowledge questions about which party controlled each chamber of Congress at the time of the survey. When combined, a full 44 percent of the sample attained the

the control condition for regulation, a stereotypical party cue condition for Medicare, and a counter-stereotypical cue condition for tax rates (or any other possible combination). Thus, rather than averaging the items, we estimate a multilevel model that controls for respondent-level heterogeneity (i.e., we include respondent-level "random effects") in general liberalism or conservatism across all issues independent of the treatments.

maximum possible level of engagement, and very few individuals were located at the low end of the engagement spectrum. As in Chapter 5, we divided the sample into "low" and "high" engagement, which is close to a 50–50 split. Unfortunately, the lack of variation in engagement significantly limits our ability to speak to effects at the lowest levels of engagement: we simply do not have enough truly unengaged respondents.[12] We thus look for a pattern consistent with an enhanced role for elite cues among the top 44 percent relative to the bottom 56 percent. However, it would not be unreasonable to expect some effect of elite cues even for the bottom group, as most of these individuals are not *actually* unengaged, but rather moderately engaged. Note that this also limits our ability to test the reversal hypothesis examined in Chapter 4. That is, we do not anticipate a reversal at "low" levels of engagement, because these citizens are moderately engaged rather than unengaged.

Our expectations are as follows. First, we expect a negative relationship between binding foundation importance and economic liberalism in the control condition, though this effect should be larger for engaged than unengaged respondents. In the stereotypical cues conditions, we expect the negative effect of binding importance to be larger in absolute value relative to the control condition, and this experimental treatment effect should be larger among engaged than unengaged respondents. Finally, in the counter-stereotypical cues conditions, we expect the negative association between binding importance and economic liberalism to decrease in absolute magnitude (i.e., toward zero), and perhaps even turn positive. Further, this change should be larger for engaged than unengaged respondents. A change of this sort in the impact of binding importance in the counter-stereotypical cue conditions would constitute strong evidence that the effect of openness responds to elite cues even when elites take positions that are opposite to their customary ideological orientations.

We break our analysis into two sets, one for the bottom 56 percent of engagement and one for the top 44 percent. The key estimates from this analysis are shown in Figure 6.3.[13] Panel A shows the estimates for the lower engagement group. In the control condition – in which no elite cues were associated with the policy positions – there is no relationship

---

[12] This is, unfortunately, a common problem with non-probability internet samples like the one used here (Chang and Krosnick 2009; see also Hillygus, Jackson, and Young 2014).

[13] For each engagement group, we estimated three separate models – one for each treatment condition – that regressed economic policy attitudes on binding importance and our standard set of controls. We used a normal model for the DV and included a random intercept for respondents to allow for clustering of the error terms due to the within-subjects design.

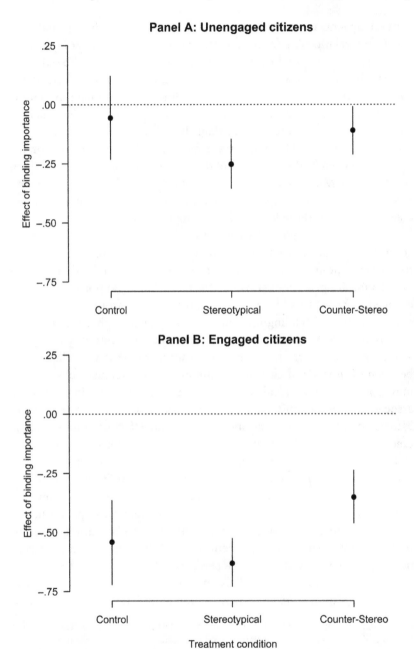

FIGURE 6.3. The moderating effect of partisan, ideological, and candidate cues on the relationship between binding foundation importance and economic policy liberalism across political engagement, 2012 CCES experiment

between openness and economic opinion.[14] Similarly, we find a small (but significant) relationship for the unengaged in the counter-stereotypical cue conditions – those in which left-leaning actors (Democrats, liberals, and Barack Obama) are associated with limited government positions. In the stereotypical cue conditions, however, we find that those high in binding importance (i.e., closed citizens) are about twenty-five points less likely to support government intervention than those low in binding importance (i.e., open citizens). This indicates a moderate treatment effect for the lower 56 percent of the engagement distribution: when Republicans, conservatives, or Mitt Romney are associated with the limited government position on the issue, respondents high in binding importance are more conservative than those low in binding importance.

Turning to the engaged 44 percent of the sample, we find that in the control condition, those high in binding importance are more opposed to government intervention than respondents low in binding importance, indicating a pre-treatment effect of binding importance among engaged citizens. This effect is quite large: moving from the 5th to the 95th percentile of binding importance is associated with a fifty percentage point decrease in support for government intervention. Given such a large preexisting relationship, it is unsurprising that the relationship between openness and economic opinion does not change substantially in response to stereotypical elite cues. That is, when right-wing cues were associated with the limited government position and left-wing cues were associated with the interventionist position, the effect of binding importance among engaged respondents is similar to the control condition.[15]

In stark contrast, there is a large treatment effect for engaged respondents assigned to the counter-stereotypical cues conditions. When left-wing cues are associated with the limited government position and right-wing cues are associated with the interventionist position, the effect of binding importance on economic preferences moves substantially toward zero. Indeed, the effect of binding importance on economic preferences is about thirty percentage points smaller than in the stereotypical cues conditions. This implies that a substantial proportion of engaged respondents shift their economic preferences in response to

---

[14] Although we cannot know for certain, this null effect may reflect a reversal such that among those who are truly unengaged, binding foundation importance is linked to economic liberalism, whereas among those who are moderately engaged, it is linked to economic conservatism. Recall that in this experiment, we cannot distinguish between those at low and moderate levels of political engagement.

[15] While the change is in the expected direction, it is rather small and not statistically significant.

the counter-stereotypical cues. This is a striking result, as it indicates that the relationship between personality and economic opinion among engaged citizens is, to a large extent, a result of elite construction rather than unconditional elective affinity (i.e., natural resonance). A skeptic of the previous experiment might argue that open citizens will only follow elite cues when they are *stereotypical* – that is, when they fit partisan expectations – but not when they are counter-stereotypical (e.g., Sniderman and Stiglitz 2012). Our findings show that this skepticism is misplaced: a substantial proportion of engaged citizens follow elite cues in a direction inconsistent with the stances typically taken by their favored group of elites. This pattern is consistent with our claim that engaged citizens care more about the expressive than the instrumental implications of economic policy conflict. Thus, rather than choosing the policy *content* that resonates with their psychological dispositions, many engaged citizens are effectively choosing the policy option associated with their cultural tribe.[16]

We end our discussion of this experiment with one final demonstration. Our CCES study was conducted in the midst of the 2012 presidential election. Therefore, we included two conditions with presidential candidate cues, one where Republican candidate Mitt Romney took limited government positions and President Obama took interventionist positions (i.e., stereotypical cues), and one where Romney took interventionist positions and Obama took limited government positions (i.e., counter-stereotypical cues). Intuitively, one might expect the effects of these treatments to be weaker than what we observed earlier (averaging over conditions) due to the intensity of campaign coverage and the corresponding clarification of each candidate's general views on the role of government. If, however, engaged citizens are primarily interested in self-expression, the salience of the campaign might exacerbate the tendency to take cues, because there is more at stake in terms of group conflict, and the candidates are the standard bearers for their respective parties.

This is exactly what we find. Looking at Figure 6.4, when Romney is associated with the limited government position and Obama takes the

---

[16] This result also suggests that moral foundations theory (Haidt 2012) provides an incomplete explanation for ideological division in contemporary American politics. Although the binding foundations of loyalty, authority, and sanctity divide left and right in terms of identity and cultural issues, this does not necessarily characterize public opinion on economic issues. To predict preferences on the latter, we must have information about two additional considerations: whether an individual is engaged in politics, and the manner in which elites are divided on an issue.

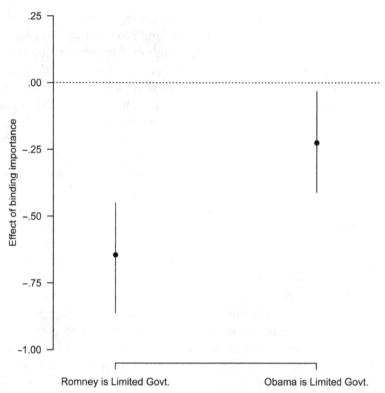

FIGURE 6.4. The moderating effect of candidate cues on the relationship between binding foundation importance and economic policy liberalism for engaged citizens, 2012 CCES experiment

interventionist position (i.e., the stereotypical cues condition), engaged citizens high in binding importance are nearly sixty-five percentage points less supportive of government intervention than those low in binding importance. However, when the experimental stimuli are reversed, such that Obama takes the conservative position and Romney takes the liberal position (i.e., the counter-stereotypical cues condition), the relationship between binding importance and economic opinion is only about one-third as large (~23 points). In other words, among engaged citizens, the counter-stereotypical treatment altered the effect of binding importance by *forty points* in the "wrong" direction. By any reckoning, this is a very large experimental treatment effect. In sum, moral foundations play an important role in structuring economic opinion, but the extent and nature of their role depends critically on both engagement and the alignment of partisan elites on the issues.

Experimental Evidence for Cultural Signaling

In this chapter and in Chapter 3, we have argued that elites bind the open-closed dimension of personality to economics, leading politically engaged citizens to express themselves through opinion-taking on bread-and-butter issues. One way this occurs is through partisan, ideological, and candidate cue-taking, as observed in the previous two experiments. However, it may also occur through the direct packaging of economic policies with *cultural signals*. This arises when elites signal their cultural orientation in close proximity to position-taking on an economic issue. In this way, even in the absence of direct partisan and ideological cues, elites can bind economics to culture and personality.

Personality and Cultural Signaling: The 2014 CCES Experiment

In our third experiment, we test this proposition and provide more direct evidence that elite cues moderate the impact of openness on economic opinion. To do this, we strip away partisan and ideological labels, and simply vary the placement of an economic policy within an overall platform containing either liberal or conservative *cultural* policies. If engaged citizens are focused on the instrumental significance of economic policy options, we should see no influence of the surrounding cultural cues, because such information is irrelevant to the instrumental desirability of a given economic policy. If, however, engaged citizens are primarily interested in signaling their cultural identifications through position taking on economic issues, the influence of openness on economic opinion should depend on the nature of the cultural signals packaged with the economic policy options.

Our first cultural signaling experiment uses data from the University of Minnesota's module of the 2014 Cooperative Congressional Election Study, administered by YouGov. This experiment is intended to capture a common occurrence in which politicians make statements or take actions that signal their cultural orientation in close proximity to statements or actions concerning an economic issue. For example, as we described in Chapter 3, a member of Congress may talk about her position on the rights of transgender people in the same message that she discusses her position on taxes. The underlying principle is simple: the cultural signal provides information about how different cultural groups line up on the economic issue, thus indirectly linking openness to economic policy judgments. In this way, cultural signals should alter the relationship between openness and economic opinion among engaged – but not unengaged – citizens.

In this experiment, respondents were presented with two hypothetical candidates, labeled only "A" and "B," each of whom took a position on three distinct issues: abortion, gun control, and one economic issue. Candidate A always supported abortion rights and gun control (thus signaling cultural liberalism), while Candidate B always supported restrictions on abortion and opposition to gun control (thus signaling cultural conservatism). For half of the respondents, the economic issue was the privatization of Social Security; for the other half the issue was financial regulation. We also introduced a variant of the stereotypical versus counter-stereotypical cue manipulation. Specifically, half of our respondents were assigned to a stereotypical-cue condition – in which Candidate A (the cultural liberal) took the interventionist position on the economic issue (i.e., opposing Social Security privatization or supporting financial regulation), while Candidate B (the cultural conservative) took the limited government position on the economic issue (i.e., supporting privatization or opposing regulation). The other half of our respondents were assigned to a counter-stereotypical cue condition in which the candidates' positions on these issues were reversed. Here, the culturally liberal candidate took the conservative economic position, and the culturally conservative candidate took the liberal economic position. Examples of the treatments presented to respondents are shown in Table 6.5.

Respondents were first asked to study each candidate's position on each issue. Following this study period, they were asked to express their own opinion on the *economic* issue only. In particular, respondents were asked, "Which candidate's position do you prefer on the issue of [Social Security privatization/financial regulation]? Candidate A or Candidate B?" We recoded these responses so that a value of "1" corresponds to support for the interventionist position, and "0" corresponds to support for the limited government position. Prior to viewing the experimental materials, respondents completed a survey that included four items measuring authoritarianism. These items were identical to those used in Chapter 4. Respondents also indicated their interest in politics and answered four political knowledge questions. As with the previous CCES experiment – and despite our inclusion of four knowledge items rather than two – we are faced with limited variation in political engagement at the lower end of the distribution. In this case, 46 percent of respondents fell in the highest interest category, and 52 percent correctly answered all four knowledge questions. Overall, 35 percent of respondents were coded at the highest level of engagement, and very few respondents fell at the lowest levels. We thus divided the sample into three engagement

TABLE 6.5. *Treatments in 2014 CCES experiment*

Instructions
"Now, you will see the issue stances of two candidates, 'Candidate A' and 'Candidate B.' Each candidate takes a position on abortion, gun control, and Social Security privatization/financial regulation.
In a minute, we will ask you for your own opinions. Right now, we would like you to carefully examine the positions of the candidates on the three issues. First, compare the two candidates on the issue of abortion. Then, compare them on the issue of gun control. Finally, compare them on the issue of Social Security privatization/financial regulation."

Example Treatments

Stereotypical Policy Condition for Social Security		
Issue	Candidate A	Candidate B
Abortion	Believes abortion is a personal choice and should be legal for any reason at all	Believes abortion should only be legal in cases of rape, incest, or where the mother's life is in danger
Gun Control	Supports a federal ban on all handguns and automatic weapons	Opposes restrictions on private gun ownership
Social Security Privatization	Opposes allowing individuals to privately invest Social Security contributions in the stock market	Supports allowing individuals to privately invest their Social Security contributions in the stock market

Counter-stereotypical Policy Condition for Financial Regulation		
Issue	Candidate A	Candidate B
Abortion	Believes abortion is a personal choice and should be legal for any reason at all	Believes abortion should only be legal in cases of rape, incest, or where the mother's life is in danger
Gun Control	Supports a federal ban on all handguns and automatic weapons	Opposes restrictions on private gun ownership
Financial Regulation	Opposes increased government oversight of large banks	Supports increased government oversight of large banks

Dependent Variable

"Which candidate's position do you prefer on the issue of Social Security privatization/financial regulation? Candidate A or Candidate B?"

categories corresponding approximately to a tertile split; our analysis focuses on the lower and upper thirds of the engagement distribution.[17] Again, it is important to remember that we are limited in what we can say about the lowest levels of engagement in this study.

We estimated models[18] separately for each engagement group and treatment condition combination, predicting support for the liberal economic policy position as a function of authoritarianism and our standard set of controls. The key estimates are shown in Figure 6.5. Panel A shows the results for the lower third of engagement and Panel B shows them for the upper third. Looking first at Panel A, we find no relationship between authoritarianism and economic opinion for unengaged citizens in either of the two cultural signaling conditions. That is, regardless of how economic policies are packaged with cultural policies, authoritarianism is uncorrelated with economic policy attitudes among those in the bottom third of the engagement scale.

Turning to engaged respondents in Panel B, we find a very different pattern. In the stereotypical cues condition, we find a large and statistically significant relationship between authoritarianism and economic opinion. Specifically, when cultural liberalism (i.e., support for abortion rights and gun control) is packaged with liberal *economic* policies, high authoritarians are about forty-five percentage points less economically liberal than low authoritarians. This is nearly identical to what we found in the partisan and ideological cues condition in the first experiment. *In the counter-stereotypical cues condition, however, this relationship disappears entirely.* That is, when economically conservative policies are embedded in the same platform as culturally liberal policies, the effect of authoritarianism is *nil*. This constitutes a forty-five percentage point experimental treatment effect, which is very large by common standards. This is exactly what we would expect if engaged citizens privilege the cultural implications of their economic policy positions. It is these expressive concerns – rather than those associated with policy content – that undergird the relationship between openness and economic opinion observed in Chapter 4 among politically engaged citizens. As the only difference between the two signaling conditions is the cultural platform accompanying the economic policies (stereotypical versus counter-stereotypical), we are in a strong position to claim that it is the association between cultural and economic policies that drives changes

[17] We also examined the middle third of engagement, but do not report the results here. These individuals look very similar to the *bottom* third.
[18] We utilized a probit link function.

Panel A: Bottom tertile of engagement

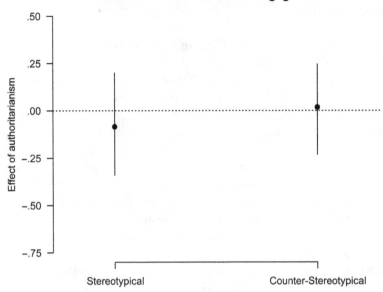

Panel B: Top tertile of engagement

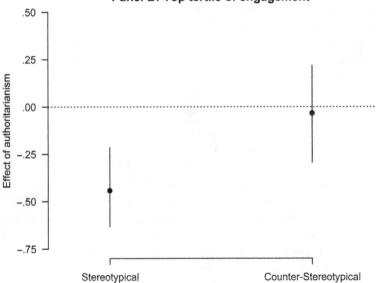

FIGURE 6.5. The moderating effect of cultural signals on the relationship between authoritarianism and economic policy liberalism across political engagement, 2014 CCES experiment

in the relationship between authoritarianism and economic preferences among engaged citizens.

Political Engagement and the Logic of Cultural Signaling: The 2015 GfK Experiment

A key assumption of our argument is that engagement is associated with a heightened concern for the cultural implications of one's policy attitudes. To further explore the role of engagement in the privileging of culture over economics, we conducted a fourth experiment focused on attitudes toward *libertarianism*. In contrast to our other experiments in this chapter, this experiment does not focus on the role of dispositional openness. Unfortunately, no personality items were available in this survey. Instead, we focus on the relationship between a composite measure of right-wing political orientation and attitudes toward libertarianism under conditions where the cultural implications of the latter are emphasized to differing degrees.[19]

Despite a departure from our usual focus on personality, we believe this experiment offers a unique opportunity to examine the importance of cultural concerns for how engaged citizens interact with elite politics.[20] Libertarianism *cross-cuts* the contemporary cleavage between the American left and right. It is defined in the abstract by a limited government philosophy, which should be appealing to the American right and distasteful to the American left. But in practice, libertarians are in conflict with the right on cultural issues and with the left on economic issues. By experimentally manipulating the relative salience of these two ideological dimensions, we can observe how the relationship between political orientation and libertarianism changes as the meaning of libertarianism changes. Importantly, we can also observe which dimension is more important to citizens' attitudes toward libertarianism. If, as we have argued, engaged citizens care most about the cultural implications of their political positions, then the relationship between political orientation and libertarianism should "follow culture" rather than economics. In other words, highlighting the economic dimension of libertarianism should be relatively unimportant to how engaged citizens evaluate libertarianism, whereas highlighting the cultural dimension of libertarianism

---

[19] Specifically, we operationalize right-wing orientation as the average of partisan and ideological identification ($r = 0.61$). We can think of citizens high and low on this measure as "sorted" partisans in Mason's (2015a) and Levendusky's (2009) terminology.

[20] Also, as we demonstrated in Chapter 5, partisanship and ideological identification are strongly tied to personality among engaged citizens.

should matter a great deal. Further, when the potential ideological conflict between culture and economics within libertarianism is made explicit, attitudes toward libertarianism should reflect the former more than the latter (i.e., culture should trump economics). This is very similar in concept to what we expected and found in the 2014 cultural signaling experiment described in the previous section.

The experiment was conducted in June 2015 by the survey research firm GfK.[21] The design included two factors. First, respondents were randomly assigned to receive one of three abstract philosophical justifications for libertarianism. The three justification treatments are shown in Table 6.6. Each explains that libertarianism is a political ideology emphasizing limited government, but the justification for limiting government varies across the three conditions. Specifically, each represents one of three primary strands of contemporary libertarian thought: natural rights, consequentialism, and public justification. We fail to find any influence of this factor on attitudes toward libertarianism, so we collapse across it in all subsequent analyses.[22]

We focus our attention on how cultural and economic position-taking influences attitudes toward libertarianism. This constitutes the second factor of the experiment. Respondents were randomly assigned to receive one of three sets of "typical" issue positions taken by libertarians, or no issues at all. In the conditions where respondents received issue positions, they saw cultural issues only, economic issues only, or both cultural and economic issues. The issues used for each treatment are shown in Table 6.6 and represent a wide array of cultural and economic policies. An overall treatment condition thus consisted of one abstract justification for libertarianism that was either presented alone or followed by a set of issue positions. The justifications and issue positions were always presented together on a single screen, with the issues below the justification. After reading the stimulus, respondents indicated their attitudes

---

[21] GfK's Knowledge Panel is an online panel of survey respondents that is representative of the entire U.S. population. They currently recruit members using a mixture of random-digit dialing and address-based sampling. Once recruited, panel members are notified by email or through their account when they are assigned to a new survey. The completion rate for the survey was 61 percent. The recruitment rate for this study reported by GfK was 13.5 percent and the profile rate was 64.6 percent for a cumulative response rate of 5.3 percent. The experiment was funded by a short-study grant from Time Sharing Experiments for the Social Sciences (http://www.tessexperiments.org/) awarded to Chris Johnston and Jonathan Anomaly.

[22] This lack of effect is interesting in its own right, and suggests that citizens are responding more to the symbol of "limited government" than the content of arguments in favor of limiting government.

TABLE 6.6. *Treatments in the 2015 GfK experiment*

Natural rights treatment
Libertarians believe that government intervention in the lives of citizens should be limited. This is because they believe that people have a natural right to self-ownership. This means that people own their bodies and their labor, and they should be free to engage in any activities they like, including activities that cause harm to themselves, as long as they do not cause direct and significant harm to other people. Libertarians believe that governments should only limit individual freedom when people's actions directly and significantly harm others.

Consequentialism treatment
Libertarians believe that government intervention in the lives of citizens should be limited. This is because they believe that society works best when people are free to make their own choices. That is, in most cases, government intervention causes more harm than good, because people know how to pursue their own interests better than the government does. Libertarians believe that governments should only limit individual freedom when the benefits to some people clearly outweigh the costs to others.

Public justification treatment
Libertarians believe that government intervention in the lives of citizens should be limited. This is because they believe that people should be treated as free and equal moral persons. This means that the natural state of affairs is complete freedom, and any restrictions on this freedom must in principle be acceptable to all reasonable people. Libertarians believe that governments should only limit individual freedom if all reasonable people could agree that the restrictions are justified

Cultural issues treatment (order of issues was randomized)
Gay couples should receive the same federal benefits as straight couples.
Adults should be allowed to sell their organs for money.
Most restrictions on legal immigration should be removed.
Women should be allowed to obtain an abortion for any reason.
The government **should not** restrict drug use by adults.
The government **should not** restrict gambling by adults.
The government **should not** restrict the sale of sex between consenting adults.

Economic issues treatment (order of issues was randomized)
Minimum wage laws should be repealed.
People should be allowed to work at any job they choose, even if working conditions are dangerous.
Taxes should be low and redistribution limited.
Businesses should be allowed to charge any prices they want for their products.
The government **should not** require certification for most occupations (e.g., hair dressers, nurses).
The government **should not** subsidize domestic industries or restrict imports from other countries.
The government **should not** restrict the interest rate banks can charge for loans or credit cards.

Dependent variable items:
 1. How well does the term "libertarian" describe your political beliefs?
 2. How positive or negative do you feel toward libertarianism?

toward libertarianism using the two items at the bottom of Table 6.6. We combined these into a single scale ($r = 0.68$).[23]

To estimate the impact of economic policy positions on attitudes toward libertarianism, we compare the relationship between right-wing orientation and libertarian attitudes in the justification only condition to the same relationship in the justification plus economic policy condition. To estimate the impact of cultural policy positions on attitudes toward libertarianism, we compare the justification-only condition to the justification plus cultural policy condition. These two comparisons represent independent effects of economic and cultural policy on the relationship between political orientation and libertarianism, respectively. We can also examine the *relative* impact of economic and cultural policies on attitudes toward libertarianism by comparing the change in the former case to the change in the latter. If, as we hypothesize, cultural policy matters more than economic policy, the change should be larger in the former than the latter. Finally, the last condition pits economic and cultural policies directly against one another, making the cross-cutting nature of libertarianism explicit. When such conflict is at the fore, do citizens follow cultural or economic policy?

The results are shown in Figure 6.6. In each panel, the y-axis represents the effect of right-wing orientation (the average of partisanship and ideology) on attitudes toward libertarianism. Positive values on the y-axis indicate that right-wing citizens feel more positive toward libertarianism than left-wing citizens. Negative values mean left-wing citizens feel more positive toward libertarianism than right-wing citizens. The x-axis is political engagement measured with a four-category political interest scale.[24] Consider Panel A, which shows the estimates for the justification-only condition (i.e., when no policy issues were linked to libertarianism). Among politically unengaged respondents, right-wing orientation is *negatively* associated with attitudes toward libertarianism. This means that unengaged left-wing citizens hold more positive attitudes toward libertarianism than unengaged right-wing citizens when libertarianism is defined abstractly in terms of support for limited government. As

---

[23] The survey also included a libertarian identity item, but this item reduced the reliability of the overall scale, because only 14 percent of respondents identify (categorically) as libertarian "generally speaking." As our interest is less in libertarian identification than attitudes toward libertarianism in the presence or absence of different cues, we exclude this item.

[24] The survey did not include any political knowledge items, but there was substantial variation across the response options for the political interest item.

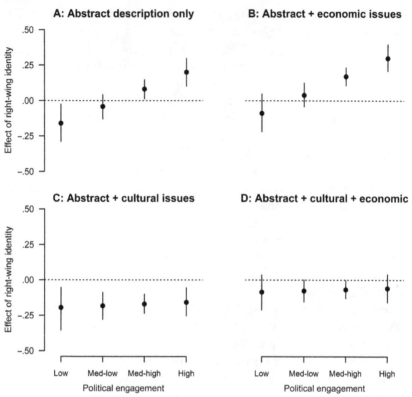

FIGURE 6.6. The moderating effect of cultural and economic issues on the relationship between right-wing orientation and libertarianism across political engagement, 2015 GfK Experiment

political engagement increases, however, this effect becomes increasingly positive. At high levels of engagement, right-wing citizens hold considerably more positive attitudes toward libertarianism than left-wing citizens. The alignment of right-wing political orientation with a limited government philosophy emerges only among politically engaged citizens. Among the unengaged, it is exactly the opposite. This interaction is consistent with what we found in Chapter 4 for limited government values and personality.

We can now compare Panel A to Panels B and C. Panel B depicts the results for the condition in which abstract justifications were paired with economic issues only. The estimates suggest very little movement – from the justification-only control condition – at any level of engagement. Thus, when libertarianism is defined along economic policy lines (in addition to abstractly in terms of limited government), there is little change (from the abstract only condition) in the link between political orientation and attitudes toward libertarianism.

Panel C depicts the results for the condition in which the abstract justifications were paired with cultural issues. Here, there is a substantial change in the relationship between political orientation and libertarian attitudes, and this movement is larger among politically engaged citizens. Specifically, among highly engaged respondents, the relationship reverses completely – from the abstract only condition – such that engaged left-wing citizens hold more positive attitudes toward libertarianism than engaged right-wing citizens. At the highest levels of engagement, the effect of political orientation changes by thirty-five percentage points, from +20 to -15. By contrast, among moderately engaged respondents, the change is much smaller, and among the least engaged there is no change at all. These findings constitute strong evidence that cultural signaling is critical to how engaged citizens evaluate libertarianism. When a limited government philosophy is presented in a highly abstract fashion, right-wing engaged citizens are supportive and left-wing citizens are opposed. When that very same philosophy is paired with cultural liberalism, however, highly engaged right- and left-wing citizens switch positions. Thus, among those who know and care about politics, the concept of "limited government" is attractive only to the extent that it maps onto one's preferred cultural orientation.

We find even stronger evidence in favor of the logic of cultural signaling by pitting economic and cultural issues directly against one another in Panel D. Recall that in this condition, citizens were presented with an abstract argument for limited government, a set of economically conservative policy positions, and a set of culturally liberal policy positions. The resulting pattern is much closer to Panel C (the cultural issues condition) than to Panel B (the economic issues condition). Indeed, despite a slight upward tick relative to Panel C, the effect of right-wing orientation remains negative at all four levels of engagement, and it is statistically significant for the middle two levels. This strongly suggests that politically engaged citizens privilege cultural issues over economic issues. When the cross-cutting nature of libertarianism is made explicit, the engaged care most about the cultural implications of their attitudes. Indeed, the difference in the effect of right-wing orientation comparing Panels B and D is large and statistically significant, while the difference in the effect between Panels C and D is minimal. That is, adding cultural policy to economic policy results in a large change, but adding economic policy to cultural policy has little effect.

In sum, the results of this fourth experiment provide further evidence for the importance of cultural signaling. When push comes to shove, the engaged are less moved by the appeal of abstract limited government values and concrete economic policy positions than by the cultural implications of their attitudes. When there are no cultural implications (Panels A and B), engaged citizens on the right- and left-wing line up as they typically do in American politics: the right prefers a limited government approach and the left prefers more intervention. But when a limited government philosophy is packaged together with cultural liberalism, the result is a robust preference reversal.

Among the *un*engaged, by contrast, the estimates across conditions are only minimally different from one another. They do vary a bit, but much less than for the engaged, and they are always negative. Indeed, compared to unengaged left-wing citizens, those on the right find the entire package of libertarianism – philosophy, economics, and culture – distasteful. If we simply average across all experimental conditions, the relationship between right-wing orientation and libertarianism among the unengaged is negative and statistically significant ($b = $ -0.12, $p < 0.05$). This is consistent with what we presented in Chapter 4. It is only through attention to elite discourse – and the pairing of a limited government philosophy with cultural conservatism in contemporary American politics – that right-wing orientation becomes positively linked to support for this political orientation. When this construction breaks down, and cultural liberalism is paired with a limited government philosophy and economic policy platform, right-wing citizens find libertarianism distasteful at *all* levels of engagement.[25]

Summary of Experimental Results

Taken together, these four experiments strongly suggest that elite cues condition the influence of personality on economic preferences by binding culture to economic policy and philosophy. Our first two experiments demonstrated that partisan and ideological cues alter the relationship between openness and economic opinion among engaged citizens, but have virtually no influence among unengaged citizens. Our second experiment included counter-stereotypical cue conditions, in which elites of the

---

[25] These results also seem consistent with those of Parker and Barreto (2014), who find that support for the Tea Party is substantially rooted in cultural factors and personality needs for social order.

right and left take economic positions opposite to their general ideological tendencies. In these cases, the relationship between openness and economic opinion among engaged citizens moved strongly in the opposite direction, suggesting that elite cues matter even when they conflict with stereotypical positions of the right and left in American politics.[26] In our third experiment, we demonstrated that cultural cues – absent partisan or ideological labels – strongly condition the influence of openness on economic opinion among engaged (but not unengaged) citizens. When interventionist economic policies are packaged together with culturally liberal policies, we see the same pattern observed in Chapter 4: engaged citizens with open personalities support the interventionist position, whereas engaged citizens with closed personalities support the limited government position. When these cultural signals are reversed, however, open and closed citizens "follow culture," effectively negating the impact of personality on political preferences altogether. In our fourth experiment, we further explored the logic of cultural signaling by providing direct evidence that engaged citizens weigh cultural information especially heavily when making political judgments. Specifically, we demonstrated that the presence of cultural issues in a description of libertarianism reverses the relationship between right-wing affiliation and support for libertarianism among engaged citizens. When cultural conservatism is paired with economic conservatism, engaged right-wing identifiers are more supportive of libertarianism than left-wing identifiers. However, when cultural *liberalism* is paired with economic conservatism, the relationship between right-wing affiliation and libertarianism changes drastically. Among the unengaged, the relationship does not significantly vary across conditions, and the overall effect of right-wing orientation on libertarianism is negative. This is similar to what we found in Chapter 4 using measures of openness as the independent variable and limited government values as the dependent variable.

Overall, these experimental results are consistent with a view of engaged citizens as primarily concerned with economics as *cultural expression* rather than as a principled commitment to an expansive or limited role for government intervention. Thus, the impact of personality on economic opinion among engaged citizens is not primarily based on an elective affinity that links the appeal of certain political ideas to particular psychological characteristics; rather, it is a relationship constructed

---

[26] These findings are consistent with previous work in political psychology (e.g., Cohen 2003; Lavine et al. 2012).

by political elites. Specifically, it is constructed on the basis of elite cues regarding the alignment between cultural symbols and economic policies.

Openness and International Trade

The advantage of our cueing and signaling experiments is tight control over political context. In these experiments, we are able to make strong causal inferences about the influence of political elites and cultural symbols in structuring the relationship between personality and economic preferences. The disadvantage of such studies is that they are artificial; in experimental design parlance, they lack a degree of external validity. Although we believe these findings are informative, it would be useful to examine the varying association between personality and economics in a more externally valid fashion. Another concern with our experimental studies is that there are large, preexisting associations between openness and economic policy liberalism among engaged citizens. As we have seen, this limits our ability to find a full reversal of the personality-policy relationship as a function of counter-stereotypical cues. While we found large counter-stereotypical treatment effects among the engaged in our second and third experiments, these simply offset the preexisting relationship rather than reverse it. Ideally, however, we would like to demonstrate that the effect of openness can indeed reverse completely when cultural liberalism is associated with a limited government orientation in the economic domain.

One approach is to look for real-world variation in the association between culture and economics. To do this, we seek to identify a set of issues pertaining to the proper role of government in economic matters, but for which the cultural associations are opposite to those we examined in Chapter 4. In particular, we seek to identify a political context corresponding to a "counter-stereotypical" association between culture and economics, so that cultural conservatism is linked to economic interventionism, and cultural liberalism is linked to limited government. We can then compare the relationship between openness and economic preferences under these circumstances to what we found in Chapter 4. Our theory suggests that when the relationship between culture and economics changes, the relationship between openness and economic opinion should change as well.

International trade may present a situation with these characteristics. Despite their disagreement on domestic social welfare issues, Democrats and Republicans in the contemporary United States are not strongly divided on international trade. Rather, trade is often treated as a "valence" issue (Stokes 1963). Politicians typically discuss trade in the context of abstract appeals to protecting American jobs, maintaining U.S. global competitiveness, and forging trade deals that will benefit the U.S. economy. For example, in the second presidential debate in 2012, both Barack Obama and Mitt Romney sought to demonstrate a "tough" approach to China's rising position as a global superpower. Romney stated, "China's been cheating over the years, one, by holding down the value of their currency, number two, by stealing our intellectual property, our designs, our patents, our technology. There's even an Apple store in China that's a counterfeit Apple store selling counterfeit goods. They hack into our computers." Similarly, President Obama stated, "When he talks about getting tough on China, keep in mind that Governor Romney invested in companies that were pioneers of outsourcing to China and is currently investing in countries that are building surveillance equipment for China to spy on its own folks. That's – Governor, you're the last person who's going to get tough on China."[27]

Republicans *and* Democrats were also critical of the Obama administration's negotiations on the Trans-Pacific Partnership (TPP) trade agreement. Senators Al Franken (D) and Olympia Snowe (R) wrote a letter to the administration in 2012 urging that the TPP negotiations include a variety of "fair trade" components, including the continuance of "Buy American" government procurement requirements and obligations to protect labor rights.[28] About two dozen Republican House members – mainly Tea Partiers – also signaled their discontent with the administration's lack of congressional consultation on the matter, creating a bipartisan coalition of criticism on the TPP.[29] More recently, both Hillary Clinton and Donald Trump expressed opposition to the TPP in the 2016 presidential debates. Elite opinion on this issue thus cuts across typical partisan boundaries, with many Republicans supporting the Obama administration and many Democrats opposing it.[30] It is therefore no surprise that the public is not sharply divided by partisanship on issues of trade. For example, in the 2012 American National Election

[27] www.npr.org/2012/10/16/163050988/transcript-obama-romney-2nd-presidential-debate.
[28] www.citizenstrade.org/ctc/blog/2012/12/03/two-dozen-us-senators-demand-labor-rights-in-the-tpp/
[29] www.motherjones.com/politics/2013/11/fast-track-authority-obama-trans-pacific-partnership
[30] www.nytimes.com/2014/01/31/business/reid-pushes-back-on-fast-track-trade-authority.html

Study, 42 percent of respondents stated that they had "not thought much about" the issue of restricting foreign imports to protect U.S. jobs, and nearly equal numbers of Democrats, Independents, and Republicans supported such restrictions.

In sum, international trade is not strongly connected to partisan orientation in the mass public. However, this does not mean that opinions on trade are random. Recent research suggests the relevance of *cultural* considerations related to ethnocentrism and nationalism, such that individuals who are particularly concerned with maintaining in-group status tend to support trade restrictions. For example, Mansfield and Mutz explain that "there is little support for free trade among people who believe the United States should take an isolationist stance on international affairs more generally or those who feel that members of other ethnic and racial groups are less praiseworthy than their own racial or ethnic group. Although such views have no direct bearing on the economic benefits of trade, they are far more predictive of trade preferences than indicators of economic self-interest" (2009: 427). In this way, mass preferences on trade issues might be conceptualized as falling along a *nationalism-cosmopolitanism* dimension, rather than the standard left-right dimension that characterizes debates over domestic economic policy (see also Hainmueller and Hiscox 2007).

This suggests that the role of openness among engaged citizens should shift when moving from domestic to international economic issues. As much previous research attests, personality traits associated with a closed orientation are strongly associated with ethnocentrism and various forms of nationalism (e.g., Adorno et al. 1950; Altemeyer 1988; Chirumbolo et al. 2004; Crowson 2009; Crowson, Debacker, and Thoma 2006; Federico et al. 2005; Golec and Federico 2004; Hetherington and Suhay 2011; Kruglanski et al. 2006; Schatz, Staub, and Lavine 1999). Conversely, traits associated with an open personality orientation are associated with cosmopolitanism. For example, citizens who score low on the need for closure and high on the Big Five trait of openness to experience are more apt to travel abroad, and to feel comfortable with and immerse themselves in foreign cultures at home (e.g., Hibbing et al. 2014a; Johnston et al. 2015; McCrae and Costa 2003).

To the extent that trade issues prime such cultural orientations, we should expect engaged citizens with open personalities to take the limited-government position of opposing restrictions on trade, and engaged citizens with closed personalities to prefer an interventionist stance in the form of economic protectionism – exactly opposite to what we observed for domestic policy in Chapter 4. Moving from domestic economic issues to those related to international trade thus entails real-world variation in the cultural meaning of support for limited government, thereby providing a complement to our experimental findings. If the relationship between openness and economic opinion reverses from the domestic to the international case, this would constitute additional evidence that economic opinion among engaged citizens is shaped more by the cultural meanings of economic policies than by principled concerns about the role of government or self-interest. As in our libertarianism experiment, when culture and economics conflict, we expect engaged citizens to privilege the former over the latter. This pattern would also reinforce the importance of elite actors in constructing the relationship between personality and economic opinion on domestic issues. That is, once strong cues from partisan and ideological elites are removed and the cultural associations of economic policy shift, engaged citizens with open personalities should prefer a free market approach, while engaged citizens with closed personalities should prefer a strong government hand.

To test this hypothesis, we examine attitudes toward economic protectionism in the 2000, 2004, 2008, and 2012 ANES surveys. In each year, respondents were asked the following question: "Some people have suggested placing new limits on foreign imports in order to protect American jobs. Others say that such limits would raise consumer prices and hurt American exports. Do you favor or oppose placing new limits on imports, or haven't you thought much about this?" The item is dichotomous, and we code it such that a value of one indicates support for restricting foreign imports and a value of zero indicates opposition to such restrictions. All four years include our four-item measure of authoritarianism and our standard measure of political engagement, all operationalized as in Chapters 4 and 5. Our general expectation is that authoritarianism will be associated with *support* for protectionism, a reversal of what we observed – among engaged citizens – for domestic forms of intervention in the economy in Chapter 4. As in Chapter 4, we also examine the potential for racial and ethnic heterogeneity in the effect of personality (unlike in our experiments, we have sufficient samples of nonwhite groups to do this here). To this end, we estimated separate models for self-identified blacks and Latinos. To maximize our sample size, we combine all four years of data.[31]

---

[31] The "imports" item is typically asked in the post-election portion of the ANES, and a substantial percentage of respondents indicate they have not thought much about the

The key quantities of interest are plotted in Figure 6.7.[32] The y-axis represents the change in the probability of supporting import restrictions as a function of authoritarianism. The full sample results (shown in Panel A) suggest a significant interaction between authoritarianism and engagement, but one that is different from what we observed in Chapter 4. Here, authoritarianism is an increasingly strong predictor of economic *protectionism* as engagement increases. This is precisely opposite to our findings in Chapter 4 for domestic economic issues. There, authoritarianism predicted a free market orientation among the engaged, but here it predicts an interventionist orientation. Further, the effect of authoritarianism is positive at all levels of engagement (though not statistically significant at the lowest levels). This pattern provides strong support for our theoretical expectations: when the cultural implications of free market ideology reverse, so does the relationship between dispositional openness and economic preferences (among engaged citizens). In the realm of international trade, high authoritarians are most supportive of government intervention, and low authoritarians are least supportive.

Panel B shows the estimates for blacks and Latinos.[33] In these two cases, there was no interaction between authoritarianism and engagement. We thus plot the "main effect," or unconditional relationship between authoritarianism and protectionism. In both cases the effect of authoritarianism is positive, but it is only significant for blacks. These estimates are also quite a bit smaller than in the full sample. Thus, as in Chapters 4 and 5, we observe heterogeneity in the influence of personality across racial groups, such that openness matters more for the full sample and non-Latino whites than for blacks or Latinos.

Summary

In the final empirical section of this chapter, we examined the relationship between authoritarianism and preferences on international trade.

---

issue, both of which limit the sample size for our analysis. However, if we look at each of the four years separately (using all available respondents), we find a similar pattern of results, but with no significant interaction between authoritarianism and engagement in 2004 and 2008. In other words, in those two years, authoritarianism has an unconditional positive influence on support for protectionism. This is consistent with our theoretical expectations. In 2000 and 2012, the interactions are significant and similar to what we report in Figure 6.7.

[32] We used a probit link function.

[33] As in Chapters 4 and 5, we also ran these analyses for non-Latino white respondents only. As expected, the results were similar to those in the full sample, so we do not report them here.

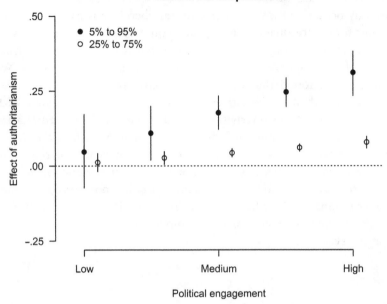

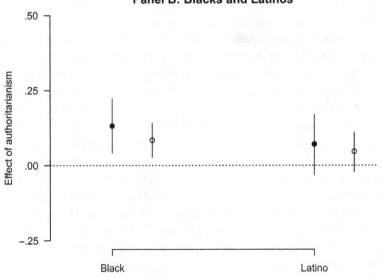

FIGURE 6.7. The relationship between authoritarianism and support for import restrictions across political engagement for the full sample and for African Americans and Latinos, 2000–2012 ANES

Issues of trade are interesting for our purposes because they represent a naturally occurring case in which cultural liberalism is associated with support for the free market and cultural conservatism is associated with government intervention. In this sense, trade issues are a naturalistic analog of our counter-stereotypical cultural signaling experiments. We predicted and found that open citizens have more positive attitudes toward trade than closed citizens. These findings are consistent with other recent work on international trade preferences that emphasize noneconomic motivations such as ethnocentrism (Mansfield and Mutz 2009). Overall, these analyses provide further evidence for the claim that the impact of openness on economic preferences varies as a function of the cultural associations of different policy positions. On issues of international trade, where cultural liberalism is associated with free market attitudes, openness promotes support for markets over government intervention.

Conclusions

In this chapter, we examined the role of political elites in shaping the relationship between personality and economic opinion. One of our primary theoretical claims is that engaged citizens seek to signal their cultural commitments through position-taking on economic issues. An important implication of this perspective is that the qualitative nature of the relationship between openness and economic opinion depends on how partisan elites package economics with culture. When Democrats, liberals, and cultural progressives line up in support of government intervention (and Republicans, conservatives, and cultural traditionalists favor limited government), traits related to openness predict support for a strong government role in the economy (as in Chapter 4). But when the left *opposes* government intervention and the right *supports* it, the relationship between openness and economic opinion shifts in the same direction. Indeed, in the experimental sections of this chapter, we provided direct evidence that elite cues alter the effect of personality on economic opinion. We randomly assigned citizens to conditions that differed only in the alignment between elites and issue positions: sometimes elites of the left advocated limited government positions (i.e., providing counter-stereotypical cues) and sometimes elites of the right advocated limited government positions (i.e., providing stereotypical cues). This subtle experimental treatment produced a dramatic change in the relationship between openness and economic preferences. In some cases, we observed experimental treatment effects on the order of forty or more percentage points. However, as our theory predicts, these treatment effects were largely limited to politically engaged citizens; the unengaged were mostly unmoved by elite cues. Overall, the results support our theoretical framework: elite actors play a critical role in determining how personality relates to economic opinion, but this role is largely felt among citizens who care most about these symbolic conflicts.

Appendix

Covariance Structure Model for Latent Openness in the 2011 YouGov Study

In 2011, we conducted a national survey through the survey firm YouGov that included three distinct measures of dispositional openness: authoritarianism, need for closure, and conservation versus openness to change. The items for authoritarianism are listed in Table 4.1. The items for the latter two traits are listed in Table 6.2. To demonstrate the deep connection among these three traits, we conducted a confirmatory factor analysis. Each indicator for each respective trait was modeled as a function of a latent variable representing its respective trait. All three latent traits were modeled as a function of a latent superordinate factor, which we conceptualize as dispositional openness. The indicators for need for closure and conservation were also modeled as a function of a latent "methods" factor that controls for differences in the use of the common survey instrument for these ten items. Specifically, each of the ten items is constrained to load equally on the latent methods factor, and the methods factor is constrained to be uncorrelated with any of the four substantive factors. With this model specification, we can examine the extent to which the three traits are derivative of a common source in latent openness. The estimates for this modeling exercise are shown in Table A6.1. They indicate strong support for a common latent source among the three traits. Both authoritarianism and conservation versus openness load very strongly on latent openness (−0.79 and −0.76, respectively). Need for closure also exceeds common standards for a good indicator of a latent trait (−0.51). Each of these coefficients can be interpreted as the expected change in the respective latent trait for a one standard deviation change in latent openness.

TABLE A6.1. *Confirmatory factor analysis estimates*

		Estimate	SE
Authoritarianism (A)			
	A1	0.54	0.03
	A2	0.57	0.03
	A3	0.57	0.03
	A4	0.38	0.03
Need for Closure (N)			
	N1	−0.55	0.03
	N2	−0.20	0.04
	N3	0.61	0.03
	N4	0.59	0.03
	N5	0.1	0.04
Conservation (C)			
	C1	0.34	0.03
	C2	−0.56	0.03
	C3	−0.45	0.03
	C4	0.54	0.03
	C5	0.64	0.03
Openness			
	A	−0.79	0.06
	N	−0.51	0.04
	C	−0.76	0.05
X^2 / df		5.41	
CFI		0.85	
TLI		0.81	
RMSEA		0.06	

Notes: Data come from a 2011 national survey conducted by YouGov. Entries are maximum likelihood estimates and standard errors. The model included an additional "methods" factor, which is not shown.

TABLE A6.2. *Estimates for the 2011*
YouGov experiment

	Control	Elite Cues
Openness	0.21 (0.23)	0.05 (0.18)
Engagement	−0.12 (0.18)	−0.48 (0.14)
Open X Engage	0.10 (0.32)	0.71 (0.27)
Age	0.09 (0.08)	0.08 (0.05)
Male	0.03 (0.03)	−0.01 (0.02)
Black	0.10 (0.06)	0.10 (0.04)
Latino	0.11 (0.05)	0.10 (0.04)
Education	0.03 (0.07)	0.05 (0.05)
Income	−0.10 (0.06)	−0.16 (0.05)
Unemployed	0.05 (0.05)	0.05 (0.04)
South	−0.03 (0.03)	−0.07 (0.02)
Intercept	0.43 (0.13)	0.57 (0.10)
R^2	0.10	0.19
N	209	424

Notes: Entries are ordinary least squares estimates and standard errors (in parentheses). The left column includes all respondents in the control (no cues) condition, while the right column includes all respondents who received partisan or ideological cues.

TABLE A6.3. *Estimates for the 2012 CCES experiment*

	Unengaged			Engaged				
	Control	Right-Wing	Left-Wing	Control	Right-Wing	Left-Wing	Obama	Romney
Binding Importance	-0.12 (0.21)	-0.57 (0.12)	-0.24 (0.11)	-1.23 (0.21)	-1.44 (0.12)	-0.80 (0.13)	-0.52 (0.22)	-1.47 (0.22)
Age	0.32 (0.09)	0.08 (0.06)	0.19 (0.06)	0.22 (0.17)	0.17 (0.12)	0.14 (0.11)	0.10 (0.18)	-0.02 (0.19)
Male	-0.10 (0.04)	0.01 (0.03)	-0.01 (0.03)	-0.04 (0.06)	-0.01 (0.04)	-0.04 (0.04)	-0.03 (0.06)	0.06 (0.07)
Black	0.01 (0.07)	0.06 (0.04)	-0.03 (0.04)	0.27 (0.13)	0.25 (0.10)	0.18 (0.09)	0.26 (0.15)	0.27 (0.14)
Hispanic	-0.02 (0.06)	0.01 (0.05)	-0.01 (0.05)	-0.02 (0.23)	0.20 (0.11)	0.03 (0.14)	-0.40 (0.35)	0.38 (0.20)
Education	0.12 (0.08)	-0.05 (0.05)	0.06 (0.05)	-0.18 (0.13)	-0.02 (0.07)	0.00 (0.07)	-0.19 (0.12)	-0.02 (0.12)
Income	-0.01 (0.11)	-0.15 (0.07)	-0.18 (0.06)	-0.19 (0.18)	-0.08 (0.10)	-0.07 (0.09)	-0.01 (0.16)	-0.03 (0.06)
Unemployed	-0.07 (0.06)	-0.02 (0.04)	0.01 (0.04)	0.12 (0.15)	0.01 (0.08)	-0.01 (0.07)	0.06 (0.11)	0.01 (0.18)
Union	0.13 (0.07)	0.08 (0.05)	-0.04 (0.04)	0.15 (0.09)	0.18 (0.05)	0.03 (0.06)	0.06 (0.10)	0.12 (0.09)
South	-0.06 (0.04)	0.01 (0.03)	0.00 (0.03)	0.04 (0.06)	-0.01 (0.04)	-0.01 (0.04)	0.00 (0.07)	0.01 (0.07)
Intercept	0.52 (0.14)	0.93 (0.08)	0.70 (0.07)	1.21 (0.19)	1.19 (0.11)	0.98 (0.11)	0.95 (0.20)	1.30 (0.20)
R^2	0.09	0.03	0.04	0.25	0.35	0.16	0.07	0.33
N	189	590	554	151	465	434	142	137

Notes: Entries are ordinary least squares estimates and standard errors (in parentheses). "Binding importance" is the relative importance of binding moral foundations to individualizing foundations. "Right-Wing" and "Romney" columns are respondents who received information that right-wing sources and Mitt Romney are in favor of limiting government's role on an issue and left-wing sources and Obama are in favor of expanding government's role. The "Left-Wing" and "Obama" columns reverse these cues. The first three columns are for respondents in the bottom 56 percent of engagement, while the right five columns are for respondents in the top 44 percent of engagement.

	Unengaged		Engaged	
	Stereotypical	Counter-Stereo	Stereotypical	Counter-Stereo
Authoritarianism	−0.27 (0.38)	0.04 (0.36)	−1.36 (0.36)	−0.09 (0.35)
Age	0.39 (0.47)	−0.42 (0.52)	−0.51 (0.57)	0.93 (0.56)
Male	−0.14 (0.23)	0.22 (0.23)	−0.38 (0.23)	0.10 (0.22)
Black	0.45 (0.33)	−0.79 (0.31)	5.05 (254.94)	0.55 (0.44)
Hispanic	0.25 (0.38)	−0.39 (0.38)	−0.58 (0.67)	−0.13 (0.52)
Education	0.61 (0.47)	−0.10 (0.43)	0.96 (0.41)	0.45 (0.41)
Income	0.36 (0.62)	0.37 (0.63)	−0.68 (0.54)	−0.58 (0.55)
Unemployed	−0.20 (0.32)	0.25 (0.34)	0.01 (0.53)	0.33 (0.54)
Union	−0.54 (0.40)	−0.44 (0.52)	0.82 (0.43)	0.20 (0.40)
South	−0.35 (0.24)	0.53 (0.23)	−0.05 (0.23)	−0.16 (0.23)
Intercept	−0.08 (0.40)	−0.19 (0.41)	0.73 (0.51)	−0.38 (0.52)
PRE	0.22	0.10	0.36	0.00
N	154	159	169	153

Notes: Entries are probit coefficients and standard errors (in parentheses). "Stereotypical" columns are respondents who received candidates taking culturally liberal (conservative) and economically liberal (conservative) positions on abortion, gun control, and either financial regulation or Social Security privatization. "Counter-stereotypical" columns are respondents who received candidates taking culturally liberal (conservative) and economically conservative (liberal) positions on these issues. "PRE" is the proportionate reduction in error. The large standard error for the "black" dummy variable in the third column is due to small sample size and partial separation. Excluding this dummy does not change the results.

TABLE A6.5. *Estimates for the 2015 GfK experiment*

	Abstract Only	Abstract + Economic	Abstract + Cultural	Abstract + Cultural + Economic
Right–Wing Orientation	−0.19 (0.08)	−0.11 (0.08)	−0.23 (0.09)	−0.10 (0.08)
Engagement	−0.18 (0.07)	−0.17 (0.06)	0.03 (0.07)	0.01 (0.07)
Right–Wing X Engage	0.43 (0.11)	0.46 (0.11)	0.04 (0.12)	0.03 (0.11)
Age	−0.07 (0.05)	−0.20 (0.05)	−0.10 (0.05)	−0.17 (0.05)
Male	0.03 (0.02)	0.05 (0.02)	0.07 (0.02)	0.06 (0.02)
Black	−0.01 (0.04)	0.08 (0.03)	−0.02 (0.04)	0.00 (0.04)
Hispanic	0.03 (0.03)	0.01 (0.03)	0.02 (0.03)	0.03 (0.03)
Education	0.02 (0.04)	0.01 (0.03)	0.06 (0.04)	0.00 (0.03)
Income	0.00 (0.05)	−0.09 (0.04)	−0.15 (0.05)	−0.03 (0.05)
Unemployed	0.03 (0.05)	0.00 (0.04)	0.00 (0.04)	−0.05 (0.04)
South	0.01 (0.02)	0.02 (0.02)	0.03 (0.02)	0.06 (0.02)
Intercept	0.51 (0.05)	0.45 (0.05)	0.53 (0.06)	0.41 (0.05)
R^2	0.06	0.14	0.11	0.07
N	489	506	469	481

Notes: Entries are ordinary least squares coefficients and standard errors (in parentheses). "Abstract Only" is the condition where respondents received only an abstract justification for libertarianism. The remaining columns are conditions that presented respondents with concrete issues as well: economic issues only, cultural issues only, or both economic and cultural issues.

TABLE A6.6. *Estimates for authoritarianism*
and import restrictions

	All Rs	Blacks	Latinos
Authoritarianism	0.14 (0.20)	0.56 (0.20)	0.28 (0.19)
Engagement	−0.96 (0.19)		
Auth X Engage	0.73 (0.28)		
Age	0.43 (0.08)	0.62 (0.22)	0.07 (0.20)
Male	−0.34 (0.04)	−0.29 (0.10)	−0.11 (0.10)
Black	0.19 (0.06)		
Latino	−0.05 (0.06)		
Education	−0.58 (0.07)	−0.32 (0.19)	−0.02 (0.20)
Income	−0.25 (0.08)	0.42 (0.23)	−0.23 (0.22)
Unemployed	−0.13 (0.08)	−0.21 (0.17)	−0.11 (0.17)
Union	0.15 (0.05)	0.20 (0.15)	0.12 (0.14)
South	0.04 (0.04)	−0.02 (0.10)	0.26 (0.11)
2004 Dummy	0.50 (0.08)	0.27 (0.24)	0.38 (0.32)
2008 Dummy	0.68 (0.07)	0.32 (0.17)	0.69 (0.23)
2012 Dummy	0.66 (0.06)	0.46 (0.16)	0.68 (0.21)
Intercept	0.39 (0.14)	−0.25 (0.23)	−0.36 (0.27)
PRE	0.19	0.08	0.04
N	5,525	794	675

Notes: Data are from the 2000–12 American National Election Studies
(ANES). Entries are probit coefficients and standard errors (in parentheses). "PRE" is the proportionate reduction in error.

7

Political Engagement and Self-Interest

In Chapter 3, we argued that politically engaged citizens are primarily motivated by expressive concerns in making judgments about economic policy, while the unengaged are more likely to think in instrumental terms related to material self-interest. We contend that engaged citizens are more likely to consider what support for a policy signals about their political and social identities, whereas unengaged citizens are more likely to consider what a policy will do for them and those they care about. This, in turn, should produce a key reversal: openness should promote support for economic intervention among the engaged, while reducing support for intervention among the unengaged. After providing evidence for the reversal hypothesis in Chapter 4, we explored the mechanisms responsible for the connection between openness and economic liberalism among politically engaged citizens in Chapters 5 and 6. The purpose of this chapter is to provide additional empirical evidence for the claim that engagement shifts political judgment from an instrumental mode to an expressive mode. In the first section of this chapter, we briefly consider contemporary views on the role of self-interest in the formation of economic policy preferences. We then reiterate our alternative framework and how it differs from the received wisdom. In the empirical sections of this chapter, we examine how various personal economic concerns relate to economic policy preferences across levels of engagement. Consistent with our theory, we find that self-interest has its strongest political effects among the *unengaged*. In contrast the impact of self-interest is much weaker among engaged citizens. Finally, as in previous chapters, we wrap things up by considering racial and ethnic heterogeneity in these effects. Importantly, we find that the overall pattern described above holds for non-Latino whites, but not Latinos or African Americans.

Self-Interest and Policy Preferences

Does self-interest provide a foundation for economic policy preferences? This is among the more contentious questions in American mass politics. Political scientists have traditionally divided into two camps. In one camp are researchers inspired by rational choice theory, who assume that citizens are motivated primarily by self-interest. For example, in a highly influential paper, Meltzer and Richard (1981) argue that citizens support redistributive policies as a function of their own place in the income distribution and the expected disincentive effects of taxation. Individuals whose incomes fall below society's mean support redistribution because they gain more than they lose, while those above the mean oppose redistribution. In a variation on this theme, Stegmueller (2013) argues that citizens choose levels of redistribution on the basis of income *expectations*. Those who expect to be wealthy in the future prefer less redistribution than those who expect to be poor. Thus, redistribution also serves as a safety net when one is at risk of losing income in the future.

Other scholars influenced by the rational choice perspective emphasize temporal dynamics and the social insurance function of redistribution (e.g., Moene and Wallerstein 2001; Rehm 2009; Sinn 1995). Iversen (2005; Iversen and Soskice 2001), for example, argues that citizens with skills specific to an occupation or industry should prefer higher levels of redistribution than citizens with transferable skills, because skill specificity implies a greater risk of sustained income loss during periods of high unemployment or rapid technological change. Citizens with general skills, by contrast, are more mobile. Similarly, Rehm (2009) argues that people in industries or occupations with high unemployment rates will prefer higher levels of redistribution as insurance against job loss. In all cases, these scholars argue that economic policy preferences are primarily rooted in instrumental concerns about personal economic well-being. Self-interest is the default assumption.

In the other camp are political psychologists who have sharply criticized the rational choice approach on empirical grounds. In a widely cited review of the literature, Sears and Funk (1991) contend that the evidence for self-interest is weak. Instead, political psychologists have emphasized the *symbolic* bases of political judgment, such as partisanship and ideological identification (Cohen 2003; Huddy, Mason, and Aarøe 2015), core social and political values (Goren 2013; Schwartz et al. 2010), national identity (Citrin and Sears 2014; Citrin, Reingold, and Green 1990), and racial prejudice and ethnocentrism (Kinder and Kam 2010; Kinder and Sears 1981; Mansfield and Mutz 2009; Tesler 2012, 2016). From the perspective of those who emphasize symbolic politics, economic policy judgments reflect citizens' long-standing affective orientations to prominent social and political symbols rather than their concrete economic interests.

Some public opinion scholars have recently taken a middle ground position, suggesting that self-interest may matter more in some circumstances than in others. In this vein, Chong, Citrin, and Conley argue that "the theoretical debate about the role of self-interest in political life should proceed by acknowledging the presence of multiple motives in preference formation. It is too simple to say that self-interest is everything or nothing" (2001: 563). In this view, the political relevance of self-interest is conditioned by *information*: citizens will exhibit self-interested policy judgment when they are able to connect their personal interests to public policy, but they default to affect-based heuristics when the implications are opaque. Chong makes this point clearly:

Self-interest is more likely to matter when people actually have a stake in a policy and can see that they have a stake. Whether they can recognize those stakes depends on the transparency of the policy, the clarity with which the policy is presented to them, and their capacity to understand the implications of the policy. When their objective interests are debatable, when the implications of a policy are hard to discern or are obscured by political persuasion, or when they are not directly affected by the policy, people will rely more heavily on general political orientations (such as ideology and partisanship) that offer guidance in the absence of other criteria. (2013: 105)

This perspective draws heavily on "bounded rationality" models of political judgment in which the weight of a given consideration depends jointly on its *cognitive accessibility* and *applicability* to the issue at hand (Higgins 1996; see also Chong and Druckman 2007). In this view, most citizens are self-interested in politics by nature, but information-poor environments make it difficult to connect one's private interests with abstract public policy debates. This idea is supported in studies that find a greater role for self-interest when the accessibility of such considerations is manipulated experimentally (Chong et al. 2001; Young et al. 1991). It also strongly implies that self-interest effects should be more evident among politically engaged citizens, as they are better equipped to discern the policy implications of their economic predicaments.[1]

We agree that the minimum conditions for self-interested policy judgment are the accessibility and applicability of self-interest-related considerations. If personal economic interests are inaccessible to the individual, objectively irrelevant to judgments about a particular policy, or if the policy is framed in such a way as to obscure its relationship to self-interest, then we expect little reliance on such considerations. Where we depart from others is in the role ascribed to political engagement. The "middle ground" view outlined by Chong (2013) and others suggests that engaged citizens are more likely than the ill-informed to recognize where their interests lie in policy debates. We demur from this view; instead, we believe that most citizens are capable of discerning their material interests in most instances. To be sure, we are not saying that it is a straightforward task to evaluate the long-run implications of different approaches to redistribution, social welfare, and regulation. Indeed, this is the subject of much debate.[2] Rather, we are simply suggesting that most citizens are capable of recognizing the *intended beneficiaries* of most economic policies and whether or not they are among them. This will not always be true – even for seemingly simple issues like tax policy (e.g., Bartels 2005) – but we think it is true much of the time. Redistribution is clearly intended to benefit the poor at the expense of the wealthy; unemployment insurance is intended to benefit the unemployed or those at greater risk of becoming unemployed; government-subsidized health insurance is intended to benefit those without health insurance and those who have difficulty affording health insurance; boosts in the minimum wage are aimed at helping those working at (or near) the minimum wage; import restrictions are targeted at industries with substantial foreign competition; mortgage income-tax deductions reduce the tax burden of homeowners; and so on. In this sense, we agree with rational choice theorists

---

[1] Another recent perspective – one we will not consider further here – emphasizes the importance of self-interest, but argues for a broader conception of what constitutes self-interest. Weeden and Kurzban (2014) in particular argue that the symbolic-politics approach has overstated its case by failing to consider more nuanced forms of self-interested political judgment. For example, they argue that individuals whose lifestyles increase the risk of unplanned pregnancies support abortion rights more than those with less "freewheeling" lifestyles. Similarly, in recent work, Chong (2013) offers a discussion of how self-interest is often defined too narrowly in political science. These points are important, but beyond the scope of our book.

[2] Consider, for example, debates over the consequences of minimum wage laws for employment rates.

that most citizens can readily identify whether they have a personal stake in the issue.

In our view, the rarity of self-interested policy judgment is due largely to *motivational* rather than *informational* deficits. In essence, it is not that citizens are unable to recognize their interests; rather, it is that material concerns are often irrelevant to the individual's goals when forming a policy opinion. As we discussed in Chapters 1 and 3, the incentive structure of mass politics generally does not promote an instrumental mindset, because citizens have little if any influence over policy outcomes. Why, therefore, would citizens spend valuable time, money, and effort promoting their narrow interests through public policy at the national level? The answer is simple: they don't. Rather, citizens engage with politics to obtain social-expressive benefits. As we demonstrated in Chapter 3, it is the politically engaged that are most likely to agree that, "In general, my political attitudes and beliefs are an important part of my self-image." Engaged citizens are also more likely to rely on symbolic factors such as partisanship and ideology in forming policy preferences. As these political predispositions are only weakly tied to indicators of economic position (e.g., income), the economic opinions of engaged citizens should better reflect these symbolic attachments than socioeconomic position. As a general matter, then, we expect the politically engaged to be *less* likely – rather than more likely – to rely on self-interest in thinking about economic issues, because they are primarily concerned with constructing a political belief system that expresses their identities and cultural commitments.

In sum, we agree with others that political engagement plays a role in moderating self-interest effects; however, we argue that it *diminishes*, rather than *promotes*, instrumental thinking. In our view, self-interest is akin to a "default" judgment style, while symbolic predispositions are used mainly by those who are motivated by a more salient set of expressive concerns. As Converse (1964) argued, the unengaged primarily rely on considerations "close to home." The engaged, by contrast, seek to construct a coherent political belief system that reflects their identities and cultural commitments. This implies that self-interested considerations are more likely to be at the "top of the head" for unengaged than engaged citizens. As we have argued, the question for the unengaged is: "How would this policy benefit me?" For the engaged, it is: "What does support for this policy say about me?"

One final issue is that of racial and ethnic heterogeneity. In Chapters 4 and 5, we demonstrated that personality has almost no effect on the political attitudes and identities of black Americans. In contrast, the dynamics for Latinos look similar to those in our sample as a whole and among non-Latino whites. For African Americans, we argued that a large "main effect" of race exists such that they tend to be liberal on economic issues and to identify almost exclusively with the Democratic Party. This sharply reduces the effect of personality on economic opinion. It is also likely to reduce the impact of income and other personal economic concerns on economic attitudes. If those who identify as black use this identity as a general heuristic for political judgment – as suggested by the concepts of "linked fate" and the "black utility heuristic" invoked by Dawson (1994) – then we should observe sharply reduced asymmetries as a function of political engagement among blacks. We expect that Latinos will fall somewhere between blacks and non-Latino whites, though as in Chapters 4 and 5, our expectations are weak.

As it turns out, our engagement-interaction hypothesis for self-interest obtains only for non-Latino whites. In contrast to Chapter 4, the moderating role of engagement on self-interest is relatively weak in models in which we utilize the full sample of respondents. Because of this, we have chosen to report all of our findings for non-Latino whites only. We then provide a sampling of our null findings for blacks and Latinos. The upshot is that we are quite confident in the importance of our motivational theory of self-interest for whites, but we have little evidence that it applies to other groups.

Empirical Tests

It is not a straightforward task to detect self-interest effects in public opinion data, as we cannot directly observe the reasoning processes that citizens use to form their judgments. Instead, we have to infer the operation of self-interest from the effects of variables that researchers identify a priori as good indicators of material concern in the context of particular policy debates. Self-interest should be most easily observed when considering variables that clearly tap the intended beneficiaries of a policy. For example, do citizens at greater risk of unemployment support unemployment benefits more than those with secure employment? Are those without health insurance – or those worried about losing it in the future – more likely to support government-guaranteed or subsidized health insurance? Are low-income citizens more supportive of redistribution and social welfare spending than rich citizens? Our general hypothesis is simple: the impact of clearly applicable, personal economic interests on policy judgments will decrease as a function of political engagement. More simply, we expect the economic policy attitudes of politically unengaged citizens will be strongly rooted in self-interest, while those of engaged citizens will not. A general pattern of findings consistent with this hypothesis will bolster our claim that political engagement shifts individuals away from an instrumental mode of policy reasoning.

Our analyses follow a similar format to those in Chapter 4. In each case, we regress a measure of economic preferences on an indicator of self-interest and its interaction with political engagement. For each analysis, we provide a plot similar to those in Chapter 4: the y-axis indicates the average difference in economic liberalism between citizens high and low on a given indicator of economic position. The y-axis thus captures a self-interest effect. The x-axis represents increasing levels of political engagement. For measures of subjective economic distress, we expect large and positive coefficients for the unengaged, which move toward zero as engagement increases. For analyses that examine the impact of household income on policy judgments, we expect large negative coefficients at low levels of engagement that decrease toward zero as engagement increases (i.e., higher-income citizens should be more economically conservative than lower-income citizens). As in previous chapters, full regression tables can be found in the chapter appendix.

Income, Redistribution, and Social Welfare

We begin by examining a straightforward proposition: poor people should prefer higher levels of redistribution and social welfare spending than rich people. We rely on four dependent variables to examine the effect of income across levels of political engagement for non-Latino whites. First, we return to our two key variables from Chapter 4: liberal economic values and support for greater spending on various forms of social welfare such as government-guaranteed health insurance, jobs, and education (see Table 4.1 for the specific items). Second, the American National Election Studies surveys have consistently asked respondents about federal government spending on a variety of different programs. We examine the two that most clearly involve redistribution from rich to poor: welfare and aid to poor people.[3] For both items, respondents received the following stem: "Should federal spending on [welfare/aid to poor people] be increased, decreased, or kept about the same?" For all four variables, we combined ANES data from 2000, 2004, 2008,

---

[3] As noted in Chapter 4, the reversal effect for openness holds for these two items as well.

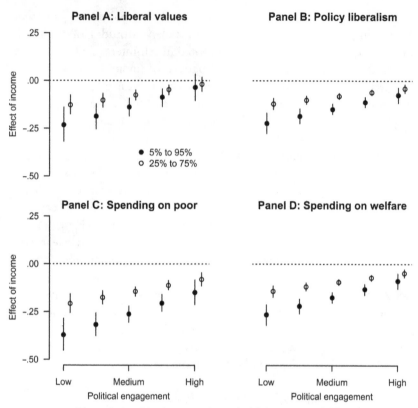

FIGURE 7.1. The relationship between household income and liberal economic values and policies across political engagement for non-Latino whites, 2000–2012 ANES

and 2012 (these studies include identical or very similar measures).[4] We examine how strongly respondents' household income predicts their opinions, and whether and how the relationship is modified by political engagement.[5]

The estimates, shown in Figure 7.1, represent the difference in economic liberalism between high- and low-income respondents at a given level of political engagement. For Panel A, it is the difference in the probability of providing two or more liberal responses to the economic values items; for Panel B, it is the percentage point difference in economic policy

---

[4] The one variable for which measures are not identical across years is the policy liberalism scale, for which the years differ somewhat. See Chapter 4.
[5] We measure engagement identically to Chapter 4. Regression models also included age, gender, race, education, employment status, union membership, and Southern residency.

liberalism; and for Panels C and D, it is the difference in the probability of supporting an increase in government spending on the poor and on welfare, respectively. Thus, each dot is the effect of income on economic liberalism at each level of engagement.

The pattern is very similar in each of the four cases, and it is consistent with our theory. Looking first at Panel A, unengaged citizens with high household incomes are considerably less likely to endorse liberal economic values than unengaged citizens with low household incomes. At the lowest levels of engagement, high-income citizens are about twenty-five percentage points less liberal than low-income citizens. The same is true for the other three variables, with even larger effect sizes. The largest effect of income occurs for unengaged citizens on the federal aid to the poor item. Here, high income citizens are about thirty-five percentage points less likely to support greater spending than low-income citizens. These large effects of income are striking, because (with a few exceptions) political psychologists have consistently argued that self-interest has only weak effects on public policy attitudes. We find just the opposite, at least among politically unengaged citizens: income is an exceptionally good predictor of support for liberal economic values, social welfare spending, and redistribution from rich to poor. The impact of income holds even for federal spending on "welfare," which political psychologists have found to be driven more by symbolic racism than self-interest among whites (e.g., Gilens 1999).

Consistent with our claim that the economic opinions of engaged citizens are expressive in nature, the effect of self-interest drops sharply as political engagement increases. Looking first at Panel A, the impact of income is cut in half at moderate levels of engagement and eliminated entirely when engagement is high. Similarly large moderating effects of engagement occur for the other three dependent variables. Consider support for aid to the poor (Panel C). The effect of income declines by more than twenty percentage points, from thirty-five points at low engagement to fewer than fifteen points at high engagement. Thus, rather than enhancing the effect of income due to the informational advantages it provides, political engagement sharply *reduces* the effect of income – in one case to statistical insignificance, and in the others to substantively small effect sizes. This finding is opposite to the "middle ground" claim that self-interest effects are stronger among more informed citizens (e.g., Chong et al. 2001). We consistently observe this pattern for a range of indicators of economic liberalism, from abstract economic values to policy opinions about redistribution from rich to poor.

Thus, contrary to a long-standing claim in political psychology, our first set of tests suggests that self-interest – as represented by household income – is an important influence on economic preferences. Consistent with rational choice theories, wealthy individuals are much less likely to support poverty programs than poor respondents, but *only* among those who are disengaged from politics. Among the politically engaged, the role of self-interest is faint.

Employment and Income Protection

The impact of income on support for redistribution and social welfare is the most obvious place to look for self-interest effects. A second straightforward hypothesis concerns the effect of employment insecurity on government-provided employment and income protection (e.g., Rehm 2009). In particular, are the insecurely employed especially supportive of government programs designed to ensure full employment or protect income in the event of unemployment? We test this possibility in two ways. First, the ANES typically asks respondents who are currently working about their employment security: "How worried are you about losing your job in the near future: a lot, somewhat, or not much at all?" In recent years, the ANES has also asked respondents the following policy item: "Some people feel the government in Washington should see to it that every person has a job and a good standard of living. Others think the government should just let each person get ahead on their own." Respondents indicated their opinion on a seven-point scale. We combined non-Latino white respondents from the 2000, 2004, 2008, and 2012 ANES, and estimated a model predicting opinions as a function of subjective employment insecurity, engagement, and their interaction. In this analysis, self-interest is indicated by a positive coefficient, with people worried about losing their jobs in the near future more supportive of guaranteed jobs and income than those who are not worried.

The results, shown in Panel A of Figure 7.2, indicate that those worried about losing their job are significantly more supportive than their secure counterparts – about twelve percentage points more – but only when political engagement is low.[6] As engagement increases, this effect is driven to insignificance. Indeed, at high and moderately high levels of engagement, there is no correspondence between employment insecurity and support for government guaranteed jobs.

[6] The employment insecurity item has only five possible categories, which is why there is only one set of coefficients, rather than both 5 percent to 95 percent and 25 percent to 75 percent effects as we have presented previously.

Next, we turn to a different dataset and a different (though related) policy issue. Specifically, our 2011 YouGov survey included an item tapping subjective employment insecurity: "So far as you and/or your family are concerned, how worried are you about your current employment situation?" Responses were recorded on a ten-point scale from "not at all worried" to "extremely worried." As described in Chapter 6, this survey also measured attitudes toward unemployment insurance: "Some people believe that we should get rid of government-provided unemployment insurance altogether. Others believe that we should greatly increase unemployment insurance. Where would you place yourself on this scale?" Responses ranged from one to seven with higher values indicating greater support for unemployment insurance. These data offer a particularly clean test, as we can be confident that a self-interested individual who feels insecure about her current job situation would support maintaining a robust unemployment insurance program.

Panel B of Figure 7.2 depicts the estimated relationship between employment insecurity and support for unemployment insurance across levels of engagement.[7] At low and moderate levels of engagement, the relationship is positive and statistically significant: unengaged citizens who are extremely worried about the security of their current employment situation are fifteen to twenty percentage points more supportive of unemployment insurance than those who are not at all worried. As engagement increases, however, this relationship falls to zero. Indeed, for moderately engaged citizens the relationship is rather small, and for the highly engaged there is no correspondence between employment insecurity and unemployment insurance attitudes.

In sum, using two datasets with two distinct measures of insecurity and two different dependent variables, we find a significant relationship between employment-related concerns on one hand and attitudes toward government-provided employment and income protection on the other. However, this relationship exists only among citizens who pay scant attention to politics. Among politically engaged citizens, employment status and support for government-provided income protection are largely unconnected.

Government-Guaranteed and Regulated Health Insurance
The government's role in regulating and providing health insurance is one of the most debated issues in American politics. For example, as we noted

---

[7] Recall that the 2011 YouGov study randomly assigned some respondents to receive partisan and ideological cues. For this analysis we use all available respondents in the dataset to maximize sample size.

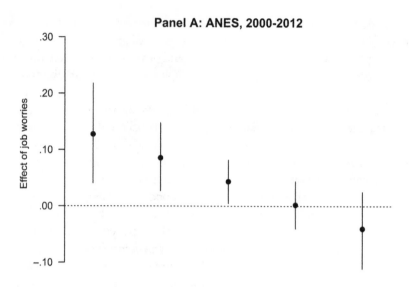

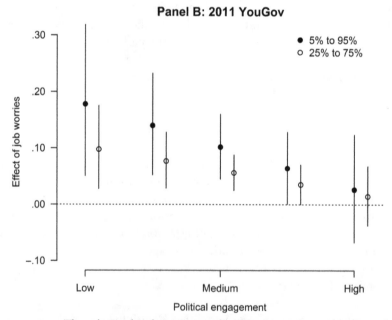

FIGURE 7.2. The relationship between employment insecurity and support for employment and income protection across political engagement for non-Latino whites, 2000–2012 ANES and 2011 YouGov

in the opening pages of this book, public discourse on the Affordable Care Act has been intensely heated. To gauge the impact of self-interest in this domain, we ask: To what extent does one's own health and health insurance status enter into these opinions? Using the 2010 ANES and our 2011 YouGov survey, we examine attitudes toward the role of government in the provision of health insurance as a function of subjective insecurity about one's own health insurance coverage. In the 2010 ANES[8] respondents were asked, "How worried are you about losing your health insurance in the next twelve months?" This item included five response categories ranging from "not at all worried" to "extremely worried." Respondents were also asked two policy items. The first read, "A new law passed in March will change the way we pay for health insurance in two ways: (1) require all Americans to buy health insurance, with the government helping to pay for those who can't afford it; and (2) require health insurance companies to cover anyone who applies for insurance, no matter what preexisting medical condition they may have." Respondents were then asked whether they favor or oppose these changes "taken together" using a branching format resulting in a seven-point scale. The second item read, "Do you favor, oppose, or neither favor nor oppose a public, government-run health insurance plan to compete with plans offered by private health insurance companies?" Again, responses were obtained using a branching format resulting in a seven-point scale. The two items were highly correlated (α =0.71), and were thus combined into a single scale with higher values indicating greater support for government regulation of the health insurance industry and government health-insurance subsidies.

In our 2011 YouGov study, respondents were asked, "So far as you and/or your family are concerned, how worried are you about your current health insurance situation?" Responses were recorded on a ten-point scale. The policy item in this study read as follows: "Some people feel there should be a government insurance plan which would cover all medical expenses for everyone. Others feel that all medical expenses should be paid by individuals through private insurance plans. Where would you place yourself on this scale?" Respondents answered on a seven-point scale anchored by the two statements given earlier.[9]

The results, shown in Panels A and B of Figure 7.3, reveal similar patterns. At low levels of engagement, citizens who are very worried about

---

[8] This sample was actually a re-contact of individuals from the 2008 ANES panel study.
[9] As with employment insecurity, we use all available respondents in this dataset, and average over conditions.

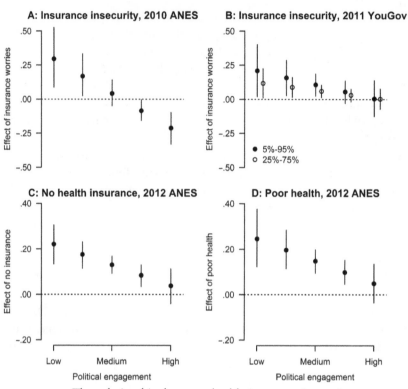

FIGURE 7.3. The relationship between health insurance insecurity, coverage, and health status and support for government-provided and -regulated health insurance across political engagement for non-Latino whites, 2010 ANES, 2011 YouGov, and 2012 ANES

their health insurance situation are considerably more supportive of government intervention in health insurance markets – by about thirty percentage points in the 2010 ANES and about twenty in the 2011 YouGov study – than citizens who are not at all worried about their health insurance. As in our previous analysis, this relationship decreases rapidly as engagement increases. One unanticipated finding in the 2010 ANES study is that at maximum engagement, health insurance worry is associated with *less* support for government intervention. We can think of two explanations for this finding. First, it could be a genuine reflection of self-interested judgment (contrary to our expectations). Although it seems intuitive that people worried about obtaining health insurance would support government regulation and subsidies, a self-interested citizen may very well believe that government intervention is not in her best interest. For example, one might believe that measures to increase competition among private insurers are to be preferred because they increase access to cheap, high-quality insurance. In this view, politically engaged citizens interpret the role of government in health insurance – as it relates to their own health insurance security – differently than the unengaged, and this is reflected in a qualitatively different relationship between insurance insecurity and health care opinions. A second possible explanation is that the negative relationship between health insurance worry and support for government intervention among highly engaged citizens reflects *expressive* concerns. Perhaps engaged citizens who strongly oppose the Affordable Care Act are more likely to report that they are worried about the stability of their health insurance than citizens who support the ACA. In other words, citizens are expressing their approval or disapproval of health insurance reform sponsored by the Democratic Party by indicating that they feel secure or worried about their own health insurance, respectively. As this study was conducted during a time of intense discussion of the Affordable Care Act, this possibility seems quite reasonable to us. Moreover, it fits our broader theoretical perspective. Nonetheless, we cannot adjudicate between these two possibilities with the data at hand.[10]

We can also examine self-interest in a different fashion in a third dataset. In the 2012 ANES, respondents were asked if they have health insurance, and whether in general their health is excellent, very good, good, fair, or poor. As our dependent variable, we rely on the same two government health insurance policy items used in Chapter 4 (see Table 4.1).[11] We regressed support for government health insurance simultaneously on engagement, these two indicators of self-interest, and their interactions with engagement. The results, shown in Panels C and D of Figure 7.3, reveal strong support for the engagement-interaction hypothesis. Among the unengaged, citizens without health insurance are more than twenty percentage points more supportive of government intervention than citizens with health insurance. However, this relationship weakens as engagement rises; strikingly, among the most engaged citizens, there is no relationship between health insurance coverage and support for government-guaranteed insurance. The same is true for subjective health status: among the unengaged, citizens who consider themselves in poor health are about twenty-five points more supportive of a strong government hand in regulating insurance markets than citizens who consider themselves in excellent health. And, as with insurance coverage,

[10] A third possibility is that this finding is merely a statistical fluke.
[11] These include support for the "health care reform law passed in 2010" and more general support for government-guaranteed health insurance over private insurance.

the relationship between health status and preferences is driven to zero among the most politically engaged citizens.[12]

In sum, the findings for health insurance policy strongly support our general thesis: contrary to the traditional skepticism of political psychologists about the political significance of self-interest, subjective worries about health insurance coverage, objective lack of coverage, and poor health status are meaningful predictors of support for government intervention in health insurance markets. Moreover, contrary to the view that self-interest effects are strengthened by political engagement, we consistently find the opposite: self-interest effects are only apparent among those who conventional wisdom holds cannot manage to tie their political shoelaces.

Racial and Ethnic Heterogeneity

We conclude our empirical investigation of self-interest with a return to the issue of racial and ethnic heterogeneity. To this point, we have examined the engagement-interaction hypothesis only among non-Latino whites. As we explained in the introduction to this chapter, we also tested the hypothesis extensively (1) using full samples, with controls for race and ethnicity, (2) for African Americans only, and (3) for Latinos only. It is clear from our investigation that the interaction holds consistently for whites, but not for any of the non-white groups. In the full sample analyses, the interactions are therefore notably smaller in magnitude. Indeed, we have even run the models for non-black, non-Latino identifiers – that is, everyone who does not identify as black or Latino – and the results are substantially weaker than for whites only.[13] Our tentative conclusion is that we find support for our interaction hypothesis only for non-Latino whites.

Before concluding, we provide a taste of these supplemental analyses by considering the conditional effect of income on our four key dependent variables in the pooled 2000–12 ANES. By combining these datasets, we have sufficient power to test for the interaction between income and engagement for both African Americans and Latinos. The estimates for these models are shown in Figure 7.4. Panels A–D provide the results

---

[12] We can be confident that among unengaged citizens this represents a true self-interest effect. Recall that in addition to subsidies for low-income individuals, one of the items in the 2012 study concerns preexisting conditions: "This law requires all Americans to buy health insurance and *requires health insurance companies to accept everyone.*" Thus, citizens without insurance – even if they are in poor health – are required to be given coverage by health insurance providers.

[13] About 8 percent of our samples are non-Latino, non-black, and non-white identifiers.

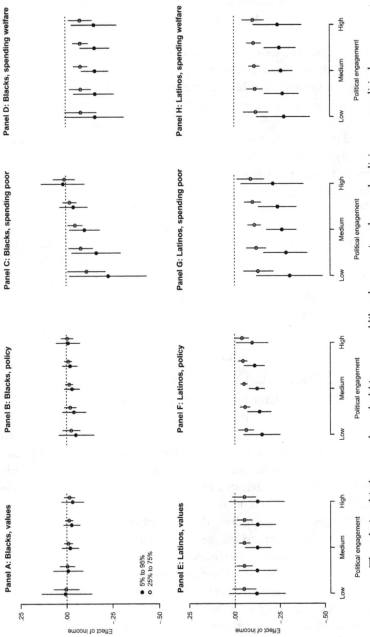

FIGURE 7.4. The relationship between household income and liberal economic values and policies across political engagement for African Americans and Latinos, 2000–2012 ANES

for black Americans for each of the four dependent variables, and Panels E–H do the same for Latinos. Looking first at African Americans, we find no effect of income at *any* level of engagement for either economic values (i.e., support for government over markets) or for our social welfare policy scale. The results are quite a bit different for federal aid to the poor and welfare spending. For the former, the engagement-interaction hypothesis is supported. When engagement is low, there is a significant effect of income in the expected negative direction, which disappears when engagement is high. Unfortunately, we cannot replicate this finding when looking at the welfare item. Here, income matters, but it does so consistently across levels of engagement.

Turning to Latinos, the results are clear and consistent: income matters, but political engagement does not modify its impact. For each of the four dependent variables, income is negatively associated with support for redistribution, and the estimates do not vary as engagement increases. Overall, then, we find little support for our interaction hypothesis among blacks and Latinos. We thus have one more reason – to add to those presented in Chapters 4 and 5 – why racial and ethnic heterogeneity must be explicitly considered when analyzing the psychological foundations of American mass opinion on economic issues.

Conclusions

In their recent book, Weeden and Kurzban argue that "reports of the death of self-interest have been greatly exaggerated" (2014: 34). They suggest that skepticism in the political psychology literature about the prevalence of self-interested policy judgment is rooted in a surprisingly small number of studies using questionable methodological assumptions. Contrary to much received wisdom, they suggest that public opinion is, to a large extent, a self-interested phenomenon. Citizens choose the policies that best promote their interests and those of close others. This argument converges with research in the rational choice tradition that has found meaningful effects of income, human capital, and labor market position on redistributive preferences.

We agree with Weeden and Kurzban that political psychologists have often exaggerated the case against self-interest; it matters more, and more often, than most think. As we have demonstrated in this chapter, self-interest is often highly predictive of economic values and policy attitudes (see also the Chapter 4 appendix). But we offer a critical caveat: self-interest matters *most* for citizens who care about politics the *least*. We provide evidence that political engagement inhibits self-interested policy judgment among non-Latino whites: rich people are much less supportive of welfare spending on the poor than poor people, but this effect is cut in half (or more) among the engaged; the tenuously employed strongly support unemployment insurance relative to the securely employed, but not when they pay a lot of attention to elite politics; and people without health insurance strongly prefer government-guaranteed insurance, unless they follow partisan debates over the issue. This pattern indicates that citizens who are most likely to participate in and influence American politics display the least self-interested – but the most expressively oriented – political attitudes. In this sense, the received wisdom in political psychology is correct in an important way: self-interest doesn't matter very much among attentive citizens; for these individuals, economic policy is largely a venue for the signaling of identity.

Our results are also inconsistent with the perspective that weak self-interest effects are due to informational deficits. In this view, political engagement should increase the impact of self-interest, as sophisticated citizens are better able to connect their private interests to complex public policy debates. Across a variety of policies, however, we find precisely the opposite. In our view, these results suggest that informational deficits are not what impede self-interested judgment. Rather, it is a deficit of *motivation*. Engaged citizens participate because they obtain expressive rather than instrumental rewards from doing so. The primacy of expressive goals leads to a tendency to ignore concrete personal concerns. Indeed, in perhaps the most striking finding of the chapter, we find no relationship between having health insurance (or not) and support for guaranteed health insurance among engaged citizens.

The results we present in this chapter also provide further support for our interpretation of the reversal effect in Chapter 4. Our primary claim is that the negative relationship between openness and economic liberalism among the unengaged is driven by instrumental, self-interested reasoning processes: closed citizens prefer government intervention to insure against the potential downside of living in a market economy, while open citizens prefer a more risk-acceptant approach emphasizing individualism and self-direction. We found evidence consistent with this theoretical claim in Chapter 4, but that evidence does not *directly* demonstrate a self-interest effect. Just as Chapters 5 and 6 provided additional evidence for expressive judgment among engaged citizens, this chapter has provided supplemental evidence for the mechanisms we believe to be operative among the unengaged. In particular, unengaged citizens appear to be primarily concerned with policy *outcomes* and their relation to personal interests, while engaged citizens largely ignore their material interests. Of course, questions remain. For example, does the pattern of policy judgment found among the unengaged reflect an active, explicit concern with the instrumental dimension of politics, or is it simply a result of the relatively low accessibility of emotionally compelling expressive concerns? That is, do the unengaged merely demonstrate self-interest "by default"? Moreover, why is the engagement interaction found only among non-Latino whites? Do the unique historical experiences of non-whites in the United States lead to a different balance between instrumental and expressive concerns across levels of engagement (e.g., Dawson 1994)?

These questions aside, the results of this chapter support our interpretation of the reversal effect described in Chapter 4, and bolster our confidence that we are on the right track theoretically. The issues addressed in this chapter deserve a book-length treatment of their own, and we have not done them justice in this short chapter. However, like Weeden and Kurzban (2014), we believe that the time is right for a reconsideration of the role of self-interest in political psychology. We hope to have contributed to this endeavor. In particular, we hope scholars will begin by considering in greater depth the varying incentives that citizens face when thinking about public policy, and how these different incentives moderate the impact of variables related to material interests on political preferences.

Appendix

TABLE A7.1. *Estimates for income and economic preferences, whites*

	Values	Policy	Poor	Welfare
Income	−0.64 (0.14)	−0.23 (0.03)	−1.08 (0.14)	−1.32 (0.14)
Engagement	−0.70 (0.11)	−0.16 (0.02)	−0.60 (0.12)	−0.44 (0.11)
Income X Engage	0.54 (0.20)	0.15 (0.04)	0.63 (0.20)	0.87 (0.20)
Age	−0.19 (0.06)	−0.01 (0.01)	−0.01 (0.06)	−0.04 (0.06)
Male	−0.30 (0.03)	−0.04 (0.01)	−0.17 (0.03)	−0.18 (0.03)
Education	−0.03 (0.06)	0.03 (0.01)	−0.16 (0.06)	0.20 (0.06)
Unemployed	0.15 (0.07)	0.04 (0.02)	0.26 (0.07)	0.34 (0.07)
Union	0.17 (0.04)	0.05 (0.01)	0.17 (0.04)	0.02 (0.04)
South	−0.11 (0.03)	−0.03 (0.01)	−0.06 (0.03)	−0.11 (0.03)
2004 Dummy	0.22 (0.06)	0.11 (0.01)	0.44 (0.06)	0.60 (0.06)
2008 Dummy	0.23 (0.05)	0.13 (0.01)	0.51 (0.06)	0.57 (0.06)
2012 Dummy	−0.11 (0.04)	0.02 (0.01)	−0.23 (0.05)	0.03 (0.05)
Intercept		0.58 (0.02)		
PRE / R^2	0.11	0.07	0.13	0.10
N	5,965	6,155	6,099	6,118

Notes: Data are from the 2000–12 American National Election Studies. All dependent variables are coded so that higher values indicate more liberal economic preferences. The estimates for values and spending on the poor and welfare are ordered probit coefficients and standard errors (in parentheses). The entries for economic policy are ordinary least squares estimates and standard errors. The sample includes only non-Latino whites. "PRE" is the proportionate reduction in error.

TABLE A7.2. *Estimates for job worries*

	ANES	YouGov
Job Worries	0.13 (0.05)	0.17 (0.07)
Engagement	−0.06 (0.03)	−0.06 (0.06)
Worries X Engage	−0.17 (0.07)	−0.15 (0.10)
Age	−0.05 (0.03)	0.13 (0.04)
Male	−0.03 (0.01)	−0.01 (0.02)
Education	0.03 (0.02)	−0.02 (0.04)
Income	−0.12 (0.02)	−0.16 (0.04)
Unemployed		0.02 (0.03)
Union	0.03 (0.01)	
South	0.00 (0.01)	−0.04 (0.02)
2004 Dummy	0.14 (0.02)	
2008 Dummy	0.33 (0.02)	
2012 Dummy	0.11 (0.02)	
Intercept	0.40 (0.02)	
R^2	0.08	0.09
N	3,174	763

Notes: Data are from the 2000–12 American National Election Studies and a 2011 national survey conducted by YouGov. All dependent variables are coded so that higher values indicate more liberal preferences on employment and income protection issues. Entries are ordinary least squares coefficients and standard errors (in parentheses). The samples include only non-Latino whites.

TABLE A7.3. *Estimates for health insurance worries*

	2010 ANES	YouGov	2012 ANES
Insurance Worries	0.29 (0.11)	0.21 (0.10)	
No Insurance			0.22 (0.05)
Poor Health			0.24 (0.06)
Engagement	−0.04 (0.05)	0.02 (0.09)	0.04 (0.05)
Worries X Engage	−0.51 (0.14)	−0.21 (0.14)	
No Insurance X Engage			−0.19 (0.08)
Health X Engage			−0.19 (0.10)
Age	0.11 (0.06)	−0.06 (0.06)	−0.01 (0.02)
Male	−0.11 (0.02)	−0.03 (0.03)	−0.01 (0.01)
Education	0.27 (0.04)	0.17 (0.05)	0.11 (0.02)
Income	−0.17 (0.05)	−0.22 (0.05)	−0.10 (0.02)
Unemployed	0.04 (0.06)	0.01 (0.04)	0.07 (0.03)
Union			0.06 (0.02)
South	−0.05 (0.02)	−0.07 (0.03)	−0.02 (0.01)
Intercept	0.47 (0.06)	0.49 (0.07)	0.35 (0.04)
R^2	0.09	0.06	0.05
N	1,201	763	3,037

Notes: Data are from the 2010 American National Election panel re-contact study, a 2011 YouGov national survey, and the 2012 ANES. All dependent variables are coded so that higher values indicate more liberal preferences on government-provided health insurance. Entries are ordinary least squares coefficients and standard errors (in parentheses). The samples include only non-Latino whites.

TABLE A7.4. *Estimates for income and economic preferences, blacks and Latinos*

	Blacks				Latinos			
	Values	Policy	Poor	Welfare	Values	Policy	Poor	Welfare
Income	0.04 (0.34)	−0.06 (0.06)	−0.86 (0.38)	−0.61 (0.32)	−0.50 (0.31)	−0.17 (0.06)	−1.02 (0.33)	−1.05 (0.31)
Engagement	0.63 (0.24)	0.04 (0.04)	−0.18 (0.27)	0.17 (0.22)	−0.32 (0.26)	−0.05 (0.05)	−0.27 (0.28)	−0.08 (0.25)
Income X Engage	−0.31 (0.52)	0.05 (0.09)	0.91 (0.57)	0.09 (0.48)	0.08 (0.51)	0.06 (0.10)	0.34 (0.54)	0.12 (0.50)
Age	0.07 (0.13)	0.00 (0.02)	−0.07 (0.14)	0.05 (0.12)	−0.32 (0.12)	0.00 (0.02)	−0.33 (0.13)	−0.18 (0.12)
Male	−0.25 (0.06)	−0.02 (0.01)	−0.14 (0.07)	0.00 (0.06)	−0.22 (0.06)	−0.02 (0.01)	−0.28 (0.07)	−0.03 (0.06)
Education	−0.18 (0.12)	−0.02 (0.02)	−0.35 (0.13)	−0.26 (0.11)	−0.28 (0.12)	−0.03 (0.02)	−0.15 (0.13)	−0.17 (0.12)
Unemployed	0.07 (0.10)	0.01 (0.02)	0.14 (0.11)	0.20 (0.09)	0.09 (0.11)	0.00 (0.02)	0.15 (0.12)	0.17 (0.10)
Union	0.03 (0.09)	0.03 (0.02)	0.01 (0.10)	−0.08 (0.08)	−0.06 (0.09)	0.01 (0.02)	−0.02 (0.10)	−0.02 (0.09)
South	−0.02 (0.06)	−0.01 (0.01)	−0.11 (0.07)	−0.16 (0.06)	−0.16 (0.06)	−0.03 (0.01)	−0.13 (0.07)	0.04 (0.06)
2004 Dummy	−0.03 (0.15)	0.00 (0.03)	0.29 (0.18)	0.10 (0.14)	0.18 (0.21)	0.10 (0.04)	0.65 (0.23)	0.71 (0.21)
2008 Dummy	−0.12 (0.12)	0.05 (0.02)	0.06 (0.14)	0.38 (0.11)	0.53 (0.16)	0.18 (0.03)	0.84 (0.17)	0.82 (0.16)
2012 Dummy	−0.11 (0.11)	−0.01 (0.02)	−0.27 (0.13)	0.08 (0.10)	0.03 (0.15)	0.03 (0.03)	0.07 (0.16)	0.20 (0.15)
Intercept		0.66 (0.03)				0.63 (0.03)		
PRE / R2	0.00	0.03	0.00	0.03	0.00	0.11	0.05	0.07
N	1,679	1,708	1,723	1,707	1,382	1,429	1,424	1,425

Notes: Data are from the 2000–12 American National Election Studies. The first four columns are for self-identified black respondents and the second four are for self-identified Latinos. Entries for economic values and spending on the poor and on welfare are ordered probit coefficients and standard errors (in parentheses). Entries for economic policy are ordinary least squares estimates and standard errors. All dependent variables are coded so that higher values indicate more liberal preferences. "PRE" is the proportionate reduction in error for the values models.

8

Personality and American Democracy

We began this book with a question: Why do Americans seem so bitterly divided over the role of government in the economy? The intuitive answer is self-interest. The economically insecure support a strong government hand in the market because they expect to benefit, while the well-off stand in opposition to protect their private economic gains. As we have noted, however, this cannot be the whole story. Standard measures of self-interest – income, job security, health insurance coverage, and the like – matter to some degree, but they fail to explain much of the variation in citizens' economic values and policy preferences, and this is particularly true for the most politically engaged citizens. Nevertheless, many people feel passionately about redistribution, social insurance, and market regulation. Where do such preferences come from, and what do they signify?

In this book, we have presented a new model of economic preference formation, one rooted in both a reinvigorated focus on the link between personality and politics and a novel perspective on the nature of political engagement. With regard to the latter, we note that citizens do not have much influence on policy outcomes through voting or expressing opinions in surveys, and thus have little instrumental reason to become deeply engaged in politics. Rather, we argue that engagement is rooted largely in the desire for *social-expressive* benefits, which make political attentiveness and participation worth the cost (Brennan and Lomasky 1994; Kahan 2016). In this view, citizens seek to express core aspects of the self through their political identities and attitudes. The upshot is that economic preferences among the participating class have come to stand for a deeper, cultural divide, reflecting a core dimension of personality we have labeled *openness*.

Along these lines, we have argued that engaged citizens choose their political "team" on the basis of cultural affinity, and then adopt the party line on a range of relatively technical issues concerning government intervention in the economy. In such a world, it is little surprise that partisan debates over issues like health insurance reform take on a heated character. In effect, for some citizens, economic policy debates have become symbolic conflicts over the status of competing cultural groups, and therefore have come to elicit the same fiery disagreement as those over gay marriage, abortion, and immigration (Hetherington and Weiler 2010). As the result of long-standing electoral imperatives among elites, the economic dimension of political conflict is now infused with a deeper conflict between two core psychological types: an open one and a closed one.

As we reviewed in Chapter 2, the literature on personality and political ideology has generally come up short in finding a connection between openness and economic preferences. For example, in their wide-ranging examination of the role of authoritarianism in American politics, Hetherington and Weiler (2010) write that "Since preferences on [New Deal] issues are not structured by authoritarianism, we wish to acknowledge that the authoritarian divide is not all-encompassing. It is a significant part of the story of American political conflict, but it is not the only part." This statement is, of course, true. No single explanation can fully account for political disagreement. However, our most important claim is that this "authoritarian divide" – one reflection of the division between the open and the closed – *does* encompass the major ideological dimensions in contemporary American politics, including conflict over traditional New Deal issues. We believe that dispositional openness is a major part of the story of left-right division on issues ranging from gay marriage, immigration, and foreign policy to taxes, health insurance reform, and Social Security privatization.

The key insight by which we arrive at this conclusion – one that has been overlooked in past work – is that personality traits can influence political attitudes in two distinct ways. On one hand, as psychologists and political scientists have noted in past research (e.g., Jost et al. 2004; Mondak 2011), they can operate on political attitudes through a direct process in which the content of a policy position provides a "functional match" to the psychological needs of an individual. We do not dispute that this occurs, and indeed this is precisely how we conceptualize the impact of personality on economic preferences among politically unengaged citizens. On the other hand, this is not the only – nor necessarily the most important – pathway by which personality and economic preferences become linked. Personality can also influence political attitudes *indirectly* through another form of affinity – namely, its influence on how citizens sort into culturally congenial political groups and learn from like-minded elite political actors. If citizens are motivated to form economic opinions that line up with elites who share their cultural affinities, and if cultural affinity is driven largely by personality, then personality may influence political attitudes independently of the substantive content of a policy proposal. For many citizens, the symbolic associations of a policy are more personally meaningful than the societal outcomes the policy aims to achieve. As Kahan (2016) has argued, politics is typically most consequential in our lives via our immediate social relationships, and our political opinions are often little more than signals of our underlying social and cultural commitments.

In this final chapter, we take stock of our empirical findings and reiterate the claims of our dual pathway model. We then turn to potential critiques of our work. Although we have worked hard to make our case, it is not beyond criticism. In this section, we address gaps in our argument, and acknowledge places where further research is needed. We conclude with a discussion of some of the broader implications of our research, including what our findings imply about when and why citizens will privilege expressive goals over economic interests (and when and why the two collide or dovetail), the evolution of partisan competition, and the quality of democratic citizenship.

Summary of Empirical Findings

Chapters 4 through 8 each tested hypotheses emerging from our theory. Taken as a whole, we believe they paint a consistent portrait of the nature of mass preferences on economic issues. We consider each in turn.

The Reversal Effect

The core dynamic highlighted by our book is the reversal of the impact of openness on economic preferences across levels of political engagement. Engaged citizens care most about self-expression. Therefore, they seek to align their economic opinions with their social identities, which emanate from variation in dispositional openness. Due to the current alignment of cultural conservatism with the Republican Party and cultural liberalism with the Democratic Party, engaged citizens with a closed personality orientation adopt a free market approach in the economic domain while open citizens adopt an interventionist approach. However, unengaged citizens care less about the symbolic dimension of partisan politics. Instead, they view economic issues through the more concrete lens of "what will this policy do for me?" As we argued in Chapters 1 and 3, this reverses the sign of the relationship between personality and economic opinion, such that unengaged closed citizens prefer the certainty- and security-enhancing policies of the economic left, while open citizens prefer the individualism and self-direction of the economic right.

In Chapter 4, we tested this claim across ten national datasets spanning twenty years of American politics. Moreover, we tapped a wide array of the most commonly used indicators of the open-closed personality dimension, including authoritarianism, need for closure, the Big Five dimensions of openness to experience and conscientiousness, openness to change versus conservation, and risk aversion. Ultimately, we subjected the reversal hypothesis to twenty-one empirical tests in various samples of the American public. Our results were highly consistent: for every indicator of openness, we found evidence for the reversal effect.

Among engaged citizens, we found a positive relationship between openness and economic liberalism in *every* full-sample test in Chapter 4: twenty-one for twenty-one. Given the mixed results of past research, this is striking. Moreover, we did not uncover mere statistical significance; the effect size for openness among engaged citizens is large. Indeed, if we compare the importance of personality to several leading explanations of economic preferences – income, race and ethnicity, employment status, union membership, and the like – openness is clearly and consistently among the best, and in many cases *the* best, predictor of economic values and policy attitudes. Quite simply, dispositional openness is a central foundation of economic opinion in American politics.

Among unengaged citizens, we found a negative relationship between openness and economic liberalism in seventeen of twenty-one tests in Chapter 4 – that is, a reversal of the relationship between personality and economic preferences. While this reversal is thus reliable and strong, it is not symmetrical across engagement. The political impact of personality is more robust among engaged than unengaged citizens. Why is this the case? We can think of three possibilities. First, people who are less interested in politics are known to hold "noisy" opinions (e.g., Converse 1965; Judd, Krosnick, and Milburn 1982). Their opinions contain more random error than those who have thought more deeply about their preferences. Some of this error may also result from the way that political novices experience the survey environment (e.g., with less diligence). It is thus reasonable to believe that the asymmetry in the robustness of the personality-politics connection is intrinsic to the nature of political engagement.

A second possibility focuses on the Big Five dimensions of openness to experience and conscientiousness, where the impact of personality among the unengaged was particularly weak. In fact, all four failures to demonstrate a full reversal effect in Chapter 4 occurred for the Big Five traits. Openness to experience and conscientiousness may therefore be weaker indicators of the general dimension of openness (despite the labeling overlap in the former case). Alternatively, it may be that the Ten-Item Personality Inventory used in our analyses – which includes only two items per trait – is insufficient to reliably tap each dimension (e.g., Credé et al. 2013). This could attenuate associations with other variables, especially among unengaged citizens whose preferences are noisy to begin with.

Finally, there may be a more theoretically interesting reason for the volatility among politically unengaged citizens. Perhaps it requires only a small amount of exposure to elite politics to "flip" the impact of openness on economic preferences. If this is the case, a closed personality should translate into economic liberalism only among those who are truly tuned out. This explanation is consistent with the failure to observe a reversal in Chapter 6, in which we were forced to rely on coarse measures of engagement with few respondents at the lowest levels. We find this to be a reasonable account of the observed asymmetry. As we have noted, the instrumentalism of the unengaged may be instrumentalism "by default." The unengaged *look* self-interested because personal concerns are what most easily come to mind when political surveys force politics upon people who typically spend little time thinking about such things. According to this account, even a small amount of exposure to elite partisan competition might be sufficient to foster political attitudes reflective of broader social identities. Thus, even relatively low levels of attention might inform citizens of the cultural gulf that defines party cleavages in contemporary American politics, thereby activating an expressive orientation to economic issues. Of course, this is merely speculative. A deeper exploration of this asymmetry is an important topic for future research.

Personality and Political Sorting
We have argued that the influence of personality on the economic preferences of engaged citizens is mediated by interactions with political

elites. Open citizens are attracted to cultural liberalism and sort into left-wing identities and information environments, while closed citizens are attracted to cultural conservatism and sort into right-wing identities and information environments. In Chapter 5, we provided extensive support for the *conditional dispositional sorting hypothesis* with respect to ideological labels, partisanship, and left- versus right-leaning information environments. Relying on a wide array of commonly studied traits – including authoritarianism, need for closure, openness to experience, conscientiousness, openness to change, and the importance of binding moral foundations – we found clear and consistent support for an interaction between dispositional openness and political engagement. In all but one of the tests conducted on full samples in Chapter 5, we found that personality influences political sorting among engaged but not unengaged citizens; the exception was the one test using moral foundations, where sorting was present among both the unengaged and the engaged but substantially stronger among the latter.[1] Indeed, openness appears to be among the strongest predictors of political sorting among engaged citizens, rivaling – and often exceeding – the influence of income and race.

In some respects, Chapter 5 is simply a replication of what previous work has found: openness promotes a left-wing political orientation (and vice versa). But the interaction with political engagement is crucial. It is simply not the case that personality strongly shapes political identity for all citizens. It is only among those who know and care about politics that openness is influential. With only a few exceptions – mainly in work by Federico and his colleagues[2] – the literature has ignored the critical role engagement plays in this regard. This lack of attention is surprising, as political engagement is among the most important variables in the study of mass politics. One obvious reason for this neglect is the use of convenience samples in psychology, where variation in engagement may be considerably lower than in representative adult samples. We hope that our findings in Chapter 5 inspire psychologists to pay more attention to the importance of political engagement in their own work – it appears to be inducing a *psychological* effect, after all – and to seek more representative samples of the population. Importantly, we expect engagement to condition the impact of openness, even when the latter is operationalized in terms of biological markers. For example, there is good reason to

---

[1] Recall, however, that our measure of engagement in this survey was coarse.
[2] See Federico et al. (2011); Federico and Goren (2009); Federico and Tagar (2014); see also Osborne and Sibley (2012).

expect that differences in physiological sensitivity to threat or differences in brain structure will interact with political engagement to predict political identification and economic preferences. Moreover, to the extent that the heritability of ideology is due to differences in deep-seated personality dispositions, we would expect heritability estimates to be largest among the most engaged citizens. These are interesting topics for future research, as they suggest a dynamic in which highly stable, partially heritable biological traits interact with the reception of elite political discourse to shape citizens' political commitments.

The Role of Elites

In Chapter 3, we argued for two primary mechanisms by which openness shapes economic preferences through citizen–elite interactions. The first is *partisan cue-taking*. As we demonstrated in Chapter 5, openness strongly shapes political sorting among engaged citizens. In Chapter 6, we demonstrated the downstream consequences of this sorting. In two experimental studies, we showed that openness structures economic opinion by determining how engaged citizens take cues from elites. Specifically, open citizens privilege information from left-wing sources, while closed citizens privilege information from right-wing sources. Personality thus structures economic opinion indirectly. Importantly, this implies a disconnect between openness and the content of economic policy among engaged citizens: openness can promote support or opposition to a strong government hand in the economy depending on how partisan elites happen to line up on the issue at a given point in time.

In our first experiment, we showed that the relationship between openness and economic liberalism strengthens substantially in the presence of partisan and ideological cues. In our second experiment, we showed that such cues can forcefully push the relationship between openness and economic opinion in the opposite direction when they are counter-stereotypical (i.e., when left-wing elites take limited government positions and right-wing elites take an interventionist approach). For example, in 2012 when Mitt Romney was depicted as opposing government intervention on issues like financial regulation, openness was strongly associated with support for intervention (as observed in Chapter 4). In contrast, when the experimental stimuli associated Barack Obama with opposition to intervention (and associated Romney with support for intervention), the effect of openness was cut by more than 50 percent. These experiments strongly suggest that among engaged citizens, the relationship between personality and economic opinion observed in Chapter 4 is in large part constructed by partisan elites as they package economic issues within a broader party platform and political coalition.

In our third experiment, we demonstrated that the role of elites extends to what we have termed *cultural signaling*: the juxtaposition of expressions of cultural identity and economic policy position-taking. In this experiment, when economic liberalism was packaged with a culturally liberal platform, openness was strongly associated with support for government economic intervention among engaged citizens (as in Chapter 4). In contrast, when economic liberalism was packaged with cultural conservatism, the effect of openness was driven to zero. This constitutes strong evidence that the relationship between personality and economic opinion among engaged citizens critically depends on the packaging of economic policy with cultural policy. In particular, citizens use information about the cultural orientation of elite actors to figure out how debates over complex economic issues map onto their broader identities and ultimately their core psychological dispositions.

An important building block of the cultural-signaling argument is that engagement prompts citizens to focus on the cultural implications of their policy attitudes. In an effort to validate this assumption and provide further support for the logic of the cultural-signaling hypothesis, we conducted a fourth experiment examining attitudes toward libertarianism. Here we showed that the relationship between right-wing political orientation and support for libertarianism depends on both engagement and whether cultural issues are made salient. When the cultural liberalism of libertarians is not salient, engaged right-wing citizens hold more favorable attitudes toward libertarianism than engaged left-wing citizens. However, when cultural issues are brought to the fore, this relationship reverses. Importantly, this experiment demonstrates that engaged citizens privilege culture over economics. That is, when the two policy dimensions were placed in direct competition, the evidence clearly indicated that culture won out, as our model would predict. More broadly, this result suggests that engaged right-wing citizens' support for – and left-wing citizens' opposition to – the abstract value of limited government is tenuous: it hinges on the packaging of this value with cultural conservatism. Indeed, among the unengaged, right-wing individuals found libertarianism distasteful regardless of whether we emphasized culture or economics. The overall attitudinal pattern for libertarianism is thus similar in structure to the reversal for personality and economic values uncovered in Chapter 4.

Finally, in Chapter 6, we exploited "natural" variation in the association between cultural conservatism and economic policy by considering international trade. In Chapter 3, we argued that closed citizens should generally be less supportive of trade because of its consequences for economic security and certainty (e.g., Ehrlich and Maestas 2011; Johnston 2014). In Chapter 6, we also argued that cultural changes associated with globalization may drive closed citizens to oppose trade (e.g., Mansfield and Mutz 2010). Since partisan elites are not strongly divided on these issues, we expected to find a positive relationship between openness and support for trade at all levels of engagement. Thus, among engaged citizens, we should observe a reversal of the relationship between openness and support for free markets when moving from domestic economic issues to international ones focused on trade. Indeed, we found that open citizens were considerably less supportive of import restrictions than closed citizens. Moreover, in contrast to what we found in Chapter 4, political engagement exacerbated this tendency, so that engaged citizens with closed personalities were the least supportive of free markets, and engaged citizens with open personalities were the most supportive. Once again, this is consistent with the idea that the impact of openness on economic opinion among politically engaged citizens operates primarily through the link between economic policy and cultural considerations. Thus, moving from the domestic to the international realm, the meaning of free markets shifts from cultural conservatism to cultural liberalism, and the effect of openness on support for markets thereby shifts from negative to positive.

Political Engagement and Self-Interest

A key element of our argument is that political engagement causes a shift in the motivation underlying the formation of economic preferences, from instrumental (when engagement is low) to expressive (when engagement is high). In our final empirical chapter, we sought to provide more direct evidence for this claim. To do so, we examined variation in the relationship between self-interest and economic policy attitudes across levels of political engagement. If expressive goals dominate instrumental ones among engaged citizens, the relationship between indicators of self-interest and policy attitudes should decline as engagement rises. Our analyses provided strong evidence in support of this claim. In Chapter 7, we explored the role of several indicators of self-interest, including household income, employment security, health insurance possession and stability, and health status. In all cases for non-Latino whites, we found these indicators of material concern to be stronger predictors of economic liberalism among unengaged than engaged individuals. As engagement increased, the impact of income and other sources of economic insecurity on economic preferences declined. This dovetails with our claim that the unengaged think about economic policy primarily in terms of "what this policy *does for* me," while the engaged are more likely to think in terms of "what support for this policy *says about* me."

Racial and Ethnic Heterogeneity

Finally, we examined whether our findings generalized across racial and ethnic groups. In Chapter 3, we argued that there are good reasons to expect dispositional openness to matter little for African Americans, and less for Latinos than for whites. Unfortunately, it is difficult to test for such heterogeneity, as national samples rarely have sufficient numbers of minority respondents to conduct appropriately powered tests of the interaction between personality and political engagement. However, we were able to leverage the repetition of items and oversamples of African Americans and Latinos in surveys from the ANES to examine racial and ethnic heterogeneity in support for the reversal hypothesis (Chapter 4), the dispositional sorting hypothesis (Chapter 5), and the self-interest hypothesis (Chapter 7).

While our results must be treated as preliminary, we draw three tentative conclusions from these analyses. First, as expected, the open-closed personality dimension is of little relevance to the economic preferences and political identities of African Americans. This should not be surprising. Blacks as a group evince considerably less variation in both partisan identity and economic opinion than whites. The latter reduces the very possibility of an impact of personality, and the former eliminates the primary pathway through which personality operates on economic opinion among engaged citizens. African Americans thus cannot be lumped in with other groups when exploring the political effects of personality. Second, the patterns for Latinos were quite similar to what our full sample analyses uncovered, though smaller in magnitude. Third, we found no evidence for an interaction between class position and engagement on economic preferences among African Americans or Latinos. This is not to say that income and other indicators of self-interest were unrelated to economic preferences; rather, these effects simply did not depend on political engagement. In sum, these findings reinforce the fact that the dynamics of mass preference formation on questions of economic redistribution vary substantially across subgroups of the electorate. They also indicate the need for scholars interested in personality and politics to pay more attention to race and ethnicity than they have to date (but see Gerber et al. 2011).

Criticisms of Our Theory and Findings

All theories are provisional, and all empirical research is a work in progress. Ours is no exception. We believe we have made a compelling case for a new perspective on the impact of personality on politics. Nonetheless, neither our theory nor our evidence is the final word on the matter. In this section, we address some potential criticisms of our work, and suggest places where other research complements our findings, where we may have fallen short, and where more work is needed.

Narrow Focus on the United States

One especially obvious criticism of our work is its exclusive focus on the American case. In part, this focus is by design: we are students of American politics, and we were interested in how the evolution of partisanship and ideology in the United States has affected the relationship between personality and economic opinion among different groups of Americans. Nevertheless, this still leaves us with the question of how well our model is likely to generalize to other contexts. On one hand, our theoretical model should be "portable" in the sense that variation in political engagement and opinion leadership by partisan elites are general features of mass politics in democratic societies. On the other hand, unique features of economic life in the United States raise reasonable concerns about whether our findings apply elsewhere. Perhaps most importantly, a wealth of evidence suggests that Americans are far less supportive of redistribution than citizens of other advanced democracies (e.g., Lipset 1997) – a difference that has been variously attributed to the predominance of individualistic values in the United States (Feldman and Zaller 1993; Hartz 1956; Kluegel and Smith 1987; McClosky and Zaller 1985) and its greater racial diversity (e.g., Alesina, Glaeser, and Sacerdote 2002). Whatever its basis, this stark difference suggests caution in generalizing any model of the dynamics of economic opinion formation in America to other contexts.

That said, recent comparative work by Malka and his colleagues (2015) suggests that similar dynamics can be found across a wide variety of political systems. Using World Values Survey data drawn from respondents in fifty-one nations, they find, as we do in Chapter 5, that openness is more strongly related to left-wing ideological affinity among engaged individuals. Malka and his colleagues also find a pattern similar to our reversal effect: in many nations, openness was linked to opposition to redistribution among the unengaged but to support for redistribution among the engaged. Moreover, consistent with our claim that openness will be linked to support for redistribution only when elites tie economic and cultural forms of conservatism together as part of the same ideological package, Malka and colleagues (2015) find that engagement produces a reversal only in nations where economic and cultural conservatism tend to co-occur. In places where this is not true, openness appears to promote a preference for limited government across levels of engagement. Thus, comparative evidence suggests that the core dynamics of our model may hold in political contexts whose economic histories and cultures differ from that in the United States.

Is Income or Education Responsible for the Reversal Effect?

One reasonable question is whether political engagement – knowing and caring about politics – is the primary moderator of the relationship between openness and economic opinion, or whether its conditioning impact is due to an interaction between openness and some other moderator we have not considered. One obvious possibility is that *income* is what really matters. Perhaps we are observing a "post-materialism" effect in which the rich concern themselves with culture and value expression, while the poor focus perforce on their personal economic interests. If income and engagement are correlated (which they are), this could be a problem for our interpretation of the reversal effect. A related possibility is that education – which is also correlated with political engagement and known to moderate the effect of personality variables (e.g., Federico and Tagar 2015; Osborne and Sibley 2013) – actually produces the reversal effect. To test both possibilities, we re-estimated the models examined in Chapter 4 for authoritarianism, need for closure, and openness to change, but with additional interactions between each trait and income and education, respectively.

The relevant estimates are shown in Table 8.1. They provide strong evidence that political engagement is the central driver of the reversal effect. In only one case does the inclusion of these additional interactions reduce the focal interaction between personality and engagement to statistical insignificance (though even here it is in the expected direction and of a reasonable magnitude). In all other cases, the interaction remains statistically significant and substantively large. Further, the interaction

TABLE 8.1. *The reversal effect with income and education interactions included*

	2000 ANES Values	2000 ANES Policy	2004 ANES Values	2004 ANES Policy	2008 ANES Values	2008 ANES Policy	2012 ANES Values	2012 ANES Policy	2008 KN	2011 WVS
Trait X Engagement	-2.13^*	-0.36^*	-1.85^*	-0.31^*	-1.74^*	$-.17$	-1.97^*	-0.36^*	-0.54^*	0.48^*
Trait X Income	$1.83^\wedge$	-0.14	$.88$	0.08	1.08^*	$.35^*$	0.11	-0.04	$-0.40^\wedge$	0.24
Trait X Education	-0.30	-0.04	$-.43$	-0.15	$-0.76^\wedge$	$-.42^*$	-1.07^*	-0.22^*	-0.34^*	0.13

Notes: Entries are ordered probit estimates for values in the 2000–12 ANES and ordinary least squares estimates for all other models. $^*p < 0.05$, $^\wedge p < 0.10$. Dispositional openness is measured with authoritarianism in the first eight columns, with need for closure in the 2008 Knowledge Networks study, and with openness to change in the 2011 World Values Survey. In this last case, higher values indicate greater openness. In all other cases, higher values indicate a closed personality.

between openness and income is significant in only two of ten tests, and in both cases the effect is incorrectly signed. Thus, the impact of personality on economic opinion is generally unaffected by income (and when it does matter, it appears to *inhibit* the reversal effect).[3] The results for education are somewhat more encouraging. Here, the interaction between personality and education is significant in four out of ten cases, and in all four cases education promotes the reversal effect. Thus, education may occasionally complement engagement in facilitating a reversal of the impact of personality on economic opinion, and may therefore play a role similar to engagement in shifting citizens' focus from instrumental to expressive.

Overall, these robustness checks suggest that political engagement – and not education or income – is primarily responsible for the reversal effect. While education promotes political engagement – and thus may work *through* engagement – it is engagement itself, whatever its source(s) may be, that most strongly and consistently accounts for the observed opinion dynamics.

Is Personality Really Exogenous to Politics?

Throughout the book we have assumed that openness in personality is exogenous to political identity (e.g., partisanship). As core psychological dispositions are broader and more fundamental than political identities, this seems like an uncontroversial assumption. To our knowledge, it is also one to which most scholars subscribe. But is it accurate? Perhaps we should not be so quick to write off the possibility that politics can shape personality. There are two ways in which the assumed causal order could be reversed: the way we *measure* personality might be endogenous to politics, and/or personality and political preferences might reciprocally influence one another.

The first possibility is a two-fold methods problem that has historically plagued work on personality and politics. The first aspect of the problem is that some personality scales include explicit political content. For example, as we noted in Chapter 4, Altemeyer's (1982, 1989) right-wing authoritarianism scale includes items about the acceptability of non-traditional lifestyles (e.g., LGBT rights). Similarly, Graham, Haidt, and Nosek's (2010) moral foundations scales include an item about patriotism and another about rich people inheriting money. This problem

---

[3] In two additional cases, the income interaction is marginally significant. In one of these cases, the interaction inhibits the reversal effect and in one case it promotes it similar to engagement.

is easily remedied by capturing motivational and cognitive orientations without making any reference to political objects and actors. For the most part, we think our measures accomplish this. For example, our measure of authoritarianism (i.e., childrearing values) was created for the explicit purpose of overcoming problems with endogeneity to political orientations (e.g., Feldman and Stenner 1998). Respondents are asked to make choices between values that are broader and more basic (e.g., being considerate versus well-behaved) than what we seek to explain (e.g., partisanship). This also seems to be the case for our measures of need for closure, the Big Five, openness to change, and risk aversion, none of which contains political content (see Tables 4.2–4.5 and 7).[4] The one serious concern in this regard is with the moral foundations questions used in Chapters 5 and 7. Although in theory basic moral principles are exogenous to political orientation – and can thus explain why people are liberal or conservative (Haidt 2013) – the items that comprise the moral foundations dimensions contain political content, as noted earlier (e.g., "I think it's morally wrong that rich children inherit a lot of money ... "). This is not to say that all of the items are problematic, but the few that do reference politics raise troubling questions about reverse causality similar to those raised by Altemeyer's right-wing authoritarianism items.

The second aspect of the measurement problem is more subtle. It involves a process whereby survey participants infer the "proper" response to personality items based on their political identities even when political content is minimal. For example, highly engaged liberals and conservatives may infer the ideologically appropriate response to a question about the trade-off between being "creative" (a stereotypically liberal trait) versus being "disciplined" (a stereotypically conservative trait). In other words, people may try to signal their political identities through responses to items on personality inventories.[5] This could inflate our estimates of the causal impact of personality on political identifications and

---

[4] One exception here may be the "tradition" item in the openness to change scale in Table 4.4.

[5] There is recent evidence for this possibility. Ludeke, Tagar, and DeYoung (2016) find that at least some of the correlation between some openness-related traits and political attitudes may be the result of citizens over-reporting traits that are socially desirable within their social networks. Ludeke and colleagues estimated the correlations among self-reported intelligence, openness to experience, conscientiousness, and political attitudes, and then re-estimated them with criterion measures of each trait (i.e., an IQ test for intelligence and peer ratings for the Big Five traits). As expected by past theorizing, they find significant and substantively meaningful correlations among intelligence, openness, and liberalism. Importantly, however, they find that citizens self-report traits consistent with their ideology *over and above* what is justified by the criterion measures

preferences. This criticism applies to virtually all work on personality and politics, and is thus an important topic for future research.

A related, yet more theoretically interesting possibility is that personality and political preferences reciprocally influence one another.[6] Although this may seem counterintuitive, we think it is possible that political identities feed back into traits, reinforcing and strengthening the initial associations. Consider the hypothetical example of someone high in openness to experience. In line with our perspective, this person – let's call her Mary – might be attracted to the ideological left for cultural reasons, and consistent with work on the social proclivities of politically engaged individuals, she mainly associates with other open liberals. If Mary's peers are more open than she is, social conformity pressures might induce Mary to engage in behaviors that are more open than she would otherwise contemplate. Through well-established behavior-to-attitude processes (e.g., Bem 1968), Mary might come to regard herself as – and over time perhaps even become – a more open person. This is an interesting possibility, and one that should be taken seriously in future research. Consider also that this is not a question of "either/or" with respect to causality. Indeed, dispositional openness is the initial impetus to political sorting. However, subsequent social interaction may cause a change in openness toward the group average. The reality may therefore be one of mutual causation, especially among politically engaged individuals for whom politics is important. Future research, perhaps using longitudinal data, will need to explore this question.

Are Engaged Citizens Instrumental or Expressive?
We have argued that economic opinion among engaged citizens is motivated by expressive rather than instrumental goals. Specifically, we claim that engaged citizens adopt the economic policy positions of favored elites as a way of expressing more affectively salient cultural commitments. In this sense, economic opinions are signals of traits and identities rather than beliefs about what policies will bring about desirable consequences for the self or society. However, it is not the only explanation for our findings. Perhaps engaged citizens are instrumentally motivated,

---

(e.g., left-wing citizens report higher intelligence than they should given their objective IQ scores). The authors conclude that this occurs because different sets of traits are seen as desirable within left and right social networks, leading people to feel pressure to conform their self-perceptions to those dispositional qualities. The conclusion is that some, but by no means all, of the correlation is due to such conformity pressures.

[6] See also Verhulst, Eaves and Hatemi (2012). These authors argue that personality traits and political attitudes are correlated due to common roots in more basic, heritable individual differences. They also find evidence that some broad personality traits may be shaped by political attitudes.

and simply use cultural considerations as low-effort cues for determining whom to trust at the elite level on matters of economics (Kahan and Braman 2007). In this view, economic issues are "hard" in the terminology of Carmines and Stimson (1981): they are technical, means-oriented, and lack the symbolic content of "easier" cultural issues like gay marriage, immigration, and race. For example, few citizens are able to navigate debates over the importance of the individual mandate in health insurance reform, or the expected effects of a minimum wage hike on unemployment. Most of us therefore rely on elite actors we deem knowledgeable and trustworthy as sources of information for making sense of economic policy (Lupia and McCubbins 1999).

This problem raises the question of *how* citizens decide whom to trust. If most of us are unable to decide this on the basis of policy information (due to lack of expertise), we must turn to easier cues, even if they are often unreliable. It is quite possible that engaged citizens use shared lifestyle, culture, and personality as cues for trustworthiness – what Caprara and Zimbardo (2005) refer to as *dispositional heuristics* (i.e., people "like me" are trustworthy on difficult political issues). In this view, engaged individuals are instrumental; they seek the best possible policy outcomes, and to do so they follow elites who share their cultural preferences. If this perspective is accurate, then the distinction between engaged and unengaged citizens is not a matter of goal type. Rather, it is simply that engaged citizens pay more attention to elite discourse, and thus make their judgments on the basis of elite guidance, while unengaged citizens do not. This interpretation of the nature of political engagement does not negate the reversal effect; it simply changes our interpretation of it (i.e., as being less about identity expression than about reasonable strategies for making sense of technical policy debates). We believe we have made a strong case for our preferred interpretation (that engaged citizens are expressively motivated), but we recognize that adjudicating between the two possibilities requires additional research.

Why Does Openness Promote Economic Conservatism among the Unengaged?

There is also explanatory ambiguity in our findings among politically unengaged citizens. We have argued that unengaged citizens with closed personalities are economic liberals because they construe economic policy debates in instrumental terms. Lacking a concern with political identity and the cultural conflicts that animate contemporary partisan debates, we argued that the unengaged think about economic issues in concrete terms related to personal benefits: How will this policy affect me and those I care about? In this view, closed citizens prefer economic liberalism for its security and certainty (a "safety net") while open citizens prefer the individualism and self-direction of the free market. Our evidence in Chapter 7 supports this claim: compared to those who know and care about politics, unengaged citizens show much stronger associations between indicators of class position (e.g., income, employment, health) and economic policy opinion. Still, our evidence is indirect. It would be useful if future research could more directly document that a self-interested thought process explains the impact of openness on economic opinion among unengaged citizens. For example, Zaller and Feldman (1993) examined the considerations that come to mind when responding to survey questions. If unengaged citizens with closed personalities are more likely than others to report concerns with economic security, this would constitute evidence for an instrumental, security-seeking pathway from personality to economic preferences.

Broader Implications

We now turn to some broader implications of our theory and findings for the study of personality and politics and for American politics more generally. What have we learned and why does it matter?

Threat Sensitivity and Uncertainty Aversion Do Not Always Promote Conservatism

Our findings suggest the need for a more nuanced understanding of how personality and political attitudes are related. As we noted in Chapter 2, the conventional wisdom posits an elective affinity between needs for security and certainty on one hand and conservative political preferences on the other (Jost et al. 2004, 2010). In particular, those with strong needs for certainty and security seek to preserve the status quo to avoid the risks associated with social change. Similarly, they are willing to sacrifice individual freedom in the name of protecting society from internal and external threats to the social order (e.g., Feldman 2004; Hetherington and Weiler 2010).

We have no quarrel with the elective affinity perspective. Indeed, our model – like almost all research on personality and politics – incorporates the idea of functional matching between psychological dispositions and political preferences. However, we claim that the path from threat and uncertainty aversion to political attitudes is not always a simple one, and that it does not always result in conservative preferences. In the cultural domain – and with respect to general predispositions like ideology and partisanship – our model dovetails with standard approaches: we expect individuals with closed personalities to gravitate toward cultural conservatism and toward ideologies and parties with a conservative cultural reputation. However, this pattern breaks down in the context of economic issues,[7] where past work shows that the connection between personality and economic opinion is weak and prone to inconsistency.[8]

We argue that there are at least two reasons for this lack of empirical support. First, by ignoring the multidimensionality of ideology, and by defining liberalism narrowly as opposition to the status quo, political psychologists have failed to consider the intuitive hypothesis that policies promoting a social safety net may – in some cases – be a strong functional match for those with a closed personality orientation (and vice versa). Indeed, political psychologists and political economists hold diametrically opposite perspectives in this regard.[9] The conflict between them seems to be rooted in the different ways that each defines the nature of mass ideology. Within political psychology, citizens are thought to view left and right in highly abstract terms related to orientations toward the status quo, while in political economy citizens are thought to form their preferences on the basis of expected material benefits. As we hope to have shown, scholars working within these two traditions would benefit from greater attention to the insights of the other.

Second, political psychologists have largely ignored the indirect effects of personality on economic opinion through political identity and information seeking. In other words, they have paid insufficient attention to the mediated pathways of preference formation highlighted by research in political science. The critical insight here is that mediation implies a potential disconnect between the needs that define a given trait and the *content* of public policy. This allows for the very same trait to be associated with a range of policy preferences, with the realized relationship

---

[7] It may break down in other issue domains as well. For example, foreign policy issues are often quite complex and may not always have a direct link to psychological dispositions, but rather may work through partisan cue-taking, as in the economic domain (Berinsky 2007). An examination of how far the indirect model of personality and political attitudes extends is a worthy topic for future research.

[8] For a review, see Hibbing et al. (2014b); Kossowska and Van Hiel 2003; Malka et al. (2014); McFarland, Ageyev, and Djintcharadze (1996).

[9] For example, compare arguments made by Jost et al. (2003) to those made by Duch and Rueda (2014).

depending on how elites construct the social meaning of the issue at a given point in time.

In sum, strong needs for security and certainty do not invariably lead to conservatism; whether or not they do so depends on issue domain, individual differences in political engagement, and the behavior of parties and partisan elites. This is most acutely the case in the economic domain, where the relationship between openness and policy preferences reverses not only in terms of outward form, but also in terms of the motives behind it. Outside the realm of cultural issues, any analysis of the political implications of personality should consider not only psychological dispositions, but the *political* processes that assign psychologically-relevant meaning to partisanship and to the issue positions offered by competing groups of partisan elites.

The Importance of the Culture War to Economic Redistribution and American Politics

Over the past few decades, the American party system has undergone a secular realignment in which changes in elite priorities have produced changes in the bases and distribution of mass party allegiances (Abramowitz and Saunders 1999; Hetherington and Weiler 2010). In particular, in an effort to exploit fissures in the New Deal coalition in the aftermath of the civil rights movement, the Republican Party championed a variety of symbolic concerns related to race and ethnicity, crime, law and order, religion, sexuality, and gender (Hetherington and Weiler 2010). In more recent years, the cultural dimension has been extended to encompass issues related to the war on terrorism that tap into similar concerns (Hetherington and Suhay 2012). In taking popular positions on these issues – which resonated with blue-collar Democrats – Republicans politicized the question of whether the government should take an active role in promoting social order, in-group cohesion, and traditional ideas about morality.

While these basic facts are not in dispute, there is disagreement about the importance of the culture wars. On one hand, some observers of American politics have maintained that cultural issues now dominate traditional economic concerns on the public agenda (Edsall and Edsall 1993; Frank 2005; Phillips 1970). According to this narrative, Republicans managed to sever the New Deal consensus by marshaling cultural anger, and by recasting political competition as a conflict between traditional versus progressive conceptions of social morality (Edsall and Edsall 1993; Huckfeldt and Kohfeld 1990). We can think of this view as one in which culture has *displaced* economics in citizens' decision calculus. On the other hand, there are scholars who doubt that such a displacement has occurred. In their view, culture has become more important relative to the past, but economic conflict retains pride of place in the mind of the average citizen. In support of this view, citizens regularly cite economic matters – by Smith's (2008) count, 73 percent of the time in Gallup surveys between 1973 and 2006 – when asked to indicate the country's most important problem. Similarly, evidence from standard voting models suggests that voters continue to attach more weight to taxes and spending than to cultural issues like abortion, gun control, or school prayer (Ansolabehere et al. 2006; Bartels 2007). These empirical realities cast doubt on the claim that the rise of cultural politics has defused the impact of bread-and-butter concerns. Indeed, in the wake of the Great Recession, recent debates over health insurance reform and the increasing national salience of inequality, it is highly unlikely that economic policy has lost relevance in American politics.

Our book takes a middle ground between these two viewpoints (see also Kahan and Braman 2006 for related arguments). While we agree that culture has not displaced economics on the public agenda, we also take issue with the idea that citizens' stated economic preferences can be treated as exogenous givens in standard models of political behavior (e.g., vote choice).[10] Moreover, we believe this is especially the case among politically active citizens. We hold that cultural orientations – and the personality traits that underpin them – *shape* economic preferences among the engaged through their influence on ideological and partisan sorting, political information seeking, and delegation. In particular, our claim is that economic opinion among engaged citizens is, in large part, endogenous to a basic cultural division in the electorate. In this view, empirical associations between economic policy attitudes and partisanship or voting behavior tell an oversimplified story, because a substantial portion of this covariation is due to the influence of party choice and partisan information seeking on policy preferences, rather than the other way around (Cohen 2004; Lavine et al. 2013; Lenz 2013; Levendusky 2010). To give a concrete example, the correlation between economic preferences and vote choice may be larger than that between authoritarianism and vote choice. However, if authoritarianism is exogenous to partisanship, and if economic preferences are, in large part, *endogenous* to partisanship and candidate choice, then we should not conclude that economic preferences are a more important influence

---

[10] See Ansolabehere et al. (2008) for an example.

on voting than personality. Indeed, in this model, authoritarianism is an exogenous *cause* of these policy preferences in a way similar to income or race. Thus, economic policy conflict is not simply about economics per se; among our most politically engaged citizens, it is also about cultural conflict. To a large extent, economic and cultural divisions are inseparable (see also Kahan 2016; Walsh 2013).

Why Do Working-Class Citizens Seemingly Vote Against Their Economic Interests?

In a similar fashion, our findings help to unpack one of the more contentious questions in mass politics: Why do many working-class individuals – and working-class *whites* in particular – support policies that seem to contradict their economic interests? In the study of American politics, this question has traditionally been answered in one of two ways: ignorance or elite-driven persuasion through the priming of racial animus. The first claim is that citizens low in socioeconomic status lack the information necessary to determine what types of policies will best represent their material interests. The second is that strategic elites have been successful in tying redistribution and welfare to minorities, leading some low-socioeconomic-status whites to abandon these policies as a function of racial resentment.

Our work speaks to this literature in at least two ways. First, our results strongly conflict with perspectives emphasizing political ignorance. In Chapter 7, we consistently found that material interest has its strongest impact among citizens *low* in political engagement, that is, those with less information. This is precisely the opposite of what the ignorance hypothesis predicts. Therefore, we reject the notion that working-class citizens oppose redistribution and social welfare because they don't know any better. Instead, we argue that politically engaged citizens simply care less about the instrumental implications of economic policy, and focus instead on how such proposals line up with their core traits, political identities, and cultural commitments. Our most informed citizens are therefore the least self-interested in the traditional sense.

This conclusion, while supported by the evidence presented in this book, is strongly at odds with a half century of theory and research in political science. From the outset of the behavioral era, political scientists have argued that a central ingredient – perhaps the central ingredient – of competent citizenship is *political knowledge* (Campbell et al. 1961; Converse 1965). As Delli Carpini and Keeter write in the introduction to their landmark book, *What Americans Know about Politics and Why it Matters*, "democracy functions best when its citizens are politically informed" (1996: 1). As a general matter, one can hardly object to this statement. Delli Carpini and Keeter (p. 218) go on to write that "knowledge is also an instrumental good that helps to enlighten one's self-interest and to translate it into effective political action" and that "if more knowledgeable citizens are better equipped to articulate their interests and better able to reward and punish political leaders for their actions, then when interest clash, less informed citizens are at a decided disadvantage" (p. 218). In the abstract, this too is difficult to disclaim. But in one respect – perhaps a narrow one – it is simply wrong. The *political* effect of knowledge is not to motivate citizens to privilege their economic interests; rather, it is to divert them away from such considerations, and to give their economic policy preferences an altogether different motivational focus. As it turns out, engaged citizens do not prioritize their pocketbooks; rather, they privilege expressive psychological goals associated with deep-seated aspects of their personalities. This means that objective economic insecurity (e.g., low income) and psychological insecurity (i.e., low openness) are in conflict: the latter pulls engaged, low-socioeconomic status citizens away from left-wing economic positions, and toward right-wing positions that predominate among their cultural affiliates.

In contrast, among less-engaged citizens, economic interests and psychological needs are better aligned: both objective economic insecurity and psychological insecurity push them in the same direction vis-à-vis attitudes toward social welfare. In both cases, insecurity predicts support for strengthening the social safety net. What is more, objective and psychological insecurity are correlated: less educated and less wealthy citizens tend to be the least dispositionally open. Among unengaged citizens who are low in socioeconomic status, this suggests that personality and economic self-interest reinforce one another. The opposite is true among low-socioeconomic-status citizens who are highly engaged, for whom psychological insecurity leads to economic preferences that may conflict with material interests.

Second, our findings speak to the implications of the symbolic politics literature for social welfare preferences among working-class whites (e.g., Gilens 2000; Tesler 2012). Gilens (1999) has made a convincing argument that welfare is racialized in American politics, such that white citizens think of blacks when they think about welfare beneficiaries, thus driving down support for many policies that might benefit them. Extending this work, Tesler (2012; 2016) has argued that racial attitudes are now an important component of attitudes toward a variety of economic policies associated with the Obama administration (e.g., health insurance reform) due to a "spillover" of racialization from evaluations of the nation's first black president to the policies he has championed.

We do not dispute these important findings, or the broader argument that many economic issues are racialized. However, our theory and findings suggest that "spillover" from non-economic to economic dimensions of policy is part of a more general phenomenon. Dispositionally closed citizens do not learn to oppose left-wing economic policies for racial reasons *alone*; rather, the effects of race reflect spillover from a more general cluster of cultural attitudes that includes gender, religion, sexuality, immigration, patriotism, law and order, fears about terrorism, and the like. Indeed, as we demonstrated in Chapter 6, the spillover of non-economic considerations onto economic policy preferences can occur in ways entirely unrelated to race, such as the priming of abortion or gun rights attitudes. Further, as we have shown in Chapter 4, the positive association between the closed personality type and economic conservatism among engaged citizens predates the Obama era by a more than a decade.

In this way, we see our work as complementing and extending the racialization thesis offered by Sears, Tesler, Gilens, and others in two respects. First, we see racialization as one component of a set of changes in American party politics that has increasingly bound the open-closed dimension of personality to political identity (Hetherington and Weiler 2009), and thereby to conflicts over the proper role of government in the economy. Second, we contend that such spillover should be especially pronounced among politically engaged individuals, as they care most about the identity-related implications of taking one policy position over another (e.g., Federico 2004; Federico and Holmes 2005; Federico and Sidanius 2002). For the unengaged, by contrast, the psychological traits underpinning racial and cultural conservatism may have opposite implications for economic preferences, namely, those in which racial conservatism coexists with support for more redistribution and a larger welfare state.

In this regard, consider Figure 8.1. These are the results from a regression model predicting support for redistribution and social welfare in the 2012 ANES. It is identical to the model estimated in Figure 4.2, Panel D. The only difference is that we substitute racial resentment – the most common measure of racial animus in the political psychology literature – for authoritarianism, and we restrict our analysis to non-Latino whites. As can be seen, the reversal pattern emerges here

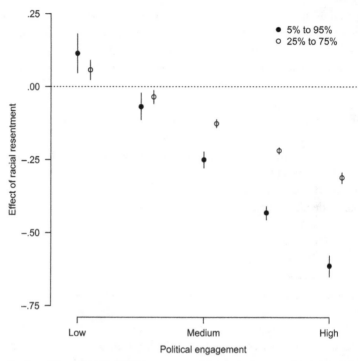

FIGURE 8.1. The relationship between racial resentment and economic policy liberalism across political engagement for non-Latino whites, 2012 ANES

too. That is, racial resentment is associated with opposition to social welfare among engaged citizens – as previous work would expect – but it is associated with *support* for social welfare among the politically unengaged. We do not think that anti-black affect is the root cause of economic liberalism in the latter case. Rather, we argue that the core personality traits that underpin racial conservatism – and a tendency toward ethnocentrism more generally (e.g., Kruglanski et al. 2006) – increase the attractiveness of liberal approaches to social welfare among politically unengaged citizens. It is only through political engagement and exposure to contemporary party politics that these traits and their associated racial and cultural attitudes become linked to economic conservatism.

Is There a Coming Realignment?
Recent political events in the United States have driven speculation about the possibility of an ideological realignment. The argument is that future

conflict between the parties will revolve around issues of nationalism and internationalism (immigration, free trade, and the role of the nation-state more generally) rather than domestic size-of-government issues that currently divide the parties. The surprising success of Donald Trump in 2016, as well as the success of populist candidates and movements in Europe, has made this view more plausible.

Our theory and evidence are consistent with the idea that contemporary party coalitions are unstable, and that Republican political entrepreneurs appealing to economic populism (rather than to markets) can be successful. First, we have argued and shown that the association between openness and support for government intervention is a distortion of a more "natural" (and opposite) relationship we consistently observe among politically unengaged citizens (see Chapter 4). The current alignment between personality and economic preferences is maintained because of the way that racial and cultural conflict became embedded in American party politics in the second half of the twentieth century, and because engaged citizens are motivated to put aside the policies they would otherwise prefer on instrumental grounds, in order to obtain the expressive benefits associated with identity politics. Second, as we demonstrated in Chapter 6, on increasingly salient issues surrounding international trade, open citizens prefer a free market approach while closed citizens prefer restrictions on markets. This is a result of closed citizens' preference for social protection and the association between free trade and cosmopolitan cultural openness.

In this view, the success of candidates like Trump – who appeal to cultural conservatism but break to some extent with the conservative line on issues of trade and social welfare (e.g., entitlement spending) – is less surprising, as they represent a more natural alignment between culture and economics when considered from the perspective of personality. These considerations suggest that the current ideological alignment of the parties may be unstable. In this vein, *New York Times* columnist David Brooks recently made an explicit case for a coming realignment along open-closed lines:

The old size-of-government question was growing increasingly archaic and obsolete. In country after country the main battle lines of debate are evolving toward the open/closed framework. If you don't like our current political polarization, wait 10 years. One way or another it will go away. When the frame of debate shifts to open/closed, sometime soon, the old coalitions will smash apart and new ones will form. Politics will be unrecognizable ... The prophets of closedness will argue that the problem is trade. The prophets of openness will argue that we need the dynamism that free trade brings.[11]

For politically engaged Americans, such an alignment of cultural and economic preferences may be hard to imagine. For decades they have been taught that an open orientation and cultural liberalism go with support for government intervention, and that a closed orientation and cultural conservatism go with support for free markets. But as we have shown, the opposite bundle of preferences is exactly what exists among the many citizens who tune out politics altogether. Realignments are obviously rare events that play out over many years, but the evidence we have presented for the reversal effect should give pause to skeptics who consider a change along the lines argued by Brooks to be unlikely. In our view, it seems like an entirely plausible way for personality, culture, and economic preferences to relate to one another.

Expressive Motivations and Simulated Representation

Our findings also raise deep questions about political representation in an era of cultural conflict. Democratic theory suggests that representatives should be broadly responsive to the preferences of their constituents (e.g., Gilens 2012). However, we have shown that our most politically active citizens care more about identity expression than they do about the content of particular economic policies. Indeed, engaged citizens do not seem to approach politics with fixed preferences and reward or punish representatives based on whether they enact policies consistent with those preferences. Rather, engaged citizens seem especially motivated to *assimilate* their own positions to those held by co-partisan elites (Achen and Bartels 2016; Lenz 2012), and in the process to stick it to the cultural out-group. In essence, the most engaged among us seem willing to give the partisan in-group broad political leeway so as to facilitate expressive psychological goals (see also Sniderman and Stiglitz 2012).

This dynamic is similar to what Shapiro and Jacobs have labeled *simulated representation*, "in which political leaders have incentives to move the public in the direction of their preferred policies, rather than engage the public in ways that respond to its wishes" (2010: 1). In this view, links among mass preferences, elite position-taking and policy output are driven by citizens' proclivity to align their own opinions with those of

---

[11] www.nytimes.com/2016/07/01/opinion/the-coming-political-realignment.html?_r=o

favored elites rather than the other way around. Representation is "simulated" because it is only apparent: it is imposed from the top down, rather than being driven by demands from the bottom up (see also Achen and Bartels 2016). Our own work is consistent with this view, and reinforces these concerns. Indeed, we find that economic opinion among those who are most likely to participate in political life is largely endogenous to political attachments rooted more in psychological dispositions and cultural affinities than in economics and material interests.

A Political Psychology True to Its Name

If nothing else, we hope our book will inspire future efforts to integrate theory and research on stable individual differences with work on the role of political context and elite opinion leadership. What we need, in the words of Krosnick and McGraw, is a political psychology *true to its name* (2002). Stable individual differences necessarily express themselves in particular social and historical contexts, and the social meaning of public opinion is defined within those contexts. Moreover, research in political science consistently indicates that political parties strongly shape how citizens understand and respond to policy disputes, and that political engagement conditions these processes (Zaller 1992). The field of personality and politics has made important contributions to our understanding of mass behavior. But its impact will be limited unless scholars fuse the psychological with the political by adopting a theoretical approach that integrates the best insights from each field. Too often, we think, the individual-differences approach in psychology is seen as competing with elite-driven approaches popular in political science (see Jost et al. 2009 for a similar argument). This is unfortunate. We believe standard theories emphasizing social and political factors benefit from a deeper understanding of the dispositional factors that structure long-standing political identities. Similarly, we believe that individual difference approaches benefit from a deeper understanding of how political processes condition the impact of predispositions. In our view, future research on personality and politics must take seriously the question of how deep-seated biological and psychological dispositions interact with political contexts to produce mass opinion. If our book makes any progress in moving the literature in this direction, it will have been a worthwhile endeavor.

References

Abramowitz, Alan I. 2010. *The Disappearing Center: Engaged Citizens, Polarization, and American Democracy*. New Haven, CT: Yale University Press.

Abramowitz, Alan I., and Kyle L. Saunders. 1998. "Ideological Realignment in the U.S. Electorate." *The Journal of Politics* 60 (3): 634–652.

Abrams, Samuel, Torben Iversen, and David Soskice. 2011. "Informal Social Networks and Rational Voting." *British Journal of Political Science* 41 (2): 229–57.

Achen, Christopher H., and Larry M. Bartels. 2006. "It Feels Like We're Thinking: The Rationalizing Voter and Electoral Democracy." Annual Meeting of the American Political Science Association, Philadelphia.

——— 2016. *Democracy for Realists: Why Elections Do Not Produce Responsive Government*. Princeton, NJ: Princeton University Press.

Adams, Greg D. 1997. "Abortion: Evidence of an Issue Evolution." *American Journal of Political Science* 41 (3): 718–37.

Adams, Thomas G., Patrick A. Stewart, and John C. Blanchar. 2014. "Disgust and the Politics of Sex: Exposure to a Disgusting Odorant Increases Politically Conservative Views on Sex and Decreases Support for Gay Marriage." *PLoS One* 9 (5): e95572.

Adorno, Theodor W., Else Frenkel-Brunswik, Daniel J. Levinson, and R. N. Sanford. 1950. *The Authoritarian Personality*. New York: Harper and Row.

Ahn, Woo-Young, Kenneth T. Kishida, Xiaosi Gu, Terry Lohrenz, Ann Harvey, John R. Alford, Kevin B. Smith, Gideon Yaffe, John R. Hibbing, and Peter Dayan. 2014. "Nonpolitical Images Evoke Neural Predictors of Political Ideology." *Current Biology* 24 (22): 2693–9.

Alesina, Alberto, and Eliana La Ferrara. 2005. "Preferences for Redistribution in the Land of Opportunities." *Journal of Public Economics* 89 (5): 897–931.

Alesina, Alberto, Edward Glaeser, and Bruce Sacerdote. 2001. "Why Doesn't the US Have a European-Style Welfare System?" *Brookings Papers on Economic Activity* (2): 188–277.

Alford, John R., Carolyn L. Funk, and John R. Hibbing. 2005. "Are Political Orientations Genetically Transmitted?" *American Political Science Review* 99 (2): 153–67.

2008. "Beyond Liberals and Conservatives to Political Genotypes and Phenotypes." *Perspectives on Politics* 6 (2): 321–8.

Allport, Gordon W. 1954. *The Nature of Prejudice*. Perseus Books Publishing.

Altemeyer, Bob. 1981. *Right-Wing Authoritarianism*. University of Manitoba Press.

1988. *Enemies of Freedom: Understanding Right-Wing Authoritarianism*. Jossey-Bass.

1996. *The Authoritarian Specter*. New York: Cambridge University Press.

1998. "The Other 'Authoritarian Personality.'" *Advances in Experimental Social Psychology* 30: 47–92.

Amodio, David M., John T. Jost, Sarah L. Master, and Cindy M. Yee. 2007. "Neurocognitive Correlates of Liberalism and Conservatism." *Nature Neuroscience* 10 (10): 1246–7.

Ansolabehere, Stephen, Jonathan Rodden, and James M. Snyder. 2006. "Purple America." *The Journal of Economic Perspectives* 20 (2): 97–118.

2008. "The Strength of Issues: Using Multiple Measures to Gauge Preference Stability, Ideological Constraint, and Issue Voting." *American Political Science Review* 102 (2): 215–32.

Arceneaux, Kevin, and Martin Johnson. 2013. *Changing Minds or Changing Channels? Partisan News in an Age of Choice*. Chicago: University of Chicago Press.

Aspelund, Anna, Marjaana Lindeman, and Markku Verkasalo. 2013. "Political Conservatism and Left–Right Orientation in 28 Eastern and Western European Countries." *Political Psychology* 34 (3): 409–17.

Bafumi, Joseph, and Robert Y. Shapiro. 2009. "A New Partisan Voter." *The Journal of Politics* 71 (01): 1–24.

Barbaranelli, Claudio, Gian V. Caprara, Michele Vecchione, and Chris R. Fraley. 2007. "Voters' Personality Traits in Presidential Elections." *Personality and Individual Differences* 42 (7): 1199–208.

Barker, David C., and James D. Tinnick. 2006. "Competing Visions of Parental Roles and Ideological Constraint." *American Political Science Review* 100 (2): 249–63.

Bartels, Larry M. 2005. "Homer Gets a Tax Cut: Inequality and Public Policy in the American Mind." *Perspectives on Politics* 3 (1): 15–31.

2006. "What's the Matter with What's the Matter with Kansas?" *Quarterly Journal of Political Science* 1 (2): 201–26.

Baumeister, Roy F., Ellen Bratslavsky, Catrin Finkenauer, and Kathleen D. Vohs. 2001. "Bad Is Stronger than Good." *Review of General Psychology* 5 (4): 323–70.

Bem, Daryl J. 1967. "Self-Perception: An Alternative Interpretation of Cognitive Dissonance Phenomena." *Psychological Review* 74 (3): 183–200.

Bennett, W. Lance, and Jarol B. Manheim. 2006. "The One-Step Flow of Communication." *The Annals of the American Academy of Political and Social Science* 608: 213–32.

Berinsky, Adam J. 2007. "Assuming the Costs of War: Events, Elites, and American Public Support for Military Conflict." *Journal of Politics* 69 (4): 975–97.

Bilsky, Wolfgang, and Shalom H. Schwartz. 1994. "Values and Personality." *European Journal of Personality* 8 (3): 163–81.

Bishop, Bill. 2009. *The Big Sort: Why the Clustering of Like-Minded America Is Tearing Us Apart.* New York: Mariner Books.

Block, Jack, and Jeanne H. Block. 2006. "Nursery School Personality and Political Orientation Two Decades Later." *Journal of Research in Personality* 40 (5): 734–49.

Bonanno, George A., and John T. Jost. 2006. "Conservative Shift among High-Exposure Survivors of the September 11th Terrorist Attacks." *Basic and Applied Social Psychology* 28 (4): 311–23.

Botvinick, Matthew M., Jonathan D. Cohen, and Cameron S. Carter. 2004. "Conflict Monitoring and Anterior Cingulate Cortex: An Update." *Trends in Cognitive Sciences* 8 (12): 539–46.

Boyce, Christopher J., Alex M. Wood, and Eamonn Ferguson. 2016. "Individual Differences in Loss Aversion: Conscientiousness Predicts how Life Satisfaction Responds to Losses Versus Gains in Income." *Personality & Social Psychology Bulletin* 42 (4): 471–84.

Brennan, Geoffrey, and Loren Lomasky. 1993. *Democracy and Decision: The Pure Theory of Electoral Preference.* New York: Cambridge University Press.

Brown, Rupert. 2000. "Social Identity Theory: Past Achievements, Current Problems and Future Challenges." *European Journal of Social Psychology* 30 (6): 745–78.

Bullock, John G. 2011. "Elite Influence on Public Opinion in an Informed Electorate." *American Political Science Review* 105 (3): 496–515.

Cacioppo, John T., Richard E. Petty, Jeffrey A. Feinstein, and W. B. G. Jarvis. 1996. "Dispositional Differences in Cognitive Motivation: The Life and Times of Individuals Varying in Need for Cognition." *Psychological Bulletin* 119 (2): 197–253.

Camerer, Colin. 2005. "Three Cheers – Psychological, Theoretical, Empirical – for Loss Aversion." *Journal of Marketing Research* 42 (2): 129–33.

Campbell, Angus, Phillip Converse, Donald Stokes, and Warren Miller. 1960. *The American Voter.* New York: John Wiley.

Caprara, Gian V., Claudio Barbaranelli, and Philip G. Zimbardo. 1999. "Personality Profiles and Political Parties." *Political Psychology* 20 (1): 175–97.

Caprara, Gian V., Shalom Schwartz, Cristina Capanna, Michele Vecchione, and Claudio Barbaranelli. 2006. "Personality and Politics: Values, Traits, and Political Choice." *Political Psychology* 27 (1): 1–28.

Caprara, Gian V., and Michele Vecchione. 2013. "Personality Approaches to Political Behavior." In *The Oxford Handbook of Political Psychology (Second Edition)*, Eds. Leonie Huddy, David O. Sears, and Jack S. Levy, 23–58. New York: Oxford University Press.

Caprara, Gian V., and Philip G. Zimbardo. 2004. "Personalizing Politics: A Congruency Model of Political Preference." *American Psychologist* 59 (7): 581–94.

Carl, Noah. 2015. "Does Intelligence Have a U-Shaped Relationship with Leftism?" *Intelligence* 49: 159–70.

Carmines, Edward G., and James A. Stimson. 1980. "The Two Faces of Issue Voting." *American Political Science Review* 74 (1): 78–91.

1989. *Issue Evolution: Race and the Transformation of American Politics.* Princeton, NJ: Princeton University Press.

Carney, Dana R., John T. Jost, Samuel D. Gosling, and Jeff Potter. 2008. "The Secret Lives of Liberals and Conservatives: Personality Profiles, Interaction Styles, and the Things They Leave Behind." *Political Psychology* 29 (6): 807–40.

Carraro, Luciana, Luigi Castelli, and Claudia Macchiella. 2011. "The Automatic Conservative: Ideology-Based Attentional Asymmetries in the Processing of Valenced Information." *PLoS One* 6 (11): e26456.

Castelli, Luigi, and Luciana Carraro. 2011. "Ideology Is Related to Basic Cognitive Processes Involved in Attitude Formation." *Journal of Experimental Social Psychology* 47 (5): 1013–16.

Chang, Linchiat, and Jon A. Krosnick. 2009. "National Surveys Via RDD Telephone Interviewing Versus the Internet Comparing Sample Representativeness and Response Quality." *Public Opinion Quarterly* 73 (4): 641–78.

Charney, Evan. 2008. "Genes and Ideologies." *Perspectives on Politics* 6 (2): 299–319.

Charney, Evan, and William English. 2012. "Candidate Genes and Political Behavior." *American Political Science Review* 106 (1): 1–34.

Chirumbolo, Antonio. 2002. "The Relationship between Need for Cognitive Closure and Political Orientation: The Mediating Role of Authoritarianism." *Personality and Individual Differences* 32 (4): 603–10.

Chirumbolo, Antonio, Alessandra Areni, and Gilda Sensales. 2004. "Need for Cognitive Closure and Politics: Voting, Political Attitudes and Attributional Style." *International Journal of Psychology* 39 (4): 245–53.

Chong, Dennis. 2013. "Degrees of Rationality in Politics." In *The Oxford Handbook of Political Psychology (Second Edition)*, Eds. Leonie Huddy, David O. Sears, and Jack S. Levy, 96–129. New York: Oxford University Press.

Chong, Dennis, Jack Citrin, and Patricia Conley. 2001. "When Self-Interest Matters." *Political Psychology* 22 (3): 541–70.

Chong, Dennis, and James N. Druckman. 2007. "Framing Theory." *Annual Review of Political Science* 10: 103–26.

Citrin, Jack, Beth Reingold, and Donald P. Green. 1990. "American Identity and the Politics of Ethnic Change." *The Journal of Politics* 52 (4): 1124–54.

Citrin, Jack, and David O. Sears. 2014. *American Identity and the Politics of Multiculturalism.* New York: Cambridge University Press.

Cizmar, Anne M., Geoffrey C. Layman, John McTague, Shanna Pearson-Merkowitz, and Michael Spivey. 2014. "Authoritarianism and American Political Behavior from 1952 to 2008." *Political Research Quarterly* 67 (1): 71–83.

Cohen, Florette, Daniel M. Ogilvie, Sheldon Solomon, Jeff Greenberg, and Tom Pyszczynski. 2005. "American Roulette: The Effect of Reminders of Death on Support for George W. Bush in the 2004 Presidential Election." *Analyses of Social Issues and Public Policy* 5 (1): 177–87.

Cohen, Geoffrey L. 2003. "Party over Policy: The Dominating Impact of Group Influence on Political Beliefs." *Journal of Personality and Social Psychology* 85 (5): 808–22.

Cohen, Geoffrey L., Joshua Aronson, and Claude M. Steele. 2000. "When Beliefs Yield to Evidence: Reducing Biased Evaluation by Affirming the Self." *Personality and Social Psychology Bulletin* 26 (9): 1151–64.

Cohrs, Christopher J., and Frank Asbrock. 2009. "Right-Wing Authoritarianism, Social Dominance Orientation and Prejudice Against Threatening and Competitive Ethnic Groups." *European Journal of Social Psychology* 39 (2): 270–89.

Conover, Pamela J., and Stanley Feldman. 1981. "The Origins and Meaning of Liberal/Conservative Self-Identifications." *American Journal of Political Science* 25 (4): 617–45.

Converse, Phillip. 1964. "The Nature of Belief Systems in Mass Publics." In *Ideology and Discontent*, Ed. David Apter. New York: Free Press.

Conway, Lucian G., Laura J. Gornick, Shannon C. Houck, Christopher Anderson, Jennifer Stockert, Diana Sessoms, and Kevin McCue. 2015. "Are Conservatives really More Simple-Minded than Liberals? The Domain Specificity of Complex Thinking." *Political Psychology*: doi:10.1111/pops.12304.

Cornwell, J. F., and E. T. Higgins. 2013. "Morality and Its Relation to Political Ideology: The Role of Promotion and Prevention Concerns." *Personality & Social Psychology Bulletin* 39 (9): 1164–72.

Costa, Paul T., and Robert R. McCrae. 1992. "Normal Personality Assessment in Clinical Practice: The NEO Personality Inventory." *Psychological Assessment* 4 (1): 5–13.

Credé, Marcus, Peter Harms, Sarah Niehorster, and Andrea Gaye-Valentine. 2012. "An Evaluation of the Consequences of Using Short Measures of the Big Five Personality Traits." *Journal of Personality and Social Psychology* 102 (4): 874–88.

Crowson, H. Michael. 2009. "Are all Conservatives Alike? A Study of the Psychological Correlates of Cultural and Economic Conservatism." *The Journal of Psychology* 143 (5): 449–63.

Crowson, H. Michael, Teresa K. Debacker, and Stephen J. Thoma. 2006. "The Role of Authoritarianism, Perceived Threat, and Need for Closure or Structure in Predicting Post-9/11 Attitudes and Beliefs." *The Journal of Social Psychology* 146 (6): 733–50.

Cunningham, William A., Marcia K. Johnson, J. C. Gatenby, John C. Gore, and Mahzarin R. Banaji. 2003. "Neural Components of Social Evaluation." *Journal of Personality and Social Psychology* 85 (4): 639–49.

Dancey, Logan, and Paul Goren. 2010. "Party Identification, Issue Attitudes, and the Dynamics of Political Debate." *American Journal of Political Science* 54 (3): 686–99.

Dawson, Michael C. 1994. *Behind the Mule: Race and Class in African-American Politics*. Princeton, NJ: Princeton University Press.

De Martino, B., C. F. Camerer, and R. Adolphs. 2010. "Amygdala Damage Eliminates Monetary Loss Aversion." *Proceedings of the National Academy of Sciences of the United States of America* 107 (8): 3788–92.

Delli Carpini, Michael X., and Scott Keeter. 1996. What Americans Know about Politics and Why It Matters. New Haven, CT: Yale University Press.

Dodd, M. D., A. Balzer, C. M. Jacobs, M. W. Gruszczynski, K. B. Smith, and J. R. Hibbing. 2012. "The Political Left Rolls with the Good and the Political Right Confronts the Bad: Connecting Physiology and Cognition to Preferences." *Philosophical Transactions of the Royal Society B* 367: 640–9.

Downs, Anthony. 1957. *An Economic Theory of Democracy*. New York: Harper and Row.

Druckman, James N., Erik Peterson, and Rune Slothuus. 2013. "How Elite Partisan Polarization Affects Public Opinion Formation." *American Political Science Review* 107 (1): 57–79.

Duch, Raymond M., Harvey D. Palmer, and Christopher J. Anderson. 2000. "Heterogeneity in Perceptions of National Economic Conditions." *American Journal of Political Science* 44 (4): 635–52.

Duch, Raymond M., and David Rueda. 2014. "The People You Are: Personality Traits as Determinants of Redistribution Preferences." Unpublished Manuscript.

Duckitt, John. 2001. "A Dual-Process Cognitive-Motivational Theory of Ideology and Prejudice." *Advances in Experimental Social Psychology* 33: 41–114.

Duckitt, John, and Chris G. Sibley. 2009." A Dual-Process Motivational Model of Ideology, Politics, and Prejudice." *Psychological Inquiry* 20 (2–3): 98–109.

Edsall, Thomas B., and Mary D. Edsall. 1992. *Chain Reaction: The Impact of Race, Rights, and Taxes on American Politics*. New York: W.W. Norton & Company.

Ehrlich, Sean, and Cherie Maestas. 2010. "Risk Orientation, Risk Exposure, and Policy Opinions: The Case of Free Trade." *Political Psychology* 31 (5): 657–84.

Eidelman, Scott, Christian S. Crandall, Jeffrey A. Goodman, and John C. Blanchar. 2012. "Low-Effort Thought Promotes Political Conservatism." *Personality & Social Psychology Bulletin* 38 (6): 808–20.

Ellis, Christopher, and James A. Stimson. 2012. *Ideology in America*. New York: Cambridge University Press.

Evans, Geoffrey, and Robert Andersen. 2006. "The Political Conditioning of Economic Perceptions." *Journal of Politics* 68 (1): 194–207.

Evans, Geoffrey, Anthony Heath, and Mansur Lalljee. 1996. "Measuring Left-Right and Libertarian-Authoritarian Values in the British Electorate." *British Journal of Sociology* 47 (1): 93–112.

Eysenck, Hans J. 1954. *The Psychology of Politics*. London: Routledge.

Federico, Christopher M. 2004. "When do Welfare Attitudes Become Racialized? The Paradoxical Effects of Education." *American Journal of Political Science* 48 (2): 374–91.

2012. "Ideology and Public Opinion." In *New Directions in Public Opinion*, Ed. Adam Berinsky, 81–103. New York: Routledge.

Federico, Christopher M., Grace Deason, and Emily L. Fisher. 2012. "Ideological Asymmetry in the Relationship between Epistemic Motivation and Political Attitudes." *Journal of Personality and Social Psychology* 103 (3): 381.

Federico, Christopher M., Emily L. Fisher, and Grace Deason. 2011. "Expertise and the Ideological Consequences of the Authoritarian Predisposition." *Public Opinion Quarterly* 75 (4): 686–708.

Federico, Christopher M., A. Golec, and J. L. Dial. 2005. "The Relationship between the Need for Closure and Support for Military Action Against Iraq: Moderating Effects of National Attachment." *Personality & Social Psychology Bulletin* 31 (5): 621–32.

Federico, Christopher M., and Paul Goren. 2009. "Motivated Social Cognition and Ideology: Is Attention to Elite Discourse a Prerequisite for Epistemically Motivated Political Affinities?" In *Social and Psychological Bases of Ideology and System Justification*, Eds. John T. Jost, Aaron C. Kay, and Hulda Thórisdóttir, 267–91. New York: Oxford University Press.

Federico, Christopher M., and Justin W. Holmes. 2005. "Education and the Interface between Racial Perceptions and Criminal Justice Attitudes." *Political Psychology* 26 (1): 47–75.

Federico, Christopher M., Corrie V. Hunt, and Damla Ergun. 2009. "Political Expertise, Social Worldviews, and Ideology: Translating 'Competitive Jungles' and 'Dangerous Worlds' Into Ideological Reality." *Social Justice Research* 22 (2–3): 259–79.

Federico, Christopher M., and Jim Sidanius. 2002. "Sophistication and the Antecedents of Whites' Racial Policy Attitudes: Racism, Ideology, and Affirmative Action in America." *Public Opinion Quarterly* 66 (2): 145–76.

Federico, Christopher M., and Michal R. Tagar. 2014. "Zeroing in on the Right: Education and the Partisan Expression of Authoritarianism in the United States." *Political Behavior* 36 (3): 581–603.

Federico, Christopher M., Christopher R. Weber, Damla Ergun, and Corrie Hunt. 2013. "Mapping the Connections between Politics and Morality: The Multiple Sociopolitical Orientations Involved in Moral Intuition." *Political Psychology* 34 (4): 589–610.

Feldman, Stanley. 1988. "Structure and Consistency in Public Opinion: The Role of Core Beliefs and Values." *American Journal of Political Science* 32 (2): 416–40.

2003. "Enforcing Social Conformity: A Theory of Authoritarianism." *Political Psychology* 24 (1): 41–74.

2013. "Political Ideology." In *The Oxford Handbook of Political Psychology (Second Edition)*, Eds. Leonie Huddy, David O. Sears, and Jack S. Levy, 591–626. New York: Oxford University Press.

Feldman, Stanley, and Leonie Huddy. 2014. "Not so Simple: The Multidimensional Nature and Diverse Origins of Political Ideology." *Behavioral and Brain Sciences* 37 (3): 312–13.

Feldman, Stanley, and Christopher Johnston. 2014. "Understanding the Determinants of Political Ideology: Implications of Structural Complexity." *Political Psychology* 35 (3): 337–58.

Feldman, Stanley, and Karen Stenner. 1997. "Perceived Threat and Authoritarianism." *Political Psychology* 18 (4): 741–70.

Feldman, Stanley, and John Zaller. 1992. "The Political Culture of Ambivalence: Ideological Responses to the Welfare State." *American Journal of Political Science* 36 (1): 268–307.

Fleishman, John A. 1988. "Attitude Organization in the General Public: Evidence for a Bidimensional Structure." *Social Forces* 67 (1): 159–84.

Frank, Thomas. 2004. *What's the Matter with Kansas? How Conservatives Won the Heart of America.* New York: Holt.

Fredrickson, Barbara L. 2001. "The Role of Positive Emotions in Positive Psychology: The Broaden-and-Build Theory of Positive Emotions." *American Psychologist* 56 (3): 218–26.

Gaines, Brian J., James H. Kuklinski, Paul J. Quirk, Buddy Peyton, and Jay Verkuilen. 2007. "Same Facts, Different Interpretations: Partisan Motivation and Opinion on Iraq." *Journal of Politics* 69 (4): 957–74.

Gelman, Andrew. 2008. *Red State, Blue State, Rich State, Poor State: Why Americans Vote the Way They Do.* Princeton, NJ: Princeton University Press.

Gelman, Andrew, and Jennifer Hill. 2007. *Data Analysis Using Regression and Multilevel/Hierarchical Models.* New York: Cambridge University Press.

Gelman, Andrew, Nate Silver and Aaron Edlin. 2012. "What is the Probability Your Vote Will Make a Difference?" *Economic Inquiry* 50 (2): 321–326.

Gerber, Alan S., Gregory A. Huber, David Doherty, and Conor M. Dowling. 2011. "The Big Five Personality Traits in the Political Arena." *Annual Review of Political Science* 14: 265–87.

Gerber, Alan S., Gregory A. Huber, David Doherty, Conor M. Dowling, and Shang E. Ha. 2010. "Personality and Political Attitudes: Relationships across Issue Domains and Political Contexts." *American Political Science Review* 104 (1): 111–33.

Gerth, H., and C. W. Mills. 1948/1970. *From Max Weber: Essays in Sociology.* London: Routledge.

Gilens, Martin. 1999. *Why Americans Hate Welfare.* Chicago: University of Chicago Press.

2012. *Affluence and Influence: Economic Inequality and Political Power in America.* Princeton, NJ: Princeton University Press.

Goldberg, Lewis R. 1990. "An Alternative 'Description of Personality': The Big-Five Factor Structure." *Journal of Personality and Social Psychology* 59 (6): 1216-1229.

Golec, Agnieszka. 2002. "Need for Cognitive Closure and Political Conservatism: Studies on the Nature of the Relationship." *Polish Psychological Bulletin* 33 (4): 5–12.

Golec, Agnieszka, and Christopher M. Federico. 2004. "Understanding Responses to Political Conflict: Interactive Effects of the Need for Closure and Salient Conflict Schemas." *Journal of Personality and Social Psychology* 87 (6): 750–62.

Goren, Paul. 2004. "Political Sophistication and Policy Reasoning: A Reconsideration." *American Journal of Political Science* 48 (3): 462–78.

2005. "Party Identification and Core Political Values." *American Journal of Political Science* 49 (4): 881–96.

2013. *On Voter Competence.* New York: Oxford University Press.

Gosling, Samuel D., Peter J. Rentfrow, and William B. Swann. 2003. "A Very Brief Measure of the Big-Five Personality Domains." *Journal of Research in Personality* 37 (6): 504–28.

Graham, Jesse, Jonathan Haidt, and Brian A. Nosek. 2009. "Liberals and Conservatives Rely on Different Sets of Moral Foundations." *Journal of Personality and Social Psychology* 96 (5): 1029–46.

Graham, Jesse, Jonathan Haidt, Sena Koleva, Matt Motyl, Ravi Iyer, Sean P. Wojcik, and Peter H. Ditto. 2013. "Moral Foundations Theory: The Pragmatic Validity of Moral Pluralism." *Advances in Experimental Social Psychology* 47: 55-130.

Green, Donald, Bradley Palmquist, and Eric Schickler. 2002. *Partisan Hearts and Minds*. New Haven, CT: Yale University Press.

Greenberg, Jeff, Tom Pyszczynski, Sheldon Solomon, Abram Rosenblatt, Mitchell Veeder, Shari Kirkland, and Deborah Lyon. 1990. "Evidence for Terror Management Theory II: The Effects of Mortality Salience on Reactions to those Who Threaten or Bolster the Cultural Worldview." *Journal of Personality and Social Psychology* 58 (2): 308–18.

Greenstein, Fred I. 1969. *Personality and Politics: Problems of Evidence, Inference, and Conceptualization*. Chicago: Markham Publishing Company.

Groenendyk, Eric. 2013. *Competing Motives in the Partisan Mind: How Loyalty and Responsiveness Shape Party Identification and Democracy*. New York: Oxford University Press.

Haider-Markel, Donald P., and Mark R. Joslyn. 2008. "Beliefs about the Origins of Homosexuality and Support for Gay Rights: An Empirical Test of Attribution Theory." *Public Opinion Quarterly* 72 (2): 291–310.

Haidt, Jonathan. 2012. *The Righteous Mind: Why Good People Are Divided by Politics and Religion*. New York: Pantheon Books.

Haidt, Jonathan, and Craig Joseph. 2007. "The Moral Mind: How Five Sets of Innate Intuitions Guide the Development of Many Culture-Specific Virtues, and Perhaps Even Modules." In *The Innate Mind (Volume 3)*, Eds. Peter Carruthers, Stephen Lawrence, and Stephen Stich, 367–92. New York: Oxford University Press.

Hainmueller, Jens, and Michael J. Hiscox. 2007. "Educated Preferences: Explaining Attitudes Toward Immigration in Europe." *International Organization* 61 (2): 399–442.

Hanmer, Michael J., and Kerem Ozan Kalkan. 2013. "Behind the Curve: Clarifying the Best Approach to Calculating Predicted Probabilities and Marginal Effects from Limited Dependent Variable Models." *American Journal of Political Science* 57 (1): 263–77.

Hannagan, Rebecca J., and Peter K. Hatemi. 2008. "The Threat of Genes: A Comment on Evan Charney's 'Genes and Ideologies.'" *Perspectives on Politics* 6 (2): 329–35.

Harmon-Jones, Eddie. 2007. "Asymmetrical Frontal Cortical Activity, Affective Valence, and Motivational Direction." In *Social Neuroscience: Integrating Biological and Psychological Explanations of Social Behavior*, eds. Eddie Harmon-Jones and Piotr Winkielman, 137–56. New York: The Guilford Press.

Hartz, Louis. 1955. *The Liberal Tradition in America: An Interpretation of American Political Thought since the Revolution.* New York: Harcourt, Brace.

Hayes, Danny, and Jennifer L. Lawless. 2016. *Women on the Run: Gender, Media, and Political Campaigns in a Polarized Era.* New York: Cambridge University Press.

Heider, Fritz. 1958. *The Psychology of Interpersonal Relations.* Hillsdale, NJ: Lawrence Erlbaum Associates.

Helzer, Erik G., and David A. Pizarro. 2011. "Dirty Liberals! Reminders of Physical Cleanliness Influence Moral and Political Attitudes." *Psychological Science* 22 (4): 517–22.

Hetherington, Marc J. 2001. "Resurgent Mass Partisanship: The Role of Elite Polarization." *American Political Science Review* 95 (3): 619–31.

Hetherington, Marc, and Elizabeth Suhay. 2011. "Authoritarianism, Threat, and Americans' Support for the War on Terror." *American Journal of Political Science* 55 (3): 546–60.

Hetherington, Marc J., and Jonathan D. Weiler. 2009. *Authoritarianism and Polarization in American Politics.* New York: Cambridge University Press.

Hibbing, John R., Kevin B. Smith, and John R. Alford. 2014a. *Predisposed: Liberals, Conservatives, and the Biology of Political Differences.* New York: Routledge.

2014b. "Differences in Negativity Bias Underlie Variations in Political Ideology." *Behavioral and Brain Sciences* 37 (3): 297–307.

Hiel, Alain V., and Ivan Mervielde. 2004. "Openness to Experience and Boundaries in the Mind: Relationships with Cultural and Economic Conservative Beliefs." *Journal of Personality* 72 (4): 659–86.

Higgins, E. Tory. 1996. "Knowledge Activation: Accessibility, Applicability, and Salience." In *Social Psychology: Handbook of Basic Principles,* eds. E. Tory Higgins and Arie W. Kruglanski, 133–68. New York: The Guilford Press.

1998. "Promotion and Prevention: Regulatory Focus as a Motivational Principle." *Advances in Experimental Social Psychology* 30: 1–46.

Hill, Seth J., and Chris Tausanovitch. 2015. "A Disconnect in Representation? Comparison of Trends in Congressional and Public Polarization." *The Journal of Politics* 77 (4): 1058–1075.

Hillygus, D. S., Natalie Jackson, and M. Young. 2014. "Professional Respondents in Non-probability Online Panels." In *Online Panel Research: A Data Quality Perspective,* eds. Mario Callegaro, Reg Baker, Jelke Bethlehem, Anja S. Göritz, Jon A. Krosnick, and Paul J. Lavrakas, 219–37. New York: John Wiley and Sons.

Hodson, G., and K. Costello. 2007. "Interpersonal Disgust, Ideological Orientations, and Dehumanization as Predictors of Intergroup Attitudes." *Psychological Science* 18 (8): 691–8.

Hogg, Michael A. 2007. "Uncertainty–Identity Theory." *Advances in Experimental Social Psychology* 39: 69–126.

Huckfeldt, Robert. 2014. "Networks, Contexts, and the Combinatorial Dynamics of Democratic Politics." *Advances in Political Psychology* 35 (S1): 43–68.

Huckfeldt, Robert, Paul E. Johnson, and John Sprague. 2004. *Political Disagreement: The Survival of Diverse Opinions within Communication Networks.* New York: Cambridge University Press.

Huckfeldt, Robert, and Carol W. Kohfeld. 1989. *Race and the Decline of Class in American Politics*. Champaign: University of Illinois Press.

Huddy, Leonie, Lilliana Mason, and Lene Aarøe. 2015. "Expressive Partisanship: Campaign Involvement, Political Emotion, and Partisan Identity." *American Political Science Review* 109 (1): 1–17.

Inbar, Yoel, David A. Pizarro, Joshua Knobe, and Paul Bloom. 2009. "Disgust Sensitivity Predicts Intuitive Disapproval of Gays." *Emotion* 9 (3): 435–9.

Isen, Alice M. 1987. "Positive Affect, Cognitive Processes and Social Behavior." In *Advances in Experimental Social Psychology, Volume 20*, ed. L. Berkowitz, 203–53. : Academic Press.

Iversen, Torben. 2005. *Capitalism, Democracy, and Welfare*. New York: Cambridge University Press.

Iversen, Torben, and David Soskice. 2001. "An Asset Theory of Social Policy Preferences." *American Political Science Review* 95 (4): 875–94.

Iyengar, Shanto, and Kyu S. Hahn. 2009. "Red Media, Blue Media: Evidence of Ideological Selectivity in Media Use." *Journal of Communication* 59 (1): 19–39.

Iyengar, Shanto, Kyu S. Hahn, Jon A. Krosnick, and John Walker. 2008. "Selective Exposure to Campaign Communication: The Role of Anticipated Agreement and Issue Public Membership." *The Journal of Politics* 70 (1): 186–200.

Iyengar, Shanto, Gaurav Sood, and Yphtach Lelkes. 2012. "Affect, Not Ideology: A Social Identity Perspective on Polarization." *Public Opinion Quarterly* 76 (3): 405–31.

Iyengar, Shanto, and Sean J. Westwood. 2014. "Fear and Loathing across Party Lines: New Evidence on Group Polarization." *American Journal of Political Science* 59 (3): 690–707.

Iyer, Ravi, Spassena Koleva, Jesse Graham, Peter Ditto, and Jonathan Haidt. 2012. "Understanding Libertarian Morality: The Psychological Dispositions of Self-Identified Libertarians." *PLoS One* 7 (8): e42366.

Jacobson, Gary C. 2010. "Perception, Memory, and Partisan Polarization on the Iraq War." *Political Science Quarterly* 125 (1): 31–56.

Jacoby, William G. 2014. "Is there a Culture War? Conflicting Value Structures in American Public Opinion." *American Political Science Review* 108 (4): 754–71.

Janoff-Bulman, Ronnie. 2009. "To Provide or Protect: Motivational Bases of Political Liberalism and Conservatism." *Psychological Inquiry* 20 (2–3): 120–8.

Janoff-Bulman, Ronnie, Sana Sheikh, and Kate G. Baldacci. 2008. "Mapping Moral Motives: Approach, Avoidance, and Political Orientation." *Journal of Experimental Social Psychology* 44 (4): 1091–9.

Johnston, Christopher D. 2011. *The Motivated Formation of Economic Preferences* (Order No. 3474556). Available from ProQuest Dissertations & Theses Global. (897963495). Retrieved from http://proxy.lib.duke.edu/login?url=http:// search.proquest.com/docview/897963495?accountid=10598.

2013. "Dispositional Sources of Economic Protectionism." *Public Opinion Quarterly* 77 (2): 574–85.

Johnston, Christopher D., Benjamin J. Newman, and Yamil Velez. 2015. "Ethnic Change, Personality, and Polarization over Immigration in the American Public." *Public Opinion Quarterly* 79 (3): 662–86.

Johnston, Christopher D., and Julie Wronski. 2015. "Personality Dispositions and Political Preferences across Hard and Easy Issues." *Political Psychology* 36 (1): 35–53.

Jost, John T. 2006. "The End of the End of Ideology." *American Psychologist* 61 (7): 651–70.

Jost, John T., Christopher M. Federico, and Jaime L. Napier. 2009. "Political Ideology: Its Structure, Functions, and Elective Affinities." *Annual Review of Psychology* 60: 307–37.

——— 2013. "Political Ideologies and Their Social Psychological Functions." In *The Oxford Handbook of Political Ideologies*, eds. Michael Freeden, Lyman Tower Sargent, and Marc Stears, 232–50. New York: Oxford University Press.

Jost, John T., Jack Glaser, Arie W. Kruglanski, and Frank J. Sulloway. 2003. "Political Conservatism as Motivated Social Cognition." *Psychological Bulletin* 129 (3): 339–75.

Jost, John T., H. H. Nam, David M. Amodio, and Jay J. Van Bavel. 2014. "Political Neuroscience: The Beginning of a Beautiful Friendship." *Advances in Political Psychology* 35 (S1): 3–42.

Jost, John T., Brian A. Nosek, and Samuel D. Gosling. 2008. "Ideology: Its Resurgence in Social, Personality, and Political Psychology." *Perspectives on Psychological Science: A Journal of the Association for Psychological Science* 3 (2): 126–36.

Judd, Charles M., Jon A. Krosnick, and Michael A. Milburn. 1981. "Political Involvement and Attitude Structure in the General Public." *American Sociological Review* 46 (5): 660–9.

Kahan, Dan M. 2015. "What Is the 'Science of Science Communication'?" *Journal of Science Communication* 14 (3): 1–12.

Kahan, Dan M., and Donald Braman. 2006. "Cultural Cognition and Public Policy." *Yale Law Policy Review* 24: 147–70.

Kahan, Dan M., Ellen Peters, Erica C. Dawson, and Paul Slovic. 2013. "Motivated Numeracy and Enlightened Self-Government." *Yale Law School, Public Law Working Paper*.

Kahneman, Daniel, and Amos Tversky. 1979. "Prospect Theory: An Analysis of Decision under Risk." *Econometrica* 47 (2): 263–92.

Kam, Cindy D. 2006. "Political Campaigns and Open-Minded Thinking." *Journal of Politics* 68 (4): 931–45.

——— 2012. "Risk Attitudes and Political Participation." *American Journal of Political Science* 56 (4): 817–36.

Kam, Cindy D., and Elizabeth N. Simas. 2010. "Risk Orientations and Policy Frames." *Journal of Politics* 72 (2): 381–96.

Kanai, Ryota, Tom Feilden, Colin Firth, and Geraint Rees. 2011. "Political Orientations Are Correlated with Brain Structure in Young Adults." *Current Biology* 21 (8): 677–80.

Katz, Daniel. 1960. "The Functional Approach to the Study of Attitudes." *Public Opinion Quarterly* 24 (2): 163–204.

Keltner, Dachner, and Jennifer S. Lerner. 2010. "Emotion." In *Handbook of Social Psychology*, eds. Susan T. Fiske, Daniel T. Gilbert, and Gardner Lindzey, 317–52. : John Wiley and Sons.

Kemmelmeier, Markus. 1997. "Need for Closure and Political Orientation among German University Students." *The Journal of Social Psychology* 137 (6): 787–9.

2007. "Political Conservatism, Rigidity, and Dogmatism in American Foreign Policy Officials: The 1966 Mennis Data." *The Journal of Psychology* 141 (1): 77–90.

Kerns, John G., Jonathan D. Cohen, Angus W. MacDonald III, Raymond Y. Cho, V. Andrew Stenger, and Cameron S. Carter. 2004. "Anterior Cingulate Conflict Monitoring and Adjustments in Control." *Science* 303: 1023–6.

Kinder, Donald R., and Cindy D. Kam. 2010. *Us Against Them: Ethnocentric Foundations of American Opinion.* Chicago: University of Chicago Press.

Kinder, Donald R., and David O. Sears. 1981. "Prejudice and Politics: Symbolic Racism Versus Racial Threats to the Good Life." *Journal of Personality and Social Psychology* 40 (3): 414–31.

Kluegel, James R., and Eliot R. Smith. 1986. *Beliefs about Inequality: Americans' Views of What Is and What Ought to Be.* New York: Aldine De Gruyter.

Knoll, Benjamin R., and Jordan Shewmaker. 2015. "'Simply Un-American': Nativism and Support for Health Care Reform." *Political Behavior* 37 (1): 87–108.

Kossowska, Malgorzata, and Alain V. Hiel. 2003. "The Relationship between Need for Closure and Conservative Beliefs in Western and Eastern Europe." *Political Psychology* 24 (3): 501–18.

Kriesi, Hanspeter, Edgar Grande, Romain Lachat, Martin Dolezal, Simon Bornschier, and Timotheos Frey. 2006. "Globalization and the Transformation of the National Political Space: Six European Countries Compared." *European Journal of Political Research* 45 (6): 921–56.

Krosnick, Jon A., and Kathleen M. McGraw. 2001. "A Comparison of the Random Digit Dialing Telephone Survey Methodology with Internet Survey Methodology as Implemented by Knowledge Networks and Harris Interactive." Unpublished Manuscript.

2002. "Psychological Political Science Versus Political Psychology True to Its Name: A Plea for Balance." In *Political Psychology*, ed. Kristen Renwick Monroe, 79–94. Mahwah, NJ: Lawrence Erlbaum Associates. Krosnick, Jon A., and Linchiat Chang.

Kruglanski, Arie W. 1989. *Lay Epistemics and Human Knowledge: Cognitive and Motivational Bases.* New York: Plenum Press.

2004. *The Psychology of Closed Mindedness.* New York: Psychology Press.

Kruglanski, Arie W., Antonio Pierro, Lucia Mannetti, and Eraldo De Grada. 2006. "Groups as Epistemic Providers: Need for Closure and the Unfolding of Group-Centrism." *Psychological Review* 113 (1): 84–100.

Kruglanski, Arie W., James Y. Shah, Antonio Pierro, and Lucia Mannetti. 2002. "When Similarity Breeds Content: Need for Closure and the Allure of Homogeneous and Self-Resembling Groups." *Journal of Personality and Social Psychology* 83 (3): 648–62.

Kruglanski, Arie W., and Donna M. Webster. 1996. "Motivated Closing of the Mind: 'Seizing' and 'Freezing.'" *Psychological Review* 103 (2): 263–83.

Lakoff, George. 2002. *Moral Politics: How Conservatives and Liberals Think.* Chicago: University of Chicago Press.

Landau, Mark J., Sheldon Solomon, Jeff Greenberg, Florette Cohen, Tom Pyszczynski, Jamie Arndt, Claude H. Miller, Daniel M. Ogilvie, and Alison Cook. 2004. "Deliver Us from Evil: The Effects of Mortality Salience and Reminders of 9/11 on Support for President George W. Bush." *Personality & Social Psychology Bulletin* 30 (9): 1136–50.

Lane, Robert E. 1962. *Political Ideology: Why the American Common Man Believes What He Does*. Oxford: Free Press of Glencoe.

Lasswell, Harold D. 1930. *Psychopathology and Politics*. Chicago: University of Chicago Press.

——— 1936. *Politics: Who Gets What, When, How*. New York: Whittlesey House.

Lavine, Howard G., Christopher D. Johnston, and Marco R. Steenbergen. 2012. *The Ambivalent Partisan: How Critical Loyalty Promotes Democracy*. New York: Oxford University Press.

Lavine, Howard, Diana Burgess, Mark Snyder, John Transue, John L. Sullivan, Beth Haney, and Stephen H. Wagner. 1999. "Threat, Authoritarianism, and Voting: An Investigation of Personality and Persuasion." *Personality and Social Psychology Bulletin* 25 (3): 337–47.

Lavine, Howard, Milton Lodge, and Kate Freitas. 2005. "Threat, Authoritarianism, and Selective Exposure to Information." *Political Psychology* 26 (2): 219–44.

Lavine, Howard, Milton Lodge, James Polichak, and Charles Taber. 2002. "Explicating the Black Box through Experimentation: Studies of Authoritarianism and Threat." *Political Analysis* 10 (4): 343–61.

Layman, Geoffrey. 2001. *The Great Divide: Religious and Cultural Conflict in American Party Politics*. New York: Columbia University Press.

Layman, Geoffrey C., and Thomas M. Carsey. 2002. "Party Polarization and 'Conflict Extension' in the American Electorate." *American Journal of Political Science* 46 (4): 786–802.

Lazarus, Richard S. 1991. *Emotion and Adaptation*. New York: Oxford University Press.

LeDoux, Joseph. 1998. *The Emotional Brain: The Mysterious Underpinnings of Emotional Life*. New York: Simon and Schuster.

Lee, Frances E. 2009. *Beyond Ideology: Politics, Principles, and Partisanship in the US Senate*. Chicago: University of Chicago Press.

Lenz, Gabriel S. 2012. *Follow the Leader? How Voters Respond to Politicians' Policies and Performance*. Chicago: University of Chicago Press.

Lerner, Jennifer S., and Dacher Keltner. 2001. "Fear, Anger, and Risk." *Journal of Personality and Social Psychology* 81 (1): 146–59.

Levendusky, Matthew. 2009. *The Partisan Sort: How Liberals Became Democrats and Conservatives Became Republicans*. Chicago: University of Chicago Press.

Lieberman, Matthew D. 2007. "Social Cognitive Neuroscience: A Review of Core Processes." *Annual Review of Psychology* 58: 259–89.

Lipset, Seymour M. 1959. "Democracy and Working-Class Authoritarianism." *American Sociological Review* 24 (4): 482–501.

——— 1996. *American Exceptionalism: A Double-Edged Sword*. New York: W.W. Norton & Company.

Lodge, Milton, and Charles S. Taber. 2013. *The Rationalizing Voter*. New York: Cambridge University Press.

Ludeke, Steven, Michal R. Tagar, and Colin G. DeYoung. 2016. "Not as Different as We Want to Be: Attitudinally Consistent Trait Desirability Leads to Exaggerated Associations between Personality and Sociopolitical Attitudes." *Political Psychology* 37 (1): 125–35.

Luhtanen, Riia, and Jennifer Crocker. 1992. "A Collective Self-Esteem Scale: Self-Evaluation of One's Social Identity." *Personality and Social Psychology Bulletin* 18 (3): 302–18.

Lupia, Arthur, and Mathew D. McCubbins. 1998. *The Democratic Dilemma: Can Citizens Learn What They Need to Know?* New York: Cambridge University Press.

Luttig, Matthew D., and Howard Lavine. 2015. "Issue Frames, Personality, and Political Persuasion." *American Politics Research* 44 (3): 448–70.

Malka, Ariel, Christopher J. Soto, Michael Inzlicht, and Yphtach Lelkes. 2014. "Do Needs for Security and Certainty Predict Cultural and Economic Conservatism? A Cross-national Analysis." *Journal of Personality and Social Psychology* 106 (6): 1031–51.

Mansfield, Edward D., and Diana C. Mutz. 2009. "Support for Free Trade: Self-Interest, Sociotropic Politics, and Out-Group Anxiety." *International Organization* 63 (3): 425–57.

Marcus, George E., John L. Sullivan, Elizabeth Theiss-Morse, and Sandra L. Wood. 1995. *With Malice Toward Some: How People Make Civil Liberties Judgments*. New York: Cambridge University Press.

Mason, Lilliana. 2015a. "'I Disrespectfully Agree': The Differential Effects of Partisan Sorting on Social and Issue Polarization." *American Journal of Political Science* 59 (1): 128–45.

2015b. "Party Polarization Is Making Us More Prejudiced." In *Political Polarization in American Politics*, eds. Daniel J. Hopkins and John Sides, 55–60. New York: Bloomsbury.

McCarty, Nolan, Keith T. Poole, and Howard Rosenthal. 2006. *Polarized America: The Dance of Ideology and Unequal Riches*. Cambridge, MA: MIT Press.

McClosky, Herbert. 1958. "Conservatism and Personality." *American Political Science Review* 52 (1): 27–45.

McClosky, Herbert, and John Zaller. 1984. *The American Ethos: Public Attitudes Toward Capitalism and Democracy*. Cambridge, MA: Harvard University Press.

McCrae, Robert R. 1996. "Social Consequences of Experiential Openness." *Psychological Bulletin* 120 (3): 323–37.

2015. "A More Nuanced View of Reliability: Specificity in the Trait Hierarchy." *Personality and Social Psychology* 19 (2): 97–112.

McCrae, Robert R., and Paul T. Costa. 1999. "A Five-Factor Theory of Personality." In *Handbook of Personality: Theory and Research*, eds. Lawrence A. Pervin and Oliver P. John. New York: Guilford Press, 139-53.

2003. *Personality in Adulthood: A Five-Factor Theory Perspective*. New York: The Guilford Press.

McDermott, Rose, James H. Fowler, and Oleg Smirnov. 2008. "On the Evolutionary Origin of Prospect Theory Preferences." *The Journal of Politics* 70 (2): 335–50.

McFarland, Sam G. 2005. "On the Eve of War: Authoritarianism, Social Dominance, and American Students' Attitudes Toward Attacking Iraq." *Personality & Social Psychology Bulletin* 31 (3): 360–7.

McFarland, Sam G., Vladimir S. Ageyev, and Nadya Djintcharadze. 1996. "Russian Authoritarianism Two Years after Communism." *Personality and Social Psychology Bulletin* 22 (2): 210–17.

McGraw, A. Peter, and Philip E. Tetlock. 2005. "Taboo Trade-Offs, Relational Framing, and the Acceptability of Exchanges." *Journal of Consumer Psychology* 15 (1): 2–15.

McLean, Scott P., John P. Garza, Sandra A. Wiebe, Michael D. Dodd, Kevin B. Smith, John R. Hibbing, and Kimberly A. Espy. 2014. "Applying the Flanker Task to Political Psychology: A Research Note." *Political Psychology* 35 (6): 831–40.

Mehrabian, Albert. 1996. "Analysis of the Big-Five Personality Factors in Terms of the PAD Temperament Model." *Australian Journal of Psychology* 48 (2): 86–92.

Meltzer, Allan H., and Scott F. Richard. 1981. "A Rational Theory of the Size of Government." *Journal of Political Economy* 89 (5): 914–27.

Miller, Patrick R. 2011. "The Emotional Citizen: Emotion as a Function of Political Sophistication." *Political Psychology* 32 (4): 575–600.

Moene, Karl O., and Michael Wallerstein. 2001. "Inequality, Social Insurance, and Redistribution." *American Political Science Review* 95 (4): 859–74.

Mondak, Jeffery J. 2010. *Personality and the Foundations of Political Behavior.* New York: Cambridge University Press.

Mondak, Jeffery J., and Karen D. Halperin. 2008. "A Framework for the Study of Personality and Political Behaviour." *British Journal of Political Science* 38 (2): 335–62.

Mutz, Diana C. 2006. *Hearing the Other Side: Deliberative Versus Participatory Democracy.* New York: Cambridge University Press.

Nail, Paul R., and Ian McGregor. 2009. "Conservative Shift among Liberals and Conservatives Following 9/11/01." *Social Justice Research* 22 (2–3): 231–40.

Nie, Norman, Sidney Verba, and John Petrocik. 1976. *The Changing American Voter.* Cambridge, MA: Harvard University Press.

Norris, Catherine J., Jackie Gollan, Gary G. Berntson, and John T. Cacioppo. 2010. "The Current Status of Research on the Structure of Evaluative Space." *Biological Psychology* 84 (3): 422–36.

Nyhan, Brendan, and Jason Reifler. 2015a. "Does Correcting Myths about the Flu Vaccine Work? An Experimental Evaluation of the Effects of Corrective Information." *Vaccine* 33 (3): 459–64.

2015b. "The Role of Information Deficits and Identity Threat in the Prevalence of Misperceptions." Unpublished Manuscript.

Olver, James M., and Todd A. Mooradian. 2003. "Personality Traits and Personal Values: A Conceptual and Empirical Integration." *Personality and Individual Differences* 35 (1): 109–25.

Osborne, Danny, and Chris G. Sibley. 2012. "Does Personality Matter? Openness Correlates with Vote Choice, but Particularly for Politically Sophisticated Voters." *Journal of Research in Personality* 46 (6): 743–51.

Oxley, Douglas R., Kevin B. Smith, John R. Alford, Matthew V. Hibbing, Jennifer L. Miller, Mario Scalora, Peter K. Hatemi, and John R. Hibbing. 2008. "Political Attitudes Vary with Physiological Traits." *Science* 321: 1667–70.

Parker, Christopher S., and Matt A. Barreto. 2014. *Change They Can't Believe In: The Tea Party and Reactionary Politics in America*. Princeton, NJ: Princeton University Press.

Parks-Leduc, Laura, Gilad Feldman, and Anat Bardi. 2015. "Personality Traits and Personal Values: A Meta-Analysis." *Personality and Social Psychology Review* 19 (1): 3–29.

Peffley, Mark A., and Jon Hurwitz. 1985. "A Hierarchical Model of Attitude Constraint." *American Journal of Political Science* 29 (4): 871–90.

Pentland, Alex. 2014. *Social Physics: How Good Ideas Spread*. New York: Penguin.

Perlstein, Rick. 2008. *Nixonland: The Rise of a President and the Fracturing of America*. New York: Simon and Schuster.

Peterson, Bill, Richard Doty, and David Winter. 1993. "Authoritarianism and Attitudes Toward Contemporary Social Issues." *Personality and Social Psychology Bulletin* 19 (2): 174–84.

Phillips, Kevin P. 1969. *The Emerging Republican Majority*. New Rochelle, NY: Arlington House.

Pierro, A., and A. W. Kruglanski. 2006. "Validation of a Revised Need for Cognitive Closure Scale." Unpublished Data. Universita Di Roma, La Sapienza.

Pietri, Evava S., Russell H. Fazio, and Natalie J. Shook. 2013. "Weighting Positive Versus Negative: The Fundamental Nature of Valence Asymmetry." *Journal of Personality* 81 (2): 196–208.

Pollock, Philip H., Stuart A. Lilie, and M. E. Vittes. 1993. "Hard Issues, Core Values and Vertical Constraint: The Case of Nuclear Power." *British Journal of Political Science* 23 (1): 29–50.

Pyszczynski, Thomas, Jeff Greenberg, Sheldon Solomon, Jamie Arndt, and Jeff Schimel. 2004. "Why Do People Need Self-Esteem? A Theoretical and Empirical Review." *Psychological Bulletin* 130 (3): 435–468.

Quattrone, George A., and Amos Tversky. 1988. "Contrasting Rational and Psychological Analyses of Political Choice." *American Political Science Review* 82 (3): 719–36.

Rank, Mark R., and Thomas A. Hirschl. 1999. "The Likelihood of Poverty across the American Adult Life Span." *Social Work* 44 (3): 201–16.

2005. "Likelihood of Using Food Stamps during the Adulthood Years." *Journal of Nutrition Education and Behavior* 37 (3): 137–46.

Rehm, Philipp. 2009. "Risks and Redistribution: An Individual-Level Analysis." *Comparative Political Studies* 42 (7): 855–81.

Riemann, Rainer, Claudia Grubich, Susanne Hempel, Susanne Mergl, and Manfred Richter. 1993. "Personality and Attitudes Towards Current Political Topics." *Personality and Individual Differences* 15 (3): 313–21.

Roccas, Sonia, Lilach Sagiv, Shalom H. Schwartz, and Ariel Knafo. 2002. "The Big Five Personality Factors and Personal Values." *Personality and Social Psychology Bulletin* 28 (6): 789–801.

Roets, Arne, and Alain Van Hiel. 2007. "Separating Ability from Need: Clarifying the Dimensional Structure of the Need for Closure Scale." *Personality & Social Psychology Bulletin* 33 (2): 266–80.

Roets, Arne, and Alain Van Hiel. 2011. "Item Selection and Validation of a Brief, 15-Item Version of the Need for Closure Scale." *Personality and Individual Differences* 50 (1): 90–4.

Rokeach, Milton. 1960. *The Open and Closed Mind*. New York: Basic Books.

Samuels, David, and Cesar Zucco. 2014. "The Power of Partisanship in Brazil: Evidence from Survey Experiments." *American Journal of Political Science* 58 (1): 212–25.

Sanford, Nevitt. 1966. *Self and Society: Social Change and Individual Development*. New York: Atherton Press.

Sargent, M. J. 2004. "Less Thought, More Punishment: Need for Cognition Predicts Support for Punitive Responses to Crime." *Personality & Social Psychology Bulletin* 30 (11): 1485–93.

Schatz, Robert T., Ervin Staub, and Howard Lavine. 1999. "On the Varieties of National Attachment: Blind Versus Constructive Patriotism." *Political Psychology* 20 (1): 151–74.

Scheve, Kenneth, and Matthew J. Slaughter. 2004. "Economic Insecurity and the Globalization of Production." *American Journal of Political Science* 48 (4): 662–74.

2006. "Public Opinion, International Economic Integration, and the Welfare State." In *Globalization and Self-Determination: Is the Nation-State Under Siege?* Eds. David R. Cameron, Gustav Ranis, and Annalisa Zinn, 51–94. New York: Routledge.

Schoen, Harald, and Siegfried Schumann. 2007. "Personality Traits, Partisan Attitudes, and Voting Behavior. Evidence from Germany." *Political Psychology* 28 (4): 471–98.

Schreiber, Darren, Greg Fonzo, Alan N. Simmons, Christopher T. Dawes, Taru Flagan, James H. Fowler, and Martin P. Paulus. 2013. "Red Brain, Blue Brain: Evaluative Processes Differ in Democrats and Republicans." *PLoS One* 8 (2): e52970.

Schudson, Michael. 1998. *The Good Citizen: A History of American Civic Life*. New York: The Free Press.

Schuessler, Alexander A. 2000. *A Logic of Expressive Choice*. Princeton, NJ: Princeton University Press.

Schwartz, Shalom H. 1992. "Universals in the Content and Structure of Values: Theoretical Advances and Empirical Tests in 20 Countries." *Advances in Experimental Social Psychology* 25 (1): 1–65.

1994. "Are there Universal Aspects in the Structure and Contents of Human Values?" *Journal of Social Issues* 50 (4): 19–45.

2007a. "Universalism Values and the Inclusiveness of Our Moral Universe." *Journal of Cross-cultural Psychology* 38 (6): 711–28.

2007b. "Value Orientations: Measurement, Antecedents and Consequences across Nations." In *Measuring Attitudes Cross-nationally: Lessons from the European Social Survey*, eds. Roger Jowell, Carline Roberts, Rory Fitzgerald, and Gillian Eva, 161–93. Thousand Oaks, CA: Sage.

Schwartz, Shalom H., Gian V. Caprara, and Michele Vecchione. 2010. "Basic Personal Values, Core Political Values, and Voting: A Longitudinal Analysis." *Political Psychology* 31 (3): 421–52.

Sears, David O. 1993. "Symbolic Politics: A Socio-psychological Theory." In *Explorations in Political Psychology*, eds. Shanto Iyengar and William J. McGuire, 113–49. Durham, NC: Duke University Press.

Sears, David O., and Carolyn L. Funk. 1991. "The Role of Self-Interest in Social and Political Attitudes." *Advances in Experimental Social Psychology* 24 (1): 1–91.

Sears, David O., Richard R. Lau, Tom R. Tyler, and Harris M. Allen. 1980. "Self-Interest Vs. Symbolic Politics in Policy Attitudes and Presidential Voting." *American Political Science Review* 74 (3): 670–84.

Settle, Jaime E., Christopher T. Dawes, Nicholas A. Christakis, and James H. Fowler. 2010. "Friendships Moderate an Association between a Dopamine Gene Variant and Political Ideology." *The Journal of Politics* 72 (4): 1189–98.

Shafer, Byron E., and William J. Claggett. 1995. *The Two Majorities: The Issue Context of Modern American Politics*. Baltimore, MD: Johns Hopkins University Press.

Shapiro, Robert Y. and Lawrence Jacobs. 2010. "Simulating Representation: Elite Mobilization and Political Power in Health Care Reform." The Forum 8 (1).

Sherman, David A., Leif D. Nelson, and Claude M. Steele. 2000. "Do Messages about Health Risks Threaten the Self? Increasing the Acceptance of Threatening Health Messages Via Self-Affirmation." *Personality and Social Psychology Bulletin* 26 (9): 1046–58.

Shook, Natalie J., and Russell H. Fazio. 2009. "Political Ideology, Exploration of Novel Stimuli, and Attitude Formation." *Journal of Experimental Social Psychology* 45 (4): 995–8.

Shultziner, Doron. 2013. "Genes and Politics: A New Explanation and Evaluation of Twin Study Results and Association Studies in Political Science." *Political Analysis* 21 (3): 350–67.

Sinclair, Betsy. 2012. *The Social Citizen: Peer Networks and Political Behavior*. Chicago: University of Chicago Press.

Sinn, Hans W. 1995. "A Theory of the Welfare State." *Scandinavian Journal of Economics* 97: 495–526.

Skitka, Linda J., and Christopher W. Bauman. 2008. "Moral Conviction and Political Engagement." *Political Psychology* 29 (1): 29–54.

Smith, Kevin, John R. Alford, Peter K. Hatemi, Lindon J. Eaves, Carolyn Funk, and John R. Hibbing. 2012. "Biology, Ideology, and Epistemology: How do We Know Political Attitudes Are Inherited and Why Should We Care?" *American Journal of Political Science* 56 (1): 17–33.

Smith, Kevin B., Douglas Oxley, Matthew V. Hibbing, John R. Alford, and John R. Hibbing. 2011a. "Disgust Sensitivity and the Neurophysiology of Left-Right Political Orientations." *PLoS One* 6 (10): e25552.

2011b. "Linking Genetics and Political Attitudes: Reconceptualizing Political Ideology." *Political Psychology* 32 (3): 369–97.

Smith, Mark A. 2007. *The Right Talk: How Conservatives Transformed the Great Society into the Economic Society*. Princeton, NJ: Princeton University Press.

Smith, M. Brewster, Jerome S. Bruner, and Robert W. White. 1956. *Opinions and Personality*. New York: John Wiley.

Sniderman, Paul M. 1975. *Personality and Democratic Politics*. Berkeley: University of California Press.

Sniderman, Paul M., Richard A. Brody, and Philip E. Tetlock. 1991. *Reasoning and Choice: Explorations in Political Psychology*. New York: Cambridge University Press.

Sniderman, Paul M., Michael B. Petersen, Rune Slothuus, and Rune Stubager. 2014. *Paradoxes of Liberal Democracy: Islam, Western Europe, and the Danish Cartoon Crisis*. Princeton, NJ: Princeton University Press.

Sniderman, Paul M., and Edward H. Stiglitz. 2012. *The Reputational Premium: A Theory of Party Identification and Policy Reasoning*. Princeton, NJ: Princeton University Press.

Snyder, Mark, and Kenneth G. DeBono. 1985. "Appeals to Image and Claims about Quality: Understanding the Psychology of Advertising." *Journal of Personality and Social Psychology* 49 (3): 586.

Somin, Ilya. 2006. "Knowledge about Ignorance: New Directions in the Study of Political Information." *Critical Review* 18 (1–3): 255–78.

2013. *Democracy and Political Ignorance: Why Smaller Government Is Smarter*. Stanford, CA: Stanford University Press.

Stangor, Charles, and Scott P. Leary. 2006. "Intergroup Beliefs: Investigations from the Social Side." *Advances in Experimental Social Psychology* 38: 243–81.

Stegmueller, Daniel. 2013. "The Dynamics of Income Expectations and Redistribution Preferences." Annual meeting of the American Political Science Association, Chicago, IL.

Stenner, Karen. 2005. *The Authoritarian Dynamic*. New York: Cambridge University Press.

Stokes, Donald E. 1963. "Spatial Models of Party Competition." *American Political Science Review* 57 (2): 368–77.

Stroud, Natalie J. 2008. "Media Use and Political Predispositions: Revisiting the Concept of Selective Exposure." *Political Behavior* 30 (3): 341–66.

Sullivan, John L., James Piereson, and George E. Marcus. 1982. *Political Tolerance and American Democracy*. Chicago: University of Chicago Press.

Sunstein, Cass R. 2009. *Republic.com 2.0*. Princeton, NJ: Princeton University Press.

Taber, Charles S., and Milton Lodge. 2006. "Motivated Skepticism in the Evaluation of Political Beliefs." *American Journal of Political Science* 50 (3): 755–69.

Tajfel, Henri, and John C. Turner. 1979. "An Integrative Theory of Intergroup Conflict." In *The Social Psychology of Intergroup Relations*, eds. W. G. Austin and S. Worchel, 33–47. Monterey, CA: Brooks/Cole.

Terrizzi, John A., Natalie J. Shook, and W. L. Ventis. 2010. "Disgust: A Predictor of Social Conservatism and Prejudicial Attitudes Toward Homosexuals." *Personality and Individual Differences* 49 (6): 587–92.

Tesler, Michael. 2012. "The Spillover of Racialization into Health Care: How President Obama Polarized Public Opinion by Racial Attitudes and Race." *American Journal of Political Science* 56 (3): 690–704.

——— 2016. *Post-racial or Most-Racial? Race and Politics in the Obama Era.* Chicago: University of Chicago Press.

Tesler, Michael, and David O. Sears. 2010. *Obama's Race: The 2008 Election and the Dream of a Post-racial America.* Chicago: University of Chicago Press.

Tetlock, Philip E. 1986. "A Value Pluralism Model of Ideological Reasoning." *Journal of Personality and Social Psychology* 50 (4): 819–27.

Thórisdóttir, Hulda, and John T. Jost. 2011. "Motivated Closed-Mindedness Mediates the Effect of Threat on Political Conservatism." *Political Psychology* 32 (5): 785–811.

Thórisdóttir, Hulda, John T. Jost, Ido Liviatan, and Patrick E. Shrout. 2007. "Psychological Needs and Values Underlying Left-Right Political Orientation: Cross-National Evidence from Eastern and Western Europe." *Public Opinion Quarterly* 71 (2): 175–203.

Tom, Sabrina M., Craig R. Fox, Christopher Trepel, and Russell A. Poldrack. 2007. "The Neural Basis of Loss Aversion in Decision-Making Under Risk." *Science* 315 (5811): 515–18.

Tomkins, Silvan S. 1963. "Left and Right: A Basic Dimension of Ideology and Personality." In *The Study of Lives*, ed. R. W. White, 388–411. New York: Atherton Press.

Tomz, Michael, and Paul M. Sniderman. 2005. "Brand Names and the Organization of Mass Belief Systems." *Unpublished Manuscript.*

Trapnell, Paul D., and Jerry S. Wiggins. 1990. "Extension of the Interpersonal Adjective Scales to Include the Big Five Dimensions of Personality." *Journal of Personality and Social Psychology* 59 (4): 781–90.

Treier, Shawn, and D. Sunshine Hillygus. 2009. "The Nature of Political Ideology in the Contemporary Electorate." *Public Opinion Quarterly* 73 (4): 679–703.

Turner, John C., Michael A. Hogg, Penelope J. Oakes, Stephen D. Reicher, and Margaret S. Wetherell. 1987. *Rediscovering the Social Group: A Self-Categorization Theory.* Basil Blackwell.

Van Hiel, Alain, Ivan Mervielde, and Filip De Fruyt. 2004. "The Relationship between Maladaptive Personality and Right Wing Ideology." *Personality and Individual Differences* 36 (2): 405–17.

Van Hiel, Alain, Emma Onraet, and Sarah De Pauw. 2010. "The Relationship between Social-Cultural Attitudes and Behavioral Measures of Cognitive Style: A Meta-analytic Integration of Studies." *Journal of Personality* 78 (6): 1765–800.

Van Hiel, A., M. Pandelaere, and B. Duriez. 2004. "The Impact of Need for Closure on Conservative Beliefs and Racism: Differential Mediation by Authoritarian Submission and Authoritarian Dominance." *Personality & Social Psychology Bulletin* 30 (7): 824–37.

Vavreck, Lynn, and Douglas Rivers. 2008. "The 2006 Cooperative Congressional Election Study." *Journal of Elections, Public Opinion and Parties* 18 (4): 355–66.

Verhulst, Brad, Lindon J. Eaves, and Peter K. Hatemi. 2012. "Correlation Not Causation: The Relationship between Personality Traits and Political Ideologies." *American Journal of Political Science* 56 (1): 34–51.

Vigil, Jacob M. 2010. "Political Leanings Vary with Facial Expression Processing and Psychosocial Functioning." *Group Processes & Intergroup Relations* 13 (5): 547–58.

Walsh, Katherine C. 2012. "Putting Inequality in Its Place: Rural Consciousness and the Power of Perspective." *American Political Science Review* 106 (3): 517–32.

Weber, Christopher R., and Christopher M. Federico. 2013. "Moral Foundations and Heterogeneity in Ideological Preferences." *Political Psychology* 34 (1): 107–26.

Weber, Max. 2002. *The Protestant Ethic and the Spirit of Capitalism: And Other Writings*. New York: Penguin.

Webster, Donna M., and Arie W. Kruglanski. 1994. "Individual Differences in Need for Cognitive Closure." *Journal of Personality and Social Psychology* 67 (6): 1049–62.

Weeden, Jason, and Robert Kurzban. 2014. *The Hidden Agenda of the Political Mind: How Self-Interest Shapes Our Opinions and Why We Won't Admit It*. Princeton, NJ: Princeton University Press.

Wells, Chris, Justin Reedy, John Gastil, and Carolyn Lee. 2009. "Information Distortion and Voting Choices: The Origins and Effects of Factual Beliefs in Initiative Elections." *Political Psychology* 30 (6): 953–69.

Wilson, Glenn D. 1973. *The Psychology of Conservatism*. New York: Academic Press.

Winter, Nicholas J. 2008. *Dangerous Frames: How Ideas about Race and Gender Shape Public Opinion*. Chicago: University of Chicago Press.

Young, Jason, Cynthia J. Thomsen, Eugene Borgida, John L. Sullivan, and John H. Aldrich. 1991. "When Self-Interest Makes a Difference: The Role of Construct Accessibility in Political Reasoning." *Journal of Experimental Social Psychology* 27 (3): 271–96.

Zaller, John. 1992. *The Nature and Origins of Mass Opinion*. New York: Cambridge University Press.

Zaller, John, and Stanley Feldman. 1992. "A Simple Theory of the Survey Response: Answering Questions Versus Revealing Preferences." *American Journal of Political Science* 36 (3): 579–616.

Index

CPSIA information can be obtained
at www.ICGtesting.com
Printed in the USA
LVHW032226210321
682036LV00001B/34